Rhinestone Cowboy

Glen Campbell
with Tom Carter

★★★★★★★★★★★★★★★★★★★★★★★★★★★★★★

Rhinestone

★★★★★★★★★★★★★★★★★★★★★★★★★★★★★★

Cowboy

★★★★★★★★★★★★★★★★★★★★★★★★★★★★★★

An Autobiography

Villard Books

New York

1994

Grateful acknowledgment is made to the following for
permission to reprint previously published material:
THE FAMOUS MUSIC PUBLISHING COMPANIES: Excerpt
from "Gentle on My Mind." Copyright © 1967, 1968
by Ensign Music Corporation. Reprinted by permission
of The Famous Music Publishing Companies. SONY
MUSIC PUBLISHING: Excerpt from "Dang Me" by Roger
Miller. Copyright © 1964 (renewed) by Tree Publishing Company. All rights administered by Sony Music
Publishing, P.O. Box 1273, Nashville, TN 37202. Reprinted by permission. WARNER/CHAPPELL MUSIC, INC.:
Excerpts from and title usage of one line from "Rhinestone Cowboy" by Larry Weiss. Copyright © 1974 by
WB Music Corp. All rights reserved. Reprinted by permission.

Library of Congress Cataloging-in-Publication Data
Campbell, Glen
Rhinestone cowboy / by Glen Campbell.
p.   cm.
ISBN 0-679-41999-3
1. Campbell, Glen, 1936– . 2. Country
musicians—United States—Biography.   I. Title.
ML420.C22A3   1994
782.42'1642'092—dc20
[B]   93-47464

Manufactured in the United States of America
9 8 7 6 5 4 3 2
First Edition

To my dad,

who taught me the values

of life before I was big enough

to know them.

Foreword

I agonized for a long time over whether I should write an autobiography, over how much of my life I wanted to reveal. I didn't want to do it unless I could do it truthfully, and I wasn't sure that I wanted some friends and members of my family to know the truth about me. I have done things of which I'm not proud.

But God has forgiven me for my transgressions, and I have forgiven myself. I realized that many people live in the same self-imposed mental and spiritual bondage in which I lived, despite my public image of the clean-cut, all-American boy next door. I was once called a singing version of Dick Clark, America's oldest teenager.

I especially didn't want my three small, impressionable children to know about my fast life in the past. However, I knew they were going to hear and read things about me eventually, so I wanted them to hear the facts, the real facts, from me.

Writing down my story was not what I thought it would be. It was much harder. Dredging up painful recollections, then putting them on paper, was traumatic. I've said things to Tom Carter, the collaborator on this book, that I've never said to my closest loved ones, knowing that he was going to tell the world.

I play six months of the year in Branson, Missouri. Tom lives in Nashville, Tennessee. The round-trip is 1,040 miles. He and I huddled for days during fifteen occasions in Branson, as well as in my home city of Phoenix, Arizona, and for a week in Reno, Nevada.

I had known this new confidant only since 1991, so it was hard to address the intimate questions posed by this comparative stranger. I'm sure people think that a writer and his collaborator become the closest of friends. Working with a collaborator, however, can be trying because the collaborator's job is to ask questions. Who wants to be around someone who is always asking questions? Tom told me he grew weary of prying, and I grew weary of responding. But we pressed on.

I have received a lot of sensational, negative, and inaccurate press during my career. This book is intended to straighten out much of the erroneous reporting. It's also intended to entertain, inspire, and maybe save a life or two. Many people, myself included, have wondered how I got through my days of self-indulgence that became self-abuse and that almost caused me to self-destruct. If my words here prevent one person from making the mistakes I made, going the way I went, then this trip back in time will have been worth it.

I'll be criticized for some of the things I've said about others with whom I was once close. There is no way to avoid that, given the tangled involvement some of those people had in my life.

Could Dean Martin write a book and not talk about Jerry Lewis? Could Paul McCartney write a book and not talk about John Lennon? Could Dolly Parton write her life story and not discuss Porter Wagoner?

I don't think anyone has ever written a memoir and told "everything." Yet autobiographies do have to face up to what the public already knows. And the public certainly knows about some of my ill-founded and headline-making relationships.

I've had heavily publicized romances with two women, one of whom I married, so I had to discuss them in the name of honest biography.

Omitting that part of my life would have left a huge and hypocritical hole in my story. My days of hypocrisy are long gone.

As you will read, I grew up incredibly poor and without much secondary education. When I was a kid, my family didn't have electric lights. I eventually would see my name glowing in electric letters taller than some of the houses in which I was raised. My good friend and business manager, Stan Schneider, grew up humbly in Brooklyn, New York. On more than one occasion, Stan and I have been in a lavish hotel suite, or stood before one of the world's natural wonders, and expressed our thankfulness and amazement for what one can do with his life in the greatest nation on earth, no matter how modest one's beginnings. That might sound like exaggerated patriotism or flag-waving, but it's true. I'm living proof.

I have been to the White House during four presidential administrations. I remember performing for former President Richard Nixon in 1971, when my career was white-hot. I was there at the invitation of the secretary of agriculture and played for many farmers.

"I never imagined that I'd be playing in the White House for a bunch of fellow farmers," I said sincerely, thinking the crowd was aware of my agricultural roots. They were not. Some took offense, and the press reported it, leaving out the word "fellow." That would not be the only time in my life when I received negative press and public criticism when my intentions were pure.

When Ronald Reagan was inaugurated, I was asked to perform for a home-state party in his honor. At the time, I lived in California, as did Reagan. I sat on the presidential platform with foreign and American dignitaries as well as various heads of state. I looked across the sea of people on the White House lawn, and again couldn't believe where I was, and thanked God that He had let me get there.

I joined legendary cowboy star Gene Autry for another visit to the Reagan White House. As Gene and I were approaching the president in a receiving line, Gene told me that he had met Reagan in Hollywood in 1938, at which time he had told the young actor that he would go far in his business if he would only get himself a good agent.

"Well, I see you finally got yourself a good agent," Gene whispered to Reagan as he shook his hand about fifty years after the advice. Reagan knew exactly what Gene was talking about. I had to laugh and feel warm about their reunion.

I remember being a guest of Kentucky governor Julian Carroll at the governor's mansion in 1975 and going with him to the Kentucky Derby. The night before the race, as everyone else in the mansion slept, four friends, my wife, and I sneaked into the main dining room and took pictures of each other at the sprawling and ornate governor's table. It was wonderful mischief that was a part of a happy childhood at age forty. The next day, we went to the race, and the governor saw to it that members of the Kentucky Highway Patrol hand-carried our bets from our private box to the betting window. It was not a world-shaking experience, but one of the memorable thousands I would never have had if I hadn't succeeded in this wonderful madness called show business.

I attend a Campbell family reunion almost every Fourth of July in Billstown, Arkansas, my hometown. My brothers and sisters, their kids, and their kids' kids make up a crowd of about seventy-five people, including friends. We eat and sing all day not far from one of the many shacks in which we grew up. On these occasions, I often can't believe where I am. And I can't believe I ever got out of there. Some of my relatives still live in the area, but in fine homes unlike the ones in which we were reared.

No matter how dire the circumstances, with faith and fortitude you can overcome them. Ten Campbell children proved it.

I have become a spokesman for my spiritual convictions. Some people who know about my wild-and-woolly days may find that outrageous. I really didn't change. God changed me, and I'll share the experience with you. This isn't one of those books in which the author keeps harping, "I found God." How could I find God? He wasn't lost. He found me. I simply let Him.

I'm not going to preach to you. I simply want to tell you what worked for me, and what I know will work for you. My spiritual experience was the simplest solution to life's most complicated problems.

The most successful song I ever recorded was "Rhinestone Cowboy." It is a tongue-in-cheek tune that gets its title from the cowboy suits that some singers used to wear, myself included. The clothes were adorned with rhinestones and spangles that reflected the spotlight.

"And I'm gonna be where the lights are shining on me . . ." the song says.

This is the story about a rhinestone cowboy whose sparkle was fading fast, but who rose to live again, and lived to tell about it.

I simply want to tell it to you.

Acknowledgments

I am indebted to a number of people whose assistance was vital to this project.

First, I must thank Tom Carter, whose writing skills made my job so much easier. I know that he has spent almost two years on this book, and I appreciate his patience. His ability to draw me out was of enormous help as I organized my own thoughts.

I must also thank Stan Schneider, who spent many hours with Tom reviewing the manuscript and adding his perspective to the book.

I would like to thank Roger Adams, Bill Maclay, Lonnie Shorr, Tom Smothers, Rob Reiner, Jerry Fuller, Carl Jackson; my family members; Thurley Burnette, my secretary; the Archives of Music Preservation; and all those others who consented to take the time to tell Tom Carter something of what they knew and know about Glen Campbell.

Thanks to Diane Reverand of Villard Books, and Mel Berger and Todd Harris of the William Morris Agency, for having faith in the project.

I have to thank Kim, my wife, who stood by me through some really rough times. In fact, there is no way to thank her enough.

Most of all I thank God, who never left me, even though I might have left him for a time.

GLEN CAMPBELL
Phoenix, Arizona
January 1994

Rhinestone Cowboy

Chapter 1

The fish and coral glistened brightly in the ice-blue Pacific water off Hawaii. At twenty-six, I had just learned to snorkel. I was on a break from a show with Jan and Dean, the Beach Boys, and Jody Miller. The sun and surf were a welcome change from the confusion of a television studio.

With each dive I plunged farther and held my breath longer. I'd bolt for the top of the ocean, exhale hard, inhale, and dive again. I was amazed at how clearly I could see even tiny grains of sand along the ocean floor. The water was like a window through which the sun shone fifteen feet beneath the surface.

Too hypnotized by God's splendor on the floor of the sea, I hadn't realized how far from shore I'd swum.

And then the bottom of the ocean just fell away.

In swimming parallel to the floor, I accidentally had swum deeper into the bowels of the earth. Suddenly, the splendor became invisible and it grew incredibly dark. Just as suddenly, I thought I was drowning.

The entire weight of the Pacific seemed to be pushing against me as I fought for the surface through water that felt like molasses. I could hear my heart beating as I peered unsuccessfully through the blackness. For an instant I thought I was turned around and wondered whether I was swimming toward the top or farther into the pockets of the deep. My lungs burned like fire, feeling as if they would rupture from the air that was expanding inside as I came to the top too rapidly.

Suddenly, I could see something that had been buried in the back of my mind for twenty-four years. When I was two years old I had wandered from the back of our house onto a low-water bridge over a creek in rural southwestern Arkansas. My sister had taken me across that bridge the day before to get some apples at a nearby store. I guess I was going for more apples. Instead, I walked right into the filthy and deep backwaters off the Little Missouri River.

And I drowned.

I had stopped breathing and my body had turned black when I was pulled from the water, according to my mother, Carrie, and my brothers. My mother had noticed my absence and instinctively ran to the water's edge. She saw one of my feet lodged in a branch of some button willows and the rest of my body underwater. Hysterical, she ran into the water that was chest-deep and unfastened me from the branch. My brothers had heard her screaming and came running.

That day in the ocean my mind snapped back to those Arkansas backwaters. I felt the sea suffocate life from me just as I did when I was a child. As I got closer to the ocean's surface, I could see the tops of tall buildings way up in the air, air I wished was inside my lungs. I was sure I was drowning again, and I felt that this time there would be no rescue.

My brother Lindell had been the second to reach me on the bank. He had taken a course in medical resuscitation only a week earlier. He rolled me onto my stomach, placed his palms on my shoulder blades, and began to pump. Eventually, I threw up water and my color returned. Lindell said that it took several minutes to revive me, but that I woke up before my mother, who had fainted on the bank.

In Hawaii, when I reached a depth to where I could wade, I staggered, choking and coughing, for the beach. I fell on the sand and lay breathing heavily for forty-five minutes. I could feel myself getting sunburned, but I didn't care. I was too glad to be alive.

I never once recalled the childhood blackout until that day in Hawaii. It's as if God called me to Heaven when I was small, decided I was too little to keep, then tossed me back for some more living.

☀☀☀

I'm like a lot of entertainers, especially the ones who sing country music or the blues: I grew up poor. I'm not talking about the kind of poverty in which someone on a limited income can't pay his bills, or gets behind on his rent, or doesn't have as many clothes as he would like and is embarrassed by the way he looks. None of that is pleasant. I went through that when I was a teenager trying to make it on my own, and right after I got married at seventeen.

The kind of poverty I knew as a boy wasn't really any kind of living. It was merely existing. We didn't just endure poverty, we wore it. You could see it in the distant, fearful stare of my parents.

On the survival scale, my family was just a step above the animals that we ate to stay alive. A few times we were hungry simply because there wasn't enough food for a family of twelve, although some of the older children had left home by the time the youngest was born. There were times I went to school and didn't go outside at recess because I was cold and had no coat.

I was born on April 22, 1936, when the rural South was reeling from the Great Depression. In the city, poor people stood in breadlines and went to soup kitchens, but there were no such luxuries in the Arkansas backwoods.

I actually entered this world outside Billstown, a community that was made up of a church and two stores. It has never been printed on any map, so I tell people I'm from Delight, four miles away. Delight has always been on the map and had a population of 290 when I was small. It's about one hundred miles southwest of Little Rock.

My dad, John Wesley Campbell, was a sharecropper. He grew crops on other people's land and shared the profits with them. Nothing was more important to our survival than the crops. I remember the panic that swept our family one spring when heavy rains washed our seeds from the ground. We replanted seven times. We'd lie in bed at night, sunburned from the day's toil, and pray that the rumbling thunder overhead wouldn't produce rain. My sisters cried, knowing what damage the storms were causing. They were brokenhearted at the thought of having to replant another man's land again by hand.

When at last the rain stopped that year, our crops faced a drought, and again there were tears inside our cabin, this time for the rain that refused to fall.

When there was no more farmwork around Billstown, we went to other places. I went to Ohio and Indiana with my brothers to pick tomatoes. My dad, Shorty, Ronald, Gerald, and I lived inside a one-room shack where my dad cooked flapjacks. He flipped the flapjacks over the rafters and caught them in a pan. We laughed and really thought we were having a good time. I insisted that I get the top bunk, but Dad said I might fall out. I didn't listen, and, of course, I fell out and hit the wooden floor like a sack of cement.

In the fall, Dad earned money every Saturday by chopping a rick of wood and taking it to Delight. We boys helped, and each was paid a nickel. We spent the coins at the picture show.

I was the youngest boy, and was Dad's last go-around in a father-son relationship. I can remember the coolness of the earth on my bare feet as I walked behind his plow, picking up the worms in the overturned earth. It didn't take a lot to amuse us in the Deep South of the 1940s.

I can still see my dad today in his bib overalls, felt hat, and long-sleeved shirt buttoned at the neck. He wore those heavy clothes all year long. Because I was his youngest boy, I bonded with him closely, especially after the other boys had gone from home. My dad and his country wisdom comprise my fondest childhood memories. Randy

Travis recorded a song about the savvy of his backwoods grandfather titled "He Walked on Water." Young Randy thought his grandfather could do anything. My young adoration for my dad was almost that naïve and passionate.

We raised almost everything we ate. We had some chickens and hogs, but a lot of our meat was wild game because we didn't have to feed the game before we ate it. We even ate turtles, gar, and eel, but never snakes.

When the spring rains backed runoff across our land, our chickens would roost on the fence posts. The awkward birds looked comical teetering on the small spaces, but my dad was not amused. He knew their eggs would drop into the water and food meant for his family would literally wash away.

Dad's cash crop was cotton. He could earn more than four dollars a day picking cotton by hand, but he had to pick more than four hundred pounds to do it. None of his sons could ever pick that much, but some of us brought in an extra two to three dollars a day. The money earned during picking season would have to last the family all year.

It never did.

Some years, it went to pay the debts we had collected the previous year. Dad never caught up with the bills when I lived at home.

Each of the six boys began helping not long after he could walk, and some of my four sisters and my mother worked the fields too.

The thorny cotton boles tore the skin right off our fingers, which would be stiff, aching, and covered with dried blood after a day of picking cotton. There was no money for work gloves.

My mother gave birth to each of her children at home. She would be back working in the fields usually within two days after delivery. We slept four in the bed when we were small, three when we were older. I tell people I never knew what it was like to sleep alone until I got married.

Sometimes in the winter we would awaken to no food. On those days, the priority wasn't going to school or even earning an income. It was simply staying alive.

We had lots of pets. I was about seven when our cat had kittens and my dad ordered me to kill them. He demanded that I put them in a burlap sack and toss the sack into the river. I was ordered to stand there and watch the sack sink, making sure the kittens had drowned.

That was hard for a little boy, and I remember shaking on the riverbank and talking to those kittens, telling them I wasn't mad at them, but we just didn't have any food. I told them that they couldn't run fast enough to catch a mouse, and that there would be lots of food for them in Heaven. I was crying so hard, I could barely muster the strength to throw the sack full of life far enough from shore to reach deep water. But I did it.

My brother Lindell tells a story about my dad's ploy to commit suicide. He told Lindell that depression had swallowed him. Dad couldn't bear the pressure of not being able to provide the bare necessities for his large family any longer. So he took a shotgun and headed into the woods. He loaded his weapon and was about to put the barrel in his mouth when he was distracted by a squirrel running down a tree branch. He shot and killed it. Almost instantly, another came down, and then another. My dad was crying and shooting his gun, and the family had eight squirrels for supper. His children had been fed for another day, and Dad lived an additional forty years.

Before I was six, when electricity came to our house, we usually ate whatever game my dad caught the same day he caught it. There was no refrigerator, and in the summer meat spoiled quickly.

The house I was born in didn't have a heating stove, only a fireplace. Zero-degree weather isn't uncommon in Pike County, and there was just no way to stay warm with only the wooden walls between us and the outside. You could put your hand on the wall and feel the coldness. We would have probably been warmer inside a log cabin, because logs are thicker than cut wood. I learned to live cold, and I hate coldness to this day. That's one reason I make my home in Phoenix, Arizona.

Another fact of country life was the ever-present danger. City children grow up on playgrounds or paved streets with light signals and policemen. They face the dangers of crime but have locked doors. We grew up in a wilderness filled with poisonous snakes and spiders, and there was no money for a doctor. My brother Lindell remembers that one kid or another always seemed to have malaria in the summertime because our windows had no glass or screens. Mosquitoes ruled the house in those thick woods.

My dad taught us how to survive early in our lives. He would take us to deep water, throw us in, and say, "Swim." He never lost one of us. I laugh about it today and tell folks that it wasn't the swimming but getting out of the sack that was hard.

He would also take us into the woods late at night and walk a few steps ahead. He would say, "Duck," and he would say it only once. The first time he said it to me, I said, "What?" and then felt a branch smack me in my face. The next time he said "Duck," I did, and the branch went over my head.

Perhaps the greatest damage to poor children is not being able to be kids. They are heaped with the responsibilities of adults before they are old enough to handle them. Their bodies become more developed than their minds, and neither has a chance to develop much. Dad couldn't wait for his kids to grow up. He needed us to pull our own weight.

That was the case with my brother Ronald, who was told to watch me when I was six months old and he was three and a half. He became bored with his crawling baby brother and put me inside a burlap sack that was filled with picked cotton. With no space or air inside I almost suffocated. My mother said my skin was white from the heat inside the bag.

My dad got a tractor, but we didn't keep it long because he couldn't afford antifreeze. He had saved a long time for that contraption, and then the engine exploded when my brother drove it in the winter. The radiator had frozen and there was no money for repairs. It was back to a mule and checkline, because he could never afford another tractor. He spent much of the rest of his working life breaking the hard Arkansas dirt with a mule and plow. Eventually, he would be competing in the agricultural market with men who owned machinery and used chemical fertilizers. The only time my dad's yield increased was when one of his dependents left home.

During our limited time with modernization, I was assigned to drive that tractor. But at ten I was too young. We were working before sunrise to avoid the heat of the day, and in the cool darkness, listening to the hum of the engine, I fell asleep. I drove the tractor right into the ditch. It's a wonder I wasn't pinned beneath the weight of the machine when it partially sank.

When I was ten, I rode in a pickup truck that turned over. When I was eleven, I was in the back of a different pickup that was hit by another vehicle. The bed of the truck I was in was torn from the cab, and a friend and I were thrown to the earth and almost run over.

Poverty and danger were as much a part of my childhood as buttermilk was. That's how it was for virtually all the rural families below the Mason-Dixon line during and after the Depression.

Another part of my childhood became very important: music and church. My mother breast-fed each of her children, which meant taking us to church and services that sometimes went on all day. Her babies heard the sound of singing voices just as early as they heard the spoken word. God and music were my spiritual mainstays, and the Campbells were spiritual people.

The first music I remember was in the Church of Christ, where they didn't allow musical instruments. The congregation sang alone. My dad and mom took all of us to church and we sat together in one row. I first learned to sing harmony inside that country sanctuary.

I had heard about a black church a few miles away in which the members sang fast music with heavy rhythms. I would hike over there, stand outside the window, rise on my bare tiptoes, and peek inside at the black folks rolling on the floor and running in the aisles. They were thoroughly caught up in the spirit and the music. It was my first experience of seeing how moving music could be to people. I had never seen so much unleashed passion and I hungered to be around the rhythm and music that I felt as much as heard coming from that impoverished clapboard church.

I also listened to music on a battery-operated console radio. Dad heard that he could get an extra two weeks out of the battery by putting it on the stove after it ran down. Once, he left it on the stove too long and the battery exploded. Battery acid sprayed all over the kitchen and eventually ate holes in the cardboard-and-paper walls.

I had been walking only a couple of years when I began to try to strum one of our family's mandolins. My fingers wouldn't reach the chords, so Dad sent away to Sears Roebuck for a three-quarter-size guitar. Our mailbox was at the Billstown Crossroads, two miles from our house, and I walked up there every day at the age of four to see if the guitar had arrived. When it finally did, you couldn't get it out of my hands.

My dad's brother, Uncle Eugene "Boo" Campbell, was the best guitar player in the family. He took an interest in my curiosity and showed me how to make chords by pulling on my tiny fingers to try to stretch them to reach all the strings. When I was older, I would play hooky from school to sneak over to Uncle Boo's to play the guitar. He would scold me, but then let me come inside, and we would play.

After electricity came to our house, we got an electric radio. I was allowed to play it only when my chores were done. I suppose there were a few times when some old cow didn't get rid of all her milk because I hurried through the milking to get back to that radio. I heard the songs of Hank Williams, Roy Acuff, Ernest Tubb, Jimmy Dickens, and other stars from the Grand Ole Opry. Pretty soon, I learned to play melodies and could reproduce the tunes.

Today, they would say I was a child prodigy. That word was never used in Billstown in 1940. They just said things like, "That boy can sure play a guitar." Words like that just made me want to practice more and more, and by the time I was eight, Uncle Boo and I had formed a band that played on local radio shows, in schoolhouses, and at church functions.

My family appeared many times in a local church event called "All Day Singin' and Dinner on the Ground," and often went to these socials in a horse-drawn wagon. I remember one Campbell family appearance for which we all rode thirty miles to the church and thirty miles back. Sixty miles in two days in a wagon made for some sore behinds. But we diluted the pain with laughter, song, and the invisible parts of a wonderful thing called love. My dad, just to entertain his kids, passed cars with his horses on that trip. You could see daylight between our rears and the floor of that wagon as we bounced over the rough and rutted roads of rural Arkansas.

In the music business, they would say I was already on the road doing one-nighters. I didn't know I'd still be on that road fifty years later.

Chapter 2

The two of them had fought the land and the heat all their lives. They thought they always would, and fatigue and frustration were running high as they prepared for another day's toil. The older man led a team of horses to the front of the wagon. Their footsteps overpowered his weary mumbling. Convinced that the other man hadn't heard him, he spoke again, this time loudly.

"Go ahead and hook up the wagon," he said, handing the horses' reins to the younger man.

"Get one of the kids to do it. I'm a man now."

"I told you to do it," the weary older man said.

"Don't you tell me nothin'. I said I'm a man now, so get one of the kids to do it."

The older man stopped short and stared at his son for a long time. He had not often had his authority challenged, and this was the first time it was openly challenged by one of his own kin.

My dad was the kind of man who spoke loudly by saying nothing at all. His silence was a kind of strategy for the fight he knew was about to come. He didn't want to fight his own offspring, but if he must, he would let his son make the first challenge.

"Have you still got those boxing gloves?" my brother Wayne asked.

My dad kept two pairs of fourteen-ounce gloves in our house for years. Ten kids made for as many disagreements any given month. When we were small, Dad settled the arguments with his belt. After the boys grew up a bit, however, he would let them fight it out rather than have to listen to them argue.

"Yes, Son," my dad told Wayne. "I still got those gloves. Reckon you want to use them on me?"

"I'm a man now, Dad," Wayne said. "You ain't got no right to make me hook up no team. That's kids' work, and I ain't gonna do it. I was hopin' you'd see it my way and I wouldn't have to hurt you."

Wayne hurt my dad more than he would ever know by disobeying him, much less challenging him to a fistfight. Wayne was eighteen and had been enrolled in a militarylike camp called Three C's. It trained young boys to work much the same way as the Works Projects Administration—the federal government's antipoverty program launched in the wake of the Great Depression.

My brother would have killed anyone else who threatened our dad and he regretted his challenge to Dad's authority many times in the years to come. He, like many of us, did things when he was young that he would never do again.

The rest of the family thought that Wayne was going to fight one of his brothers when he went inside the house to get the gloves. The yard soon filled with curious Campbells, who were astonished to see that Wayne was going to fight Dad. None of us could believe our eyes. None of us wanted to. One of my sisters pleaded with Wayne not to go through with it, and my mom began to cry softly at the sight of what was about to happen between her son and her husband. For country folk, at that time, the family was all any of us had. Next to God, it was the most important thing in the world. We were taught that it was about as much of a sin to disobey your parents as it was to disobey God.

My dad stood without emotion, staring directly into the frightened face of his son, who had left home as a boy and was about to find out if he had returned as the man he thought he was.

"Go ahead, Son," Dad almost whispered. "Take the first swing."

Dad told us later that he knew Wayne would come with his left, his strongest hand. And he did. His full swing whistled louder than my sisters' gasps.

Dad ducked to his knees, leaving Wayne off balance with his chin extended. Wayne's swing had cleared Dad's head by a foot. Dad's right fist shot upward before he even straightened his legs, knocking Wayne down.

I think Wayne was unconscious before he hit the ground.

"I should have just put on one glove," my dad said. "That's all I got to use."

He turned to walk away before his spellbound children. My mother put her hands over her mouth, and the children silently cheered him. Dad was still the indisputable head of his family.

Then Dad spun on his heels. "Carrie," he said to Mom, his voice still controlled, "when Wayne wakes up, tell him to hitch up the team."

She did, and Wayne did, then and whenever he was asked thereafter.

I don't know how our family would have reacted had Wayne won. I don't think my dad's pride could have withstood the shame. He might have interpreted the loss as meaning that he shouldn't remain head of the family. I don't know who would have replaced him. It was hard enough being a Campbell child. There wasn't one of us who wanted to provide for the whole clan.

✶✶✶

I was the last boy still living at home when I decided to challenge my dad's rule. Having learned by example, I intended to outsmart him rather than overpower him. My efforts would prove to be ridiculous.

I recall all this because of its later significance. I was reared in a household in which one faced outrageously harsh punishment if he challenged parental authority. Some of my brothers and sisters tried it only once, and most never tried at all.

Dad and I had an early harvest of cotton in 1949. The boles were picked clean maybe a week earlier than usual. He told me on a Friday morning that I could hire out to somebody else on Saturday and use whatever I earned to see a picture show in Delight.

On Saturday morning my dad said, "I've changed my mind, Glen. It rained all day Friday and we didn't get to work like I wanted. So you'll have to stay at home today and help me after all." If I had asked to go to the show and he had said no, I could have lived with it. But because my dad had made the offer and then taken it back, I became overly annoyed.

Now, I knew that, according to the Bible, the Lord giveth and the Lord taketh away. But, as important as my dad was, he wasn't the Lord, and I didn't think it was fair for him to make me stay at home after he told me I could go. After all, hadn't he always taught me to keep *my* word? Why shouldn't he?

I asked myself that question all morning, but I couldn't ask Dad. We weren't allowed to talk back.

So I hid under the house.

I don't know what I thought I would tell him about where I'd been once I turned up. Maybe I didn't think that far ahead. I can remember only lying on my stomach with my heart in my mouth, struggling to hold my breath as my dad's feet walked slowly around the house.

"Glen! Glen!" he yelled.

I didn't answer.

Suddenly, I saw the worn leather on his brogan boots aim toward me. On my belly I was eye level to his feet. And the boots kept coming closer. I was sure he was going to lean down and see me. The idea of being caught eye-to-eye by the man I feared most was terrifying. I whirled around madly to scramble out on the other side of the house. My pulse was racing and I thrashed around in the dirt under the house's floor. I could hear my family's footsteps above me, and prayed they wouldn't hear me below.

How could I have ever dared to try to hide from my dad? Nothing, I was positive, could be worse than having to confront him.

Except coming nose-to-nose with a giant chicken snake.

The snake was probably an average size, which is about three or four feet long. It raised its beady eyes directly at me. Snakes "feel" with their tongues, and perhaps he was "feeling" my body. The snake and I were so close, I thought I felt his lightning tongue flick my cheek.

I've never felt such a surge of panic and energy, from that day to this. I was terrified of facing my dad, but I would rather have faced Goliath than stay under that house with that snake, which, at that moment, I was sure was a python or a cobra that had found its way across the ocean to Arkansas.

And so I started out, bolting through scrap lumber, Mason jars, and other debris that had accumulated over the years under a household of twelve. In my hysteria, I thrust myself upright. Trouble was, I was still under the house, and my head hit the floor above me. I was screaming like a panther all the while and swimming madly in the dirt, groping for daylight at the edge of our house. Again I raised up, and again my head crashed into a beam that held up the floorboards. I must have shot my head up eight or ten times before I got out of there. I'm sure I slammed my forehead into every beam between the snake and the edge of the house.

Up above, people inside the house began screaming. My sisters became hysterical, not knowing what was making so much commotion under the house. They later told me they thought it was a wild animal.

By now, my dad was on his knees, squinting under the house at his youngest boy, who was fighting the fight of his life.

"Run! Snake! Run!" I warned.

My dad's face disappeared from the ground about the time I reached the edge of the house. I saw one of his boots lift upward past the bottom of the house. I was curious, even in the midst of my panic, as to why he was standing on one foot. Was he going to try to stomp that snake when it shot out from under the house?

These thoughts were only flashes. Mostly I could think about nothing other than the expected piercing pain of that reptile's fangs.

My forehead was bleeding from the many times I had battered it against the floor beams. I glanced once again at my dad's one visible boot. I was still looking downward when my head cleared the edge of the house. One more thrust and I would be clear enough of the frame to stand up and run as fast as I could from the snake. I knew that when snakes bite they don't let go easily. I could see myself running at full tilt with that thing gripping my calf with its teeth.

And still my dad was balanced on one foot.

As my head was extended from under the house, it must have looked like a turtle's protruding from its shell. Then my dad put his boot across the back of my neck.

I don't know which hurt most—the pain he was inflicting, or the pain I imagined was being inflicted by the snake, which I never saw again. There was no chance of my talking back, since my mouth was filled with Arkansas soil.

"What were you doing under there?" he yelled.

I could feel tears streaking down the dirt smeared into my face. I confessed everything, babbling about how I had hidden from him to avoid work. By now the whole family was outside. One sister was holding a gun to shoot whatever varmint had made such a ruckus under the floor.

"Whatever in the world was he doing under there?" they kept saying.

My dad beat me with a checkline. I thought he would wear out the leather, which was strong enough to hold two horses onto a wagon. He beat me a long time.

It was the second hardest whipping I ever got, second only to the one

I received when I ran smack through a screen door while chasing my sister Jane. There was no money to buy screen wire, and we faced an even greater onslaught of flies because of my rowdiness.

Another hard pummeling came not for being disobedient but for bad judgment. My brother and I were caught smoking corn silks in the barn by our dad. He beat us within an inch of our lives. He was overcome with fury.

"I ain't givin' you this here whippin' for smokin'," he said. "I'm a givin' it to you for smokin' in the barn."

That barn contained the hay and animals that were our livelihood. Had we burned it down, we would have eliminated the small family income we had. But a kid doesn't think about things like that when he's experimenting, as I was.

I'm in favor of spanking my children, if it's warranted. I would never, however, beat my children as though they were mad animals. They say that children who are whipped will grow up to whip their children. I'm not sure that's true.

I don't resent my folks for whipping us as they did. It showed me that they cared about how we were raised, about our knowing right from wrong. I feel sorry for kids whose parents don't care what they do or what they become.

Hard physical punishment was as much a part of my rearing as religion was. With nine brothers and sisters, plus my friends at school whose parents believed the way mine did, I suspect I saw a kid take a serious licking almost every day until I was old enough to shave. I saw kids harshly beaten at school by the teachers, and whipped again at home for having gotten whipped at school. Modern disciplinary theories, such as positive reinforcement or loss of privileges, were unknown. Besides, trying to punish those tough farm kids by anything but physical means would have made them laugh.

That kind of discipline made young people very physical and aggressive. Rough practical jokes often gave real pain to the victims. Boys often got together and hoisted an outhouse off its hole in the ground.

When a would-be user approached the privy at night, he walked right into the waste-filled hole. It was a cruel joke that was as much a part of country life as the slaughtering of animals, which I learned to do by the time I was ten.

I could cut a hog's throat without thinking twice about it, slice the skin from its carcass, scrape the waste from the meat, and cut it into pieces. I carried the parts to my mother for cooking as casually as I drew water from our well, filled with rainfall and runoff from our roof.

Whenever we dropped a bucket into the well, we bounced it several times at the end of a rope to clear away the dead bugs floating on top of the water. The water, of course, was filled with rotting bug parts that we couldn't see, but we thought nothing about drinking it. I had a friend whose grandfather put live catfish into his family's well so that the fish could eat the dead bugs. The old man never considered that his drinking water was filled with catfish poop. It's a wonder we all didn't get typhoid fever.

When I saw a kid with conspicuous bruises on his back and arms, I thought nothing about it. I just figured he'd been beaten by a parent or been in a hard fight. Most disagreements between buddies were settled with fists. When they fought, they fought to win.

My last go-around with hard violence was in the fourth grade. After that I never hit anyone again in my entire life because I hurt my hand badly and realized that I might never be able to play my guitar again. That last fight happened because a boy cheated me in an Easter egg hunt. To add insult to injury, he stuck his tongue out at me. My teacher, a hearty old woman named Miss Grace, left the room for an instant, all the time I needed to coldcock the guy right in the nose. I didn't think about what I would do when Miss Grace returned and asked the boy why he was bleeding all over her floor.

"Glen, did you mean to hit him?" she asked.

"No," I said, "I meant to knock him out."

That was more sass than she wanted to hear. I knew I would get a whipping from her, but, as I said, she couldn't hand out anything I hadn't already had.

In a movie I'd once seen one of the Little Rascals insert a plate into his pants before he got a spanking. For the thrashing I was about to receive, I would need an entire set of dishes. Instead, I used a thin speller, which was a pulp-paper book about the size of a pocketbook. I quickly stuffed it into my britches. I couldn't have gotten away with it if Miss Grace had used her hand. I knew she would use a weapon, and she did, laying into me with a foot-long steel ruler.

I screamed, danced, and moaned for dear life. But I never felt a thing.

★★

Chapter 3

*7*he first time I quit school was when I was in the seventh grade. I still think it was the right thing to do. I was going to be left back a grade because I had no interest in school, didn't care where Czechoslovakia was, and knew enough about mathematics to count the money I wasn't making. Staying in school meant living at home, where things became slightly easier for my folks when one of their kids moved out.

My uncle Boo had learned that musicians could make a buck in Wyoming in 1951. He thought we could play the nightclubs out there. That's all I needed to hear. No more farming and no more school. Just making music—and getting paid for it!

Leaving home was a significant and emotional event for a country boy during the 1950s, the last days of America's innocence before the beginning of the popularity of television. My life was my family, and it was the only life I knew. To leave home was to give up life as I knew it.

My brothers left home one by one before me. When they came back to visit, they had no hesitation about punching me or other horseplay, the only affection they ever showed. But when my brothers found out

I was leaving, they began to drop by more often. They offered to let me hang out with them or wear their clothes—things they'd never done before. My sisters were glad to see me go because I was one less mouth to feed, and yet, in the days preceding my departure, they seemed to want to cook the things I liked. My dad, who was not especially emotional or expressive, unexpectedly got up from the table when talk turned to my going. My mother smiled through tear-moistened eyes.

I wanted to be a man about going, so I didn't show any signs of my feelings. The day I left I was prancing with excitement, head up, back straight. But my heart was breaking.

Uncle Boo and I traveled by bus for about three days and nights from Delight, Arkansas, to our first job in Casper, Wyoming. We could have made it faster, but had to stop many times for transfers. We stood on bus-terminal loading docks in blinding snowfalls, wearing thin jackets and clinging to battered suitcases and soggy lunch sacks. We were in pain, but for us, the road to Wyoming was the route to a career. That road would prove to be a crooked journey. I laugh about it today, but there were times back then when I couldn't even force a smile.

Our first engagement was at Casper's something-or-other bar. I was fifteen. We played for a week for no salary, just tips placed in a jar at the edge of the bandstand. The money was paltry, yet my share was more than I had ever earned in my life.

I remember the thrill of looking across a sea of bobbing heads as people danced and swayed to our music. How different the smoke-filled room felt compared to the wholesome church programs we had played back in Arkansas. I got excited seeing folks become regular fans who returned to the dance hall nightly because they liked our music. I remember the charge of hearing people ask me to play something the way I had played it the night before.

I remember the police coming to arrest me because I was underage. Right off I could tell they had no interest in dancing or listening.

"Do you have custody of the boy?" a policeman wanted to know.

"Sure I do," Boo said. "His daddy told me I could bring him. He's my nephew, and I brung him up here from Arkansas so we could play music."

That wasn't good enough. The officer wanted to see the custody papers. Boo had never heard of such a thing. So the police indirectly fired me. We found out later that Uncle Boo had been turned in by the owners of the nightclubs whose customers we were stealing. It didn't seem fair, but it was better than going to jail, so Boo promised the lawmen that he would never let me play inside that nightclub again.

We moved on to several other nightclubs in rural Wyoming, where the scene was sometimes repeated. The places were usually rough bars next to dance halls. The customers weren't allowed to bring liquor onto the dance floors, so they drank fast and hard in the bars, then ran to the dance halls. They danced until they felt themselves beginning to get sober, then dashed back to the saloon for another liquid fix.

It was an exciting time, although Uncle Boo kept close reins on me. I was a naïve farm boy who not only didn't know anything but didn't suspect anything.

One time, I wondered why there were so many pretty girls in a place we were playing. I didn't understand why they were so dressed up, looking so fancy when they just seemed to sit around by themselves. A few men came by, but they never stayed very long, and when they left, they didn't take the girls with them.

I had never heard of a house of prostitution until I played in one. Uncle Boo finally figured out what was going on and explained it all to me. If the police didn't want me playing where folks drank whiskey, I wondered what they would think about me playing for the girls who were doing that! I thought hard, but I didn't think long. Uncle Boo and I were out of that place in two days.

I really enjoyed playing a sheepherders' bar in Thermopolis, Wyoming, because the customers were such heavy tippers. But that stop was also cut short, because they found out I was a minor.

Uncle Boo and I were just two guys from Arkansas playing with musicians we picked up, but, believe it or not, we quickly developed a following. Part of that following, however, always included some police officers. Rival nightclub owners kept calling the police on the Southern guys who were stealing their customers.

We brought with us the last thing nightclub owners wanted—attention from the law. Word of the "heat" that followed us quickly spread from club owner to club owner in that sparsely populated state. Soon, no one wanted to give us a job playing music.

Our big dream of making it was short-lived. We were broke, unemployable, stranded, and farther from home than either of us had ever been. Wintertime in Arkansas had been cold. Wintertime in Wyoming was mean, with blinding snow that swirled into six-foot drifts. Sometimes, the temperature got as warm as 10 below. At that time I had not yet heard musicians talk about "paying their dues," and later would learn that that's what I was doing.

Uncle Boo went from door to door looking for work. At home, no matter how bad things got, we could always work the land, even in the winter, when we cut wood. In Wyoming, there was more land than I had ever seen, but there wasn't anybody working it. There were big ranches, but Uncle Boo and I sure weren't cowboys.

So we dug ditches. Two thousand miles from home, we wore holes in our shoes stomping shovels in the Wyoming ground, which stayed frozen long after folks had planted their crops in Arkansas. We fought that foreign earth just long enough to get the bus fare to Albuquerque, where we were sure my dad's sister and her husband, Dick Bills, would give us enough money to get back to Arkansas. We should have thought twice. It would be a long time before I would forgive Uncle Dick for turning down relatives when they were in need.

Once again, Uncle Boo and I faced an impossible situation. Whatever else we had been, we had always been musicians, because we had always had our instruments. But now we were forced to pawn them. We hocked two beat-up guitars for enough bus fare to get from Albuquerque to Delight. Eventually, my mom and dad sent money to my aunt Judy so that she could get our guitars out of hock.

When I arrived home I couldn't have been more lovingly received had I been the prodigal son. Although my leaving had made for one less mouth to feed, I was made to feel that my folks hadn't wanted me to leave home at all.

If I had ever wondered about my parents' capacity to share, the wonder was erased when I came home to find two people visiting them. In the rural South back then, when folks came a long way to visit, they often stayed a long time and they ate a lot.

Boyd and Loma Hardy had lost a son in World War II and they seemed to shine up to me, as if I were his replacement. They had some land to farm in New Mexico and asked me if I would go with them to work it. I needed the job and those folks needed me, so I took them up on their offer. While in New Mexico I enrolled in the tenth grade. I skipped the eighth and ninth and became a high school sophomore because I was needed on the basketball team. Teachers and neighbors urged me to return to school because the team needed a fifth man to fill out the squad. Without me, there would have been no season. I don't know what would have happened if a player had been injured. However, I was a terrible basketball player. I didn't finish the season, and the team's win-loss record was 0–5.

I didn't learn a lot that year. I didn't even learn how to play basketball. All I could think about was playing music. I got a job playing on Friday and Saturday nights at the Coon Hollar Club in Regina, New Mexico, with a singer named Texas Slim. I used Mr. Hardy's guitar.

I quit the classroom forever in December 1952 and had to look for day work that would support my nighttime career. I wound up in Houston working with my brothers and dad as an insulator's helper on a construction site. My job was to mix the "mud," the adhesive for the guys laying the insulation. Three men were needed to do the job I was trying to perform by myself. I couldn't keep up and quit within a week.

I landed a job at a Texaco service station, where I mashed my thumb changing a tire. I realized I could ruin my guitar playing forever at that place, so I quit that too.

Nothing, but nothing, was going to come between me and my ultimate goal, not even basic needs.

I started playing with Ronnie McKinney and a couple of other guys. Ronnie was a singer and rhythm guitarist and we played the Ace of Clubs, the Pilot Inn, and some other bars as I went through the motions, but I knew I was going nowhere.

Then I got a call from my uncle Dick Bills in Albuquerque. He had a band, and others in the family had told him that I really could sing and play. They told him he should hire me because I was good and not to worry about family ties.

At first, I was afraid to go. He, after all, was the man who had refused to give me bus fare back to Arkansas when I was desperate. I thought he would leave me stranded if I ever played on the road with him, but I took the job anyway. In the long run he proved to be a nice and supportive man and I worked with him for about eight years.

Uncle Dick had his own radio show, and back then that seemed like big-time show business to me. I played the noon show five days a week. I also played six nights a week in the fistfights set to music that were erroneously called dances. He also had a Saturday morning television show for children, and I played there too.

To this day, people still come up to me and without fanfare start singing:

> Ridin' down the trail to Albuquerque
> Saddle bags all filled with beans and jerky
> Headin' for K-Circle B, the TV ranch for you and me
> K-Circle B in Albuquerque.

That I can sing those lyrics four decades later shows what an impact that show had on me.

We played a lot of cowboy dances when we weren't working the clubs, traveling as far as west Texas, eastern Arizona, southern Colorado, and throughout New Mexico. It was a very big deal for a kid my age to be traveling that far, making music and earning a living.

We often crammed five musicians plus our instruments into an old car, drove all day, played the show, then drove all night back to Albuquerque in time for one of our home shows. It was more than uncomfortable to be so crowded in a car with no air-conditioning during southwestern summers. Those 100-degree days, and sometimes 100-degree nights, were a way of life.

I was playing an armory one night in Espanola, New Mexico, with Uncle Dick when a group of Mexicans and cowboys got into a brawl, something that happened between them at almost every dance we played. They didn't just square off and slug each other, but picked up anything that wasn't nailed down, and some things that were. People were getting knocked out all over the place and the blood flowed as if it came out of a sprinkler system.

In seconds, bottles and boards were flying up onstage. The musicians were sitting ducks in a shooting gallery, but we just kept playing, and playing louder. The first rule: Whenever a fight breaks out, play louder! I never understood why, unless it was to let the unconscious hear the band.

Pretty soon, it was too dangerous, even for seasoned saloon players like us, and I leaped from the bandstand and hid under it, shielding my guitar with my body, to protect the new Zephyr Deluxe Epiphone. I would have preferred a broken jaw over a broken guitar. Meanwhile, the kicking, biting, and slugging continued.

The next day, I read that seventeen people had been arrested, and eleven were hospitalized.

✶ ✶ ✶

Eventually I got my own band organized—the Western Wranglers—at a club called the Hitching Post. I remember once seeing my steel-guitar player, John Arvin, get hit in the head with a bottle and bleed all over his instrument, but he just kept on playing louder. The violence finally became so outrageous that the management was forced to hire a policeman with a loaded gun to stand in the doorway. Just try to have a good time at the point of a gun barrel.

Another time, a young Mexican named Little Joe walked in, sat down at the Hitching Post bar, and got into a loud argument with another man who said, "Little Joe, follow me outside and I'll shoot you."

Little Joe walked outside with his hands clenched into fists, and returned with them covering a bullet wound. He eased onto his stool and asked bartender Frank Ruiz if he could have a whiskey and an ambulance. They were provided, in that order.

Little Joe, ordinarily a night customer, was gone for three weeks during a hospitalization for a bullet that went through him, narrowly missing some vital organs. The night of the day he was released from the hospital, he returned to the bar to start another fight.

Moving back to New Mexico was different this time. I didn't go with a relative and I didn't live with one. I lived alone, in a motel. No matter how far away from home I had traveled, no matter how desperate I had been, I had always had at least one relative with me. Now I had four walls and one bad case of the blues.

I played in a bar with Uncle Dick, then walked across the road to my room, which was no more than a glorified cell. There was no television, no telephone, and it didn't matter. I had no one to call. I had a mountain of memories of life back in Arkansas and I climbed onto them every night. There is no cure for one of man's most painful experiences—homesickness—except to go home.

I wasn't about to do that.

One night I entered the old adobe motel owned by Tiny Weatherford, so named because he weighed about three hundred pounds. His wife, whom everyone called "Mrs. Tiny," pulled me aside.

"Campbell," she said, "you from Delight, Arkansas?"

I stared at her.

"Well, no, ma'am," I said shyly. "I'm actually from Billstown, but Billstown ain't on the map. So I tell people I'm from Delight."

"Well"—she paused—"I'm from Billstown."

"You're from Billstown, Arkansas?" I said.

"Yep," she said, and she meant it.

"Did you ever know Carrie Stone?" I asked.

"Went to school with her every day of my life."

"You know Wes Campbell?" I said.

"You mean one of them mean Campbell boys from Pisque?"

"That's him!" I shouted. "Well, they got married and I'm their son!"

She had gone to school with my mother in a community of about thirty people a thousand miles away. From that day she took me under her wing, but her care was not without a price. She applied a code of discipline to me, on the brink of my manhood, that was as strict as anything I had faced as a boy.

I obeyed.

Mr. Tiny was the bouncer at and once owned the Chesterfield Club, across the street. When he couldn't work, Mrs. Tiny filled in for him. She weighed about 240 pounds. She had owned nightclubs herself in her time and knew how to handle drunks. And she knew how to handle a lonesome teenage boy who had an interest in her daughter.

"I don't want you messin' with my daughter," she said.

I knew she was serious. She literally vowed to "bust my head" if I did.

She also didn't want me "messin' " with other women. At sixteen, I endured her bed checks, making sure I had no guest in the motel room that I was paying for, free and clear, from a salary of eighty dollars a week, the largest income I'd ever had in my life.

"Better not be no girls in here," she'd say, and barge right into the room, never waiting to see if I was dressed. She had a passkey. I couldn't lock her out, and wouldn't have tried. She would have kicked down the door.

I had friends for life in Mr. and Mrs. Tiny. Years later, I was playing the Las Vegas Hilton on New Year's Eve and Mrs. Tiny flew from Albuquerque to see me. Between shows, she decided to play some blackjack.

A drunk man next to her began to curse out loud, and it offended her deeply.

"I'll have you know that where I come from, men don't talk like that around ladies," she said.

"Oh, yeah?" said the drunk. "Well, up yours."

Mrs. Tiny never spoke a word, but calmly rose from her stool, walked over to the unruly man, and knocked him on his rear end right in the lobby of one of the swankiest hotels in Las Vegas. Security guards came from all directions and jerked the drunk from the floor. He thought they were going to throw out Mrs. Tiny, but instead they gave him the bum's rush.

"What are you doing?" the guy kept yelling. "She hit me."

The other gamblers applauded when Mrs. Tiny sat down and continued her game.

Chapter 4

★★★

I was developing a regular following at the Chesterfield Club in Albuquerque because of the exposure I was getting on television and as a nightclub singer. Singing in Uncle Dick Bills's band, at fifteen, marked the first time I encountered people who knew my songs by title and me by name.

I felt pretty important when people came by just to see me and say things such as, "I heard you sing 'San Antonio Rose' last week, and I brought my girlfriend out tonight so she could hear your version."

Up to now I had felt like a faceless entertainer, a fixture on the stage, like a microphone or an instrument. Self-confidence wasn't my strong suit.

I began to be aware of one regular customer, a pretty, young girl named Diane. I don't remember what she wore, although I recall my own wardrobe of cowboy shirt and trousers, string tie, and Western hat.

Diane was always with her mother whenever she was inside the club, as the house rules stipulated. Her mother was a friend of my uncle Dick, and I recall visiting with Diane regularly, but I can't remember how long I waited before asking her for a date. I do remember how old she was when she told me she was pregnant. She was fifteen.

I had broken Mrs. Tiny's rule and sneaked her into my motel room.

Diane was the first girl with whom I had ever had sex, and, according to the calendar, she got pregnant the first time we slept together. I had not used protection because I had never heard about it. My dad had given his children the tired, old lecture about the birds and the bees. He told us how we could make babies. He never told us how we could prevent making them.

I had known firsthand what it was like to be a traveler moving on a wing and a prayer; I had known hunger and cold, but I hadn't really known what it was like to be a man. Diane's pregnancy changed me from an aging child to a young grown-up. It eliminated forever my carefree days of adolescence.

Living in Mrs. Tiny's hotel, I had barely been able to provide for myself. Suddenly, I was expected to provide for three. My terror was exceeded only by my guilt. I had gotten a girl pregnant out of wedlock. My act was a direct contradiction to my conservative religious upbringing. I felt like a man branded with the symbol of sin. I just knew God was mad at me, and thought a lot more about His anger than His compassion. At a time when I needed to think clearly, my mind was clouded. I felt like a sinner's sinner.

Sex among teenagers was strictly forbidden in 1954. The phrase "free love" hadn't yet been coined. Society sat in judgment of any boy and girl who fell from Grace, regarding them as bad people who gave in to evil, not loving people who yielded to weakness.

The only thing I felt I could do to redeem myself in the eyes of God and society was to "do the right thing" by Diane and marry her. So I asked.

She said yes. Her mother said no.

It was as if her mother didn't want to acknowledge that her teenage daughter was pregnant. She all but forbade me to see Diane, and sent her to school just as she had before the pregnancy. She put her in tight jeans and, for a while, Diane continued to live with her parents while I lived in Mrs. Tiny's hotel. Perhaps her mom was practicing denial, and the reality of what had happened was, for her, too grim to face.

I got a one-bedroom apartment on Second Street North. Diane quit school and moved in with me. We were married by a judge at the Bernalillo County Courthouse with her dad as the only witness. There had been no maid of honor or groomsman present. The only ceremony was the frightened blinking of two teenagers looking upward at a judge's bench. He concluded our wedding and went on to his next case. We went to an apartment with no curtains.

We began the nervous countdown that all couples undergo while awaiting their firstborn. Meanwhile, I played in the smoky Chesterfield Club until closing time, then dragged myself home to Diane, who would be asleep from the fatigue of carrying a baby when she was little more than a child herself. Or she might be awake from the discomfort that comes from being pregnant, and the mental pain that comes from not being ready.

I feared the arrival of the baby and fatherhood and I felt guilty about my fear. I also feared for our impoverished state while we awaited the baby's arrival. We had no baby blankets, baby bed, diapers, or any of the other things the baby would need.

Glen Travis Campbell, Jr., was born several weeks early. He died a few days later. His lungs were not developed, and my first child never left the hospital until he went to a mortuary.

A few months earlier I had been a wide-eyed teenager filled with wanderlust. Now I was a man, against my will, who was carrying the weight of the world on his shoulders. And I was crumbling. The man who wanted to earn a living as a musician didn't even have the money for his only child's funeral. My father-in-law paid for it, and I'll always be grateful.

I cried for days over the death of my son. My parents, brothers, and sisters were a thousand miles away. I was thinking like an immature teenager whose mind was altered with grief. I remembered that my life had not been so hard until I married Diane, so I partially blamed her for everything. My thinking was unfair, but people are often unfair when their heart is breaking. I also blamed myself, thinking that I was being punished for having had sex before I was married. My Christian beliefs, at that point in my life, instilled more guilt than wisdom in me.

Then the temperament of our marriage changed. Diane began to attach more importance to her mother than to me. She spoke her mother's name more than mine. Everything in her life seemed to be points of reference centered around her mother.

I was trying to build a life for two struggling youngsters whose union had known life's greatest trauma, the death of an offspring. Diane was living in our house, but her home seemed to be with her mother. Any young husband would find that difficult. Diane, by now, was disapproving of virtually everything I did, and told me so. I expected her to defend me, yet she consistently sided with her mother.

As I look back on my first two marriages, I think I can cite a reason for their failures. I was the male, but not the man, of those households. I should have taken command more than I did. I was too passive, and often let the women run over me. They got their way, but they probably also lost respect for me.

I got along better with Diane's dad than I did with her. He was an Indian trader, and I used to drive him to the reservations in New Mexico. I was amused at how crafty he was, negotiating the prices of his beads and blankets to customers, whom he always left satisfied. I marveled at the way he could talk fast, but never at the expense of his integrity. He reminded me of my own rearing, in that I was taught that everybody has a job, and he or she is expected to do it. I thought that was how everybody was and, at seventeen, had no idea that some folks didn't actually carry out their duties. I certainly didn't think anyone lied. I was very naïve.

I didn't even realize what truly bad shape our marriage was in at

Christmastime in 1957, when Diane refused to go to Houston with me and our baby daughter, Debby. Imagine a wife not wanting to be with her husband and child at Christmastime, the ultimate family season.

So I started out across the December desert from New Mexico to Texas with a car that was sixteen years old and a daughter that was sixteen months old. I was armed with a few dollars, a spare tire, and a sack filled with diapers.

That was a lonely Christmas for me, even though I was with family and friends. There was a chill in the air that seemed to echo the loneliness I was feeling inside. I just thought my wife didn't want to be with me. It never dawned on me that she wanted to be with someone else.

On another occasion, she went with me all the way back to Arkansas and then didn't want to enter my parents' house. She sat in the car alone, blowing the horn, demanding that I come outside. She wanted to race back to New Mexico, and I was deeply embarrassed in front of my people. I remember forcing smiles and making excuses for Diane. My mom and dad didn't buy it, I'm sure, but they were too kind to press me.

One day a policeman friend asked to talk to me. I could see in his eyes that something heavy was on his mind.

"Glen," he said, "I don't know how to tell you this, but your wife is cheating on you."

I wasn't sure what he meant by cheating, and wondered if he was accusing my wife of stealing money from me. How, I wondered, would he know?

"Glen, there is another man in her life."

"What do you mean?" I thundered. I had plenty of criticisms about my wife, but that was not among them, and I sure wasn't going to let an outsider say something like that about her.

"Glen," he went on, "I was on patrol the other night and came on a car illegally parked. I walked up to it and caught the driver with your wife. I saw her with my own eyes."

So I confronted her. I asked her where she was at such and such a time and date. She gave an alibi. Then I presented her with a copy of the cop's citation. I don't recall if it listed her name, but it had enough information to make her confess to having been with a man at night in a parked car. I lost my temper and, for a split second, part of my mind. In my fury I pinned Diane against the wall and put my hand around her throat. I had been working out for weeks and was stronger than I had ever been. I lifted her off the floor by her head and drew back to hit her.

But I didn't. Instead, I ordered her to pack her things and get out, and that's what she did, taking the baby with her. I was left with the noon radio show, the Saturday morning television show with my uncle, the nighttime singing job, debts, an ugly and empty apartment, and the memories of what almost was.

Shakespeare wrote that it's better to have loved and lost than never to have loved at all. In 1958, I'm not sure you could have convinced me that was true.

I had dropped out of school and left my home. I was living the stories about which country songs are written. It didn't help that I was singing many of those tear-jerking ballads to throngs of equally lonely people.

I had undergone a two-year crash course in enough misery to last a lifetime. But, I would find, there were more heartaches down the line for Glen Campbell from Billstown.

Many more.

✮✮

Chapter 5

I don't want to talk about Glen Campbell for his book," said Billie Jean Campbell, my former wife. "I don't even want my name in it. Put my name in it and I'll sue you."

The words were spoken via telephone to Tom Carter, who helped me write this book. I had asked Tom to call Billie for information regarding our sixteen-year marriage. She told Tom that I had been a bad father and blamed me for one of our children's legal problems. The child was awaiting sentencing on a forgery conviction in California that Billie said related to his drug problem. She said that was my fault too.

She went on to say that I had neglected my children from each of my marriages. She said I gave them nothing but money and accused me of trying to buy their love.

She even refused to help Tom construct the chronology of our relationship. She wouldn't tell him how or where we met. She told him that she was tape-recording her conversation with him and added that she was prepared to sue him and me if I even told people we had been married.

I can't tell people. They already know.

I'm truly sorry that she felt the way she did. I won't debate her accusations, although I certainly could. I'll only say that the things I do and the things I once did are not the same. I am a new man inside my old body. I have been forgiven by God for my transgressions, and hope that Billie and others I might have wronged have forgiven me too. (Billie died on February 2, 1993, of cancer. I'll discuss that later.)

There is no way I can write about my history and not talk about the woman to whom I was married longer than any other. Billie was a good person, and very strong-willed. She was a devoted mother with whom I had differences regarding our children's discipline. I should have been more assertive as a husband and father.

I met the former Billie Jean Nunley in 1959 while playing at the Hitching Post in Albuquerque. After my divorce, I was in no hurry to become seriously involved with anyone. I sure wasn't looking for a wife when I began to notice a girl named Nancy who came into the club often and was usually accompanied by Billie.

Knowing Billie as I later did, I suspect she began flirting with me simply out of meanness toward Nancy. Billie was quite spirited, as anyone who knew her would agree.

Billie had recently moved to Albuquerque from her home in Carlsbad, New Mexico, after graduating from a beauty school. She used to prance in front of the bandstand to get my attention, and I knew it. I thought she wanted me to ask her to dance, so I did, and she declined. I asked several times before she consented.

I tried to see her outside the club, but she resisted that too. I asked many times to take her home before she finally let me.

She lived with her sister, Peggy, and I thought I could get in good with Billie by picking up points with Peggy. So I began to drop by their place regularly to help out with household chores. That spring I mowed their lawn more times than I care to count.

Billie still didn't want to go out with me. Nancy was dating a guy in my band and one night we all went over to Billie's house after the club closed. Billie got out of bed and made coffee and she and I wound up talking almost until daylight. That was our first real conversation.

I knew Billie liked me and I was frustrated because she didn't respond to my attention as quickly as I had wanted. I thought she should appreciate that I was willing to get involved with her even though I thought I never would again with anyone.

A short time into our courtship, Billie returned to Carlsbad to see her parents. I got wind that she was also going to see an old boyfriend and I became jealous. I persuaded Nancy to come along with me to drop in on Billie unannounced.

I got off work at one A.M. Sunday at the Hitching Post, drove the 280 miles, and arrived at daylight and asked Billie's mother to wake her up. I spent the day with Billie, drove back to Albuquerque, then played a full show Monday night. I traveled almost six hundred miles and was awake about thirty-six hours just to be near her. Young love generates a lot of energy.

When Billie returned to Albuquerque, we began to date regularly. A lot of folks might not think some of the things we did were overly romantic. We hunted and fished together, and I suppose there isn't a lot of sentimentality associated with cleaning game. But I had come from the country and had brought my habits with me.

I asked Billie to marry me a few weeks after meeting her. I knew she thought I was rushing things, but I felt deeply for her. She said she would have to think about it. That made me wonder about her feelings. I didn't have to think about a thing and neither should she, I thought.

Billie finally said yes, and I took the weekend off from the Hitching Post to get hitched. We drove to Las Vegas, and on September 20, 1959, we were married. We stayed at the Desert Inn, and when we were checking out I tried to pay for our lodging with a payroll check from the Hitching Post. The hotel refused to accept it. I had no other money, and walked out of the hotel without paying my bill. However, I didn't feel bad about it because I had made a sincere effort to pay.

Years later I played the Desert Inn and told them I still owed them eighty-five dollars for lodging in 1959. The management never collected.

Neither Billie nor I had ever been to Las Vegas. I was astonished at the sight of the towering hotels and the sea of flashing lights. Until then I had seen nightlife only in smoky cowboy bars with their low ceilings and plain decor.

As a musician I was used to being ignored by the dancing and drinking crowd. In Las Vegas, customers actually listened to the music. They sat still and paid attention to the lyrics and arrangements. The first show I saw there was Bobby Darin's, and I was so envious of him. He sang "Splish Splash" and "Mack the Knife," two of his big hits. He wore a tuxedo and appeared with a full orchestra. His whole presentation rang of class. I never dreamed then that I would someday play the major Vegas show rooms with a full orchestra and light show.

I remember watching Darin's guitar player and thinking that I could play as well as he could. I returned to Albuquerque with renewed determination to make it as a guitarist. Norm, a steel guitarist playing the bars around Albuquerque, was an avid fan of Django Reinhardt, the world's foremost jazz guitarist, who had died in 1953.

I would go to Norm's house and listen to those Reinhardt tapes for hours. Norm thought I was going to wear them out, so he agreed to let me take them to a radio station to have them reproduced.

I was consumed by Reinhardt's chord changes and arrangements and tried to analyze and reproduce his techniques. I strained to hear every detail on the scratchy recordings, which were made in the late 1930s. Many of these records have been duplicated on compact disc today. The quality isn't good, but nobody cares. Reinhardt was a guitarist's guitarist, and many of his fans were actually students who were so mesmerized by his style that they overlooked the recording quality.

I focused solely on guitar, determined to become the world's best player. Singing, for me, was only incidental. If someone had told me then that my biggest hit records would be vocals, I would have been astonished, and probably disappointed.

Playing at the Hitching Post lost its appeal after I saw Las Vegas. First, there was my new inspiration, which compelled me to focus on Reinhardt and try things I never had before on the guitar. And then there was my marriage. I didn't like Billie working days, since I got to see her only a little while before I went to work nights. I wanted our schedules to be more compatible.

I remembered the guitarist in Vegas, who was one of the best or he wouldn't have been in the orchestra. I figured he did recording-session work in California. If he could do it, I was sure I could do it too. I hadn't seen him play anything that I couldn't play.

And so I began my discussions with myself. Should I go to Holly-wood and try to make it in the major leagues? I was twenty-three and in love—in love with my new wife, and in love with my music. I didn't see why I couldn't have both.

I thought Billie could work as a hairstylist in Los Angeles and figured she could keep us from starving if I didn't get work right away.

Soon, we would take the plunge.

I went exploring in Hollywood with Jerry Jackson, a friend who worked at Albuquerque's KLOS, a station with various musical for-mats. His boss leased a car for him and we arrived in Hollywood in style, in a 1958 four-passenger Thunderbird.

Upon rolling into town, I was as wide-eyed as I had been upon my arrival in Las Vegas. I was speechless seeing the traffic, which was bumper-to-bumper back then, before the completion of the city's elab-orate freeway system. Palm trees waved gracefully in the ocean breeze, in stark contrast to the rigid cacti of New Mexico. The girls were blond, the men were muscular, and everyone was tan. I know that's an exaggeration, but the whole city and everyone in it looked like a giant movie set filled with actors.

Hollywood then was the recording capital of the nation. New York City had undergone a recording heyday in the 1940s and through the

1950s with cabarets, Tin Pan Alley, and saloon crooners. By now, 1960, the legendary Sun Records studio in Memphis, Tennessee, had slowed down after producing such stalwart rockabilly singers as Johnny Cash, Jerry Lee Lewis, Carl Perkins, Roy Orbison, and, of course, Elvis Presley.

Many of those same artists, including Elvis, had gotten into the movies in Hollywood, and into audio recording in Hollywood studios.

The deeper Jerry and I drove into Los Angeles, the more my enthusiasm mounted. Jerry, who was considering making an album himself, had connections that enabled us to watch a recording session. Although I had been in television and radio stations before, some of which had primitive recording facilities, that day with Jerry marked the first time for me in a major recording studio where records were made for major labels. I was awestruck.

Recording then wasn't as complicated as it is today, when every instrument and every vocalist has a microphone. In 1960, many singers shared one microphone, and so did many musicians. Nonetheless, the place looked complicated to me, with its shiny chrome microphones and miles of cables. The studio control room had more knobs than a jet fighter. I couldn't imagine how the engineer knew which knob to turn when. (Today's boards, by comparison, have perhaps a thousand more dials and knobs than I saw in 1960.)

When the session began, I watched intensely. Many of the guitarists had backgrounds in jazz and did not use a capo—a mechanical device that fits on the guitar neck to help the player make chords. Yet, the chords they were forming left open strings to achieve the sound that they wanted.

I wouldn't have done it that way, and thought I could do some of the runs and chord progressions a little bit better than what I'd heard there.

I stayed in Hollywood about two weeks, scouting nightclubs to be sure I could get a job. That was my final requirement before I made the decision to return to New Mexico for Billie and our move.

There were a lot of musicians around Albuquerque who rushed to get my old job at the Hitching Post. My group disbanded, but not before the management offered us a thirty-five-dollar weekly raise to stay. The offer was too little too late.

I bid farewell to fans and friends who had supported me in the nightclubs, my daily radio show, and the Saturday morning kiddie program.

I owned a late-model Dodge that was, unbeknownst to me, worn out. I later discovered that the dealer from whom I had bought the car had disconnected the odometer and used it as a towing vehicle for stranded cars and trucks. There was no telling how many miles were actually on the car, and how hard they had been acquired.

So I got rid of it. I had three hundred dollars, Billie's 1957 Chevrolet, a trailer with all our belongings, and a puppy I had bought to keep her company while I was playing at the Hitching Post. The car, girl, dog, and I set out for the Golden State. We looked like a modern version of the Okie migration to California during the Great Depression.

We went through the desert in the daytime with no air-conditioning and tied water bottles to the grill to keep the car from overheating. I had heard nightmarish stories about motorists getting stranded under the scorching southwestern sun.

In Los Angeles, Billie and I checked into a cheap motel and began our search for a house. We found a modest and somewhat ugly place for $105 a month. The most we had ever paid in Albuquerque was $65. The landlord wanted a month's rent in advance, so that cut severely into my $300 nest egg.

I thought I had landed a paying job in a grimy club and I wanted to celebrate. Billie's birthday was August 1, about two weeks after we arrived in California. I spent almost all the money I had left for her birthday.

I started work the next day in Anaheim, a Los Angeles suburb. It wasn't far away, but it took a long time to drive to the club.

I worked two weeks without the pay I desperately needed. I would go home each night and Billie and I would juggle our funds to stay alive for the check we thought was coming.

It never did. My first paying job in the world-famous entertainment mecca of Los Angeles didn't pay me a thing. The club owner simply ripped off the band and me. I couldn't sue him because I didn't have a contract or the money to hire a lawyer. Anyway, my scared and desperate mind wasn't thinking that way.

Billie and I were a step away from the street. We ate fast-food tacos for fifteen cents sometimes three times a day. Billie cooked beans, and we often had those for breakfast, lunch, and dinner.

Billie searched hard for a job in a beauty shop, but to no avail since she didn't have a California license. She could have gotten one after passing a test, but there was a fee for the test and the books needed to prepare for it. We couldn't afford it.

They say nothing puts stress on a young marriage like financial pressure. If that's true, our fledgling marriage must have been tested to the limit. I was looking frantically for a job in a strange and fast city where I didn't even know how to look up a street address.

Billie at last got a job and I hated it that she found employment before me. After all, it had been my idea to come west to pursue my career. I had no career, and Billie had a job that was totally unrelated to her profession. She was a cashier in a bank, and the second day on the job had to ask her boss for an advance on her salary. The money was as welcome in our household as the manna from Heaven that fed the Old Testament Israelites.

We were still broke, I was still unemployed, and we would occasionally go hungry. But we were as low as we would ever go again.

The only direction left was up.

✩✩✩

Chapter 6

*W*hile still in Albuquerque I had gone to a concert at a civic auditorium starring The Champs, a group with which I would get a job in October 1960. Jimmy Seals and Dash Crofts, who later became famous on their own as Seals and Crofts, were also members of The Champs. The band was known for its biggest hit, "Tequila." The Champs opened for Jerry Fuller, who had recorded hits such as "Tennessee Waltz" and "Betty, My Angel." I went backstage that night in Albuquerque to ask for Fuller's autograph. He eventually became one of my best friends, and he still teases me about once asking for his signature.

Following the concert, I had to sing at my nightclub engagement, and Jerry came along. He liked what he heard, and he too encouraged me to move to Los Angeles. I eventually stayed with him in L.A. very briefly before I moved Billie to the West Coast. He and I hustled jobs singing demonstration tapes for other artists. He got ten dollars for each song and I got twenty dollars because I also played guitar.

Jerry went on to write and produce some big records for some big artists, including Rick Nelson. Fuller tells a story about having written

Rick's biggest hit, "Travelin' Man." He actually wrote the song for Sam Cooke and took it to Cooke's producer. The guy played it and the sound leaked into a room next door in which Rick's bass player was hanging out. He walked into the producer's office and said, "Where is that song about travelin'? I'd like to play it for Rick."

The producer had already thrown it away. He dug it out of the trash and said, "Here, you can have the thing."

A giant record was almost thrown away—literally.

Fuller, Dave Burgess, and I sang background on all of Nelson's master recordings after "Travelin' Man," replacing the Jordanaires. I also played lead guitar on many of Rick's hits before going on tour with him in 1964.

Fuller and I had many interesting experiences during my early California days. He found a group in a San Diego bowling alley called Gary Puckett and the Union Gap. I was listening to the radio one day and heard a song called "Woman, Woman." I called the disc jockey, who happened to be Bob Kingsley, today's host of the nationally syndicated *American Country Countdown.* I asked him if I could have the song, which had been recorded by country singer Jimmy Payne. Kingsley told me to come get the record, as there was no interest in it among his listeners. Fuller produced the song on the Union Gap, and it became a million-selling record.

Fuller would eventually repay me when his record label turned down a song he produced on the Union Gap. He called me in 1969 and offered me the rejected tune.

"Do you want a hit?" he said.

That's how I acquired "Dreams of the Everyday Housewife." The music business was sometimes as easy as it was fun in those days.

Jerry was like a lot of talented people—diversified. He had his writing, singing, and producing interests, but he also developed an interest in motion pictures. He had earlier decided that he wanted to be a Hollywood stuntman.

One night, I went with Jerry to North Hollywood's legendary

Palomino Club. I was singing with the band when Fuller decided he would use the occasion to rehearse his stuntman skills. But he didn't bother to tell me. He instead enlisted the help of his brother, who I didn't know and who probably couldn't see through the smoke-filled dance hall. Jerry told his brother to hold his hand near the side of his face.

"I'll swing and hit your hand," Fuller later told me he had said. "It will sound and look as if I hit you in the face. This is how it's done in the movies."

So the "fight" broke out. Fuller threw his fake punch, and his brother, on cue, retaliated. But his brother had been drinking. Instead of hitting Fuller's hand beside his face, he hit him directly in the mouth.

Blood flew.

"I could see my career going down the tubes," Fuller said in the spring of 1993. "My lip had busted wide open and I was still trying to be a singer."

I saw the "fight" from the stage and jumped over the footlights.

"I really thought old Glen was going to take up for me," Fuller said. I had left the band in mid-song, and they just kept playing, curious about where their lead singer had gone.

By now, Fuller had charged into the men's room. I was right behind him. He thought I had followed him in there to chase away his assailant. I spun him around, looked squarely into his bloody face, and threw up everywhere.

I could have never had a career as a bouncer.

When Fuller got me the job as a Champ, I was given a bright red suit and told to have it altered to fit. I calmly took the garment to the car, and waited until we were in motion before I began to scream with excitement. I hadn't wanted to seem too eager. I was actually going to play in a "name" group with a hit record. And I was going to be paid a whopping one hundred dollars a week. I had been in Los Angeles for three months. The good news was that I would have a steady check. The bad news was that I would have to be out of town and away from my new bride, but I had no other choice. I left Billie in the strange city to which I had brought her.

I had known what it was like to work nights while my wife was home alone, but at least I was in the same city and could return to her after work. Going back to roach-infested motels instead of returning to my own modest home every night was awful.

We didn't get very far ahead saving money. Whenever I would get a couple of days off, I would spend whatever money I had on a plane ticket home. That pretty much depleted me. The Champs were organized by a guy who took 40 percent of the group's income, leaving the remaining 60 percent to be split five ways among us, and we had to pay out our own expenses. I found out real quick that the "big time" could pay small money.

I was incredibly trusting during my early days in the music business. People either didn't pay me at all or they didn't pay me my just due.

The little money that Billie and I had left over went to my little girl, Debby, back in Albuquerque.

My first exposure to screaming audiences happened with The Champs. Live rock 'n' roll really released something in teenagers back then, and I used to wonder how anyone in the crowd could hear anything from the stage.

Today's electronic equipment is refined and can project music above audience noise. But 1960s audiences could scream above any sound system we had. Monitors weren't especially good either. It was seat-of-your-pants showmanship.

We played a circuit, moving from one auditorium to the next, following other successful rock shows. I remember being in Clear Lake, Iowa, in the same hall in which Buddy Holly had just played before he boarded the doomed flight with the Big Bopper and Ritchie Valens.

We drove a leased car and pulled a trailer from show to show, putting 105,000 miles on the 1959 Pontiac in nine months. We'd travel all night—five bodies cramped together with musical instruments. We often rented one motel room for all of us, where we took showers if it had one and baths if it didn't. Then it was back to the car for more miles and music.

I quit that grind in May 1961, when Billie was four months' pregnant. We went through a stressful summer awaiting the birth while I played odd jobs here and there.

We suffered a lot of anxiety about how we were going to provide the baby's bare essentials, and were relieved when a friend agreed to give Billie a baby shower. Billie went to the party and became sick. She was taken to the hospital, where she gave birth to our first child on October 8, 1961.

Kelli Glen was born six weeks early with a lung disorder and spent her first night in an incubator. That night in the waiting room thirty-three years ago, I could not help thinking about my first child, who didn't live long enough to leave the hospital. I paced and prayed all night.

I was not overly spiritual at the time, but there is a scripture, Proverbs 22:6, that says, "Train up a child in the way he should go; and when he is old, he will not depart from it." Due to my rearing, I have never forgotten how to pray. There have been times when I felt my prayers never penetrated the ceiling. I have prayed when I've been discouraged, drunk, and disoriented. But I prayed nonetheless. I'm convinced that although my prayers weren't always answered, they were always heard. God has not always done things according to my timetable, but I know now He's never been late.

At daylight, hours after our child's birth, a doctor told Billie and me that the baby would live.

We had no health insurance, and the medical bills, in the face of no income, were staggering. I would listen to the baby cry and become restless, wanting to work and provide for my family. But the only work I could find was looking for work.

I became so desperate that I called the skid-row bars near what was then the downtown Los Angeles bus station. They were filthy old dumps filled with rummies who liked country music. The old men were mostly drunk, so their musical tastes weren't very discriminating. The bar owners didn't have to hire good musicians, so they didn't.

I could earn about as much there as I could playing just for tips. I would rather have worked at a car wash than to shop my talent in those dives. Working men's honky-tonks had been one thing. Bars whose inhabitants slept at the Rescue Mission were another. I returned from a day of going in and out of those joints not knowing where I would work, but knowing where I wouldn't.

I heard about a job on a Los Angeles television show called *Cal's Corral.* I had visions of a show similar to the one I did in Albuquerque with my uncle Dick Bills's band, and later my own. I expected the Los Angeles show to be more slick in its production, since Los Angeles was the second largest city in the nation and the home to international show business.

I was wrong.

The show's comedy value surpassed its musical quality. People tuned in just to laugh at some of the would-be singers.

The whole idea behind moving to Hollywood had been to advance my career. I realized that I might erase my chances of ever being taken seriously as a guitarist if I became identified with that show. As badly as I needed the little money that the program paid, I was smart enough to look at the long term, so I quit.

I did another nonpaying gig in Santa Fe Springs, California, and then reunited with a couple of players from the old Champs. We put together a band and got a job in Van Nuys, a Los Angeles suburb, at the Crossbow. It turned out to be the best steady job I had had since Albuquerque.

The club had a good reputation for talent, and many stars had played there on their way up, including Elvis Presley. The clientele wasn't rough, the salary was a livable wage, and, best of all, I could come home nights to my young family. It would be a lie to say that my life was financially rosy from that day forward, but my job at the Crossbow marked the end of my heavy dues-paying days. It would be a long time before I would be rich, but I would never again wonder if there would be a next meal, or have to live on a diet of beans three times a day, as Billie and I had done.

Shortly afterward, I went to work during the day at American Music, a song publishing company. One of its staff writers went on to become one of the most successful record producers in country, rock 'n' roll, and popular music. His name is Jimmy Bowen.

Bowen would eventually produce Dean Martin, Frank Sinatra, Reba McEntire, George Strait, and others, including myself. He is currently the president of Liberty Records, whose biggest star now is Garth Brooks.

He and I were little more than struggling songwriters and demonstration-tape producers in 1961, although he had played in a successful rock 'n' roll band with Buddy Knox, and had had a hit record of his own called "I'm Sticking with You." Bowen sang the song at New York City's world-famous Apollo Theater, and was one of the first white artists to appear there.

Bowen and I were supposed to write and record songs to entice celebrity artists to record them. I was pretty good at it because I had studied many singers so intensely. I could impersonate them, so we could target our songs and pitch them right at the artist we wanted.

My ability to sing like Marty Robbins, for example, eventually landed a few Robbins cuts for the company. I still like doing impersonations, and have thought about incorporating them into my show, since so many folks enjoy them. In 1991 I recorded the soundtrack for a feature-length animated film called *Rock-a-Doodle,* in which I sang like Elvis Presley. Some folks thought an old Elvis recording had been resurrected and set to animation.

Being a staff writer at American was a new experience—writing by the clock. I went into an office of sorts almost every day and wrote, whether or not I was inspired. A lot of successful songwriters don't approach the craft with that kind of practicality, and instead write only when they're in the mood. Most of contemporary songwriting is done the way Bowen and I did it in 1961, particularly in Nashville, where writers for the big publishing houses are expected to sit down and write for a certain number of hours each week in an office.

The first song I wrote that became a hit was co-written with Jerry Capeheart and titled "Turn Around, Look at Me." I eventually recorded the song myself and even sang it on Dick Clark's *American Bandstand*. It is a well-structured song, but Bowen had completely forgotten about it until recently, when he was interviewed about me. He wrote down the title and said he might produce it with one of his young artists. I've never received any royalties due me for that hit, but I did record it for my gold-selling album in 1968 that featured "By the Time I Get to Phoenix."

There is a footnote to the story about "Turn Around, Look at Me." The song became a strong regional hit in California, where I was asked to do radio and television interviews to promote the record. Interviewing was new to me, and I was coached through the process by Mike Borchetta, one of the best record-promotion men in town.

Mike put me in front of a television camera, I answered questions, and the whole thing went fine, except that my fly was open. Mike noticed, and told the producer he wanted me to tape the interview again, with my trousers zipped.

Nothing would convince the guy.

"We'll just edit the video," the producer said. "I'll see that the screen is just a head-and-shoulders shot, and no one will know about his open fly."

The guy lied.

Mike and I played golf after the interview and returned to our hotel later that night to watch my interviewing premiere. There, for all the world to see, was my shirttail protruding through my open zipper.

In 1961, I was again victimized by my trust in others. It still hadn't settled into my mind that not everyone does what he says he's going to do. I took the word of an official at American Music that I would be paid what was duly mine. I'm not sure I even wrote under a contract.

I took instead small weekly advance payments against future royalties—royalties that I would never be paid.

The best thing by far that came out of my days at American Music was my friendship with Bowen, which lasts to this day. He has produced my records for numerous labels. He also used me as a guest artist on many demonstration and master sessions in the early 1960s, including Frank Sinatra's legendary "Strangers in the Night."

Jimmy can hear a potential hit song with incredible accuracy and he is open to improvising. He doesn't believe in doing something one way merely because that's how it was done previously. He is one of the music industry's biggest assets in that he remains in charge while unafraid to accept suggestions from those who are not.

He swears that I used to drive by the studios in the early 1960s, and if I saw enough cars in the parking lot to indicate that a recording session was under way, I would stop in and get a seat in the session, even though I hadn't been scheduled. I don't remember that, but the story is indicative of Bowen's flexibility.

One of my favorite Bowen stories happened later, when he was my producer for Capitol Records. I decided to record "Amazing Grace," the spiritual standard that is my favorite song of all time. I've closed my live show with that number for twenty years, and still sing it to this day. I wanted to record that masterpiece and end the song with an instrumental section on bagpipes. I told Bowen what I wanted to do. I venture that the suggestion marked one of the first times anyone had used bagpipes on a song for a major record label. Bowen shook his head and said, "Pretty unorthodox," but he also said we could use bagpipes.

Bowen has nicknames for his friends, and mine was "Arkie," obviously because I'm from Arkansas. People who hire the musicians for a recording session are called contractors. Bowen used Don Lanier, a guitar player, whom he called "Dirt."

"Dirt," Bowen said, "Arkie wants a bagpipe player. Can you find one?"

Dirt scanned the directory of union musicians and found only two bagpipe players in all of Los Angeles.

"Do you want the young one or the old one?" Dirt asked Bowen.

"The young one," Bowen replied.

The next day, a seventy-six-year-old bagpipe player showed up.

Daniel Hood was the real thing. He wore a Scottish cap, a clan plaid, and kilts, and although he belonged to the musicians' union, we wondered if he had ever made a record. Perhaps not, as there was little call for bagpipe players in any 1970s commercial-music format.

Bowen explained that I wanted to sing the song and then let the bagpipe fade gradually into silence.

The old man somehow got the idea that it was his job to make the sound fade. He didn't realize it would be done electronically by the engineer in the control room.

I sang my part, the background singers were magnificent on the high bridge, and then the bagpipe player began to wail. He did his verse, and then it was time for his instrument to be faded out. At that point, he walked to the studio door, opened it, and went out playing down the hall and into the parking lot. He was marching and blowing away. He thought he should simply walk away from the microphone to achieve the fading effect.

The kicker is that it would have worked, except that everyone in the studio fell down laughing and their noise leaked onto the tape. We had to do the whole thing over again.

I visited later with that old man, and he taught me how to play bagpipes. We recorded the song again in two weeks with me on the wind instrument. The result was a Capitol album that sold more than a million copies.

Another example of Bowen's willingness to try anything that works was a session I did with Buddy Greco in the 1960s for an album whose title was *Buddy Greco Sings the Beatles.*

Greco wanted to know who would sing harmony and Bowen suggested me.

"Who'll play rhythm?" Greco asked.

"Glen Campbell."

"Who'll play lead?" Greco continued.

"Glen Campbell."

"Who'll do the acoustic fill?" he asked.

"Glen Campbell."

Greco wanted to "improve" on the Beatles' melodies, and was getting irritated because I had such a big part in his record. Bowen placed us side by side in the studio and put the sheet music Greco had written on my music stand.

I don't read music. I picked up my sheet music and unknowingly set it back upside down. Greco was wailing away on his melody and disagreeing with my harmony, and then he saw my inverted sheet music. He called Bowen aside and told him to kick me off the session because I couldn't read.

"Yes, he can," Bowen said. "He can read English, and, after all, that's the language we're recording in."

Greco persisted, but Bowen told him that he was running the session and that I was the best harmony singer in L.A. He even told him I could harmonize with the sound of a backfiring truck.

The studio time clock was running, and Greco was then a much bigger star than I, but Bowen stood firm for me simply because he believed in me. He exhibited the kind of professionalism and friendship that was a rarity to me during my foot-wetting days in Los Angeles.

Chapter 7

★★★

I began to work less at American Music because my association with Jimmy Bowen brought me more studio work. Songwriting, despite the paltry advances against royalties, was, by its nature, a risk. You couldn't make big money unless you wrote a big hit. I don't know how many scores of songs I wrote at American, but I never received a single royalty check that I know of.

"Turn Around, Look at Me" was my biggest song, but it was not followed by very many memorable tunes. Many were recorded by other singers, at least as album cuts. My staff-writing days were more than thirty years ago, and the person who cheated me is probably broke by now or has found a way to hide his money. He knows who he is, and knows that I know what he did to me.

Anyway, I'm happy with the way my career turned out. Who knows, if I had been paid fairly for my writing, I might have foolishly spent my entire career as a staff songwriter. What a loss that would have been for me in light of all that began to happen five years later, when I had stopped pushing songs and started singing and playing.

While I was a full-time studio musician I worked for a jingle company and recorded radio and television commercials. I was paid a small salary and received a residual each time one of my commercials aired, in relation to the number of markets in which the commercials played.

I played and sang about all kinds of household products, from water bottles to room deodorizers. Barry Manilow did the same thing in his early career, and came up with the commercial for McDonald's that went, "You deserve a break today." My biggest jingle "hit" was a Lady Clairol ditty, the lyrics of which were, "Is it true blondes have more fun?" It aired on the networks during prime time and sponsored some of the most popular television shows of the early and middle 1960s.

In 1991, I was on Bob Costas's interview show, and he aired the old black-and-white television spot. The commercial shows girls on a California beach wearing two-piece but concealing swimsuits, because modesty was still in vogue back then. The camera zooms in on a cute brunette, forlorn on a beach because a blonde next to her is getting all the male attention. She uses a Lady Clairol bleach, and the next scene shows her again on the beach, but this time blond and surrounded by muscular men. You can hear my tenor voice singing the high refrain while a bass singer intones, "Look at her go, look at her go." That voice belongs to Leon Russell.

Leon, who was struggling as hard as I to forge a career, became one of the most celebrated rock 'n' roll players of the 1970s. He starred with Joe Cocker in the successful motion picture *Mad Dogs and Englishmen,* and wrote hit songs for the Rolling Stones, Joe Cocker, the Carpenters, and others. His "A Song for You" and "Delta Lady" became rock standards. "A Song for You" was rereleased as recently as the spring of 1993 by Ray Charles.

Leon's straight-ahead rock 'n' roll tours drew sell-out crowds in America's and the United Kingdom's biggest stadiums. He starred with Bob Dylan and George Harrison in the *Concert for Bangladesh,* a motion picture and soundtrack whose proceeds went to relief efforts for victims of natural disaster in that third-world country. He billed himself as the "master of time and space" and grew waist-length hair that draped over aviator sunglasses. His entire persona was mysterious and intriguing.

In 1963, Leon Russell was an average-looking guy who was trying to stay alive doing whatever he could until he could do something better in the Southern California entertainment scene.

★★★

I recorded another commercial, "Hoffman's Famous Cup of Gold," for the Hoffman's Candy Company. A friend was staying with me temporarily after trying his luck in the record industry in Nashville. He needed something to do, and I needed another voice, so I asked him to help me with the commercial. He was awaiting the release of his first record from Nashville, and was biding his time and stretching his money, hoping for a hit. Nashville had not been overly kind to him. He worked as a hotel bellhop there to stay alive while struggling to get a record deal.

He delivered a corny narration about relaxing in a rocking chair, then I sang, "It's Hoffman's famous cup of gold and peanut clusters. / Hoffman's candies make your taster tingle 'cause they're made with a lot of good stuff."

Pretty goofy, but it must have sold a lot of candy. I made twelve hundred dollars each time that commercial aired in a region, and it aired in twenty regional markets. The checks were the largest residuals I had ever seen, and were a great relief, helping to pull me out of debt.

I didn't make as much as my friend did from his first record, which came out about six weeks after he did the commercial with me. The song was called "Dang Me," and sold more than a million copies in a few days for Roger Miller.

He went on to write and record genuine American standards, such as "England Swings," "In the Summertime," and others, including his biggest hit, "King of the Road." Roger eventually hosted his own network television show and was a staff writer for thirty-five years for

Tree International, the largest country-music publishing house in the world. But he was literally singing for peanuts (and toffee) when we cut the candy commercial.

Roger was an impish practical joker with a rapid-fire mind. He kept me, and others around me, laughing constantly. His humor was as intelligent as it was funny. People liked him, and because he played pranks on them, they played them on him.

✶✶✶

In 1961 I met a talented man of another variety. Stan Schneider helped me with my income-tax return that year. He has prepared my return annually ever since. He eventually became my business and personal manager. He runs my affairs to this day. Our relationship's longevity is a testament to his skill and integrity. He is one of the most honest men I've ever known.

I met a lot of outstanding talent on my way up. There probably never was a time when I brushed shoulders with more legends than when I worked as a studio musician. I played for scale—sixty-five dollars for a three-hour session and sometimes double as the session leader. I was employed by such successful record producers in Hollywood as Jimmy Bowen and Quincy Jones.

It took me a while to fall into the clique of studio players, but once I did my talent sustained me, and my telephone rang regularly. In 1963, my instrumentals and vocals were heard on 586 recorded songs. Each of the sessions, with a few exceptions, was recorded "live," meaning there was no electronic overdubbing. Records today are usually recorded one voice or instrument at a time. In the mid-1960s, we played and sang simultaneously during the recording.

Quincy Jones first used me to play a goofy acoustic lead guitar similar to Miller's in "Dang Me." The song was for the soundtrack of the motion picture *In the Heat of the Night*. A policeman drops a dime into a jukebox and I sing, "Bow-legged Polly and a knock-kneed Paul." It was my first soundtrack recording, and it was certainly among the less distinguished, but it got me into the Jones family of players. He called me to play several times afterward.

I was still trying to get accustomed to being around some of America's music legends. I would try to act cool around them, as though I were not overly impressed, but the fact is I was often envious and starstruck. I had to act like an associate, not a fan, when I played with these greats. Many times, the star would enter the studio and the recording would begin without any conversation. Some of these people were just being respectful of the studio clock, whose ticking translated into money. Others didn't talk to the musicians simply because they were snobs.

One of my earliest thrills came when Bowen called for me to play rhythm guitar in a Frank Sinatra session. I had been in Hollywood about three years, but there was still more Arkansas than California in me. Being indirectly summoned by Sinatra was like a soldier being summoned by General George Patton. I tried but failed to contain my awe. I wasn't intimidated, just overwhelmed.

Sinatra has been at the top of the entertainment world since 1942, when Benny Goodman introduced him as an "added attraction" at the Paramount Theater in New York City. In show business, there is no arguing with tenure. His dreamy voice was vocal satin.

I was one of four guitarists, and the only one to play in E-flat with a capo. "Strangers in the Night" was to become a classic. We rehearsed the song fifteen times before Sinatra arrived. Either he was late, or Bowen had told him a later time than he had told the rest of us. No one dared to inquire.

We recorded only three versions, or "takes," when Bowen stopped the session and selected the first rendition. The multimillion-copy version of that song was recorded on the first take. Bowen is a master.

There were perhaps thirty musicians in the studio that day, including a string section, so who should wind up standing right next to Sinatra's singing booth? Me.

I couldn't take my eyes off him. I couldn't believe that I was in the same room, much less that I was playing for him. Each time I looked at him he was already looking at me. I thought that he was impressed with my playing, and that he was taking note that I was the only guitarist using a capo. I was positive I had impressed him, particularly after I saw him talking to Bowen and looking in my direction after the session.

"Bowen," I asked, "was Frank talking about me?"

"Yes."

"What did he say?" I asked anxiously.

"He wanted to know who the fag guitar player was. Frank said you never stopped looking at him, and he thought you were lusting."

Sinatra, except to say hello, didn't talk to many people in the studio that day. When I met him again years later, he told me he had forgotten the faces of the musicians at that "Strangers in the Night" session, perhaps his second-most popular song after "My Way."

There were two singers with whom I worked whose sessions could be called "loose." Bobby Darin was a big star of the day, and Elvis Presley was the biggest star of all time, so they took liberties in the recording studio, with no regard to production costs.

I was very impressed with Elvis. First impressions are the most lasting, and Elvis made his on the national consciousness in 1956 as a hip-swinging ambassador of rock 'n' roll on *The Ed Sullivan Show.* So much attention was paid to Elvis's popularity and gyrations that his singing talent was often overlooked. He had tone, power, and range, and he combined all three to deliver a song with feeling. I think history will record Elvis Presley as one of America's great vocalists.

I knew him in his predrug days, when he was dynamic. I played with him on the soundtrack for *Viva Las Vegas,* a motion picture co-starring Ann-Margret. The recording sessions would sometimes last all day, after which Elvis would go to a nearby nightclub, where he met his cronies who had also been working on the movie.

One of the most impressive things about Elvis was how much he remembered. I had met him five years earlier in Albuquerque and he actually recalled it. A million miles and a hundred songs had passed through his life since our initial meeting, but he recalled it in precise detail. I was flattered.

"How could I forget it, man?" he said. "I thought I was going to die."

Elvis had played in a then-new armory in 1957 as the opening act for Faron Young. I was still playing the noon radio show and Faron came over to plug his Saturday night concert with some new kid named Presley. He invited my band and me to the show.

Elvis was dynamite, that night in Albuquerque, with just a drummer, Bill Black on bass, and Scottie Moore on guitar. The lush records he would later make with full-blown orchestras were good, but not nearly as overpowering as the sound of the raw young Elvis with skeletal accompaniment, shaking and spewing an infant sound called rock 'n' roll.

The girls wouldn't stop screaming at the end of his set.

"We want Elvis! We want Elvis!" the chant continued.

That night was the one and only time Elvis opened for Faron Young. On every other show on the tour, Elvis closed the program simply because the hysterical crowds wouldn't let another artist follow him.

After the Albuquerque show, my uncle Dick Bills and I visited Elvis in his dressing room. The police struggled out front to restrain the girls who had been worked into a frenzy, wanting desperately to get in to see Elvis.

Suddenly, we heard the sound of glass breaking as one girl, then another and another, tried to come through the armory windows. The newspaper carried a big story the next day describing how several of the young women had been seriously cut in the struggle.

Elvis had already encountered hysterical fans, but never before ones who jeopardized their own safety just to touch him, which is what he recalled five years later when we talked about the Albuquerque date in 1957.

★★★

Don Costa, who was Sinatra's arranger for a long time, asked me to play on a country album being recorded by Steve Lawrence and Eydie Gorme. I hadn't met Costa at the time, but the sheet music was put into place and the session began without a word of introduction.

I had never played on a session in which the conductor didn't count off the song, but Costa just lifted his baton and began waving, and the musicians began to play. So did I.

All the players looked closely at the sheet music, which might as well have been ancient Hebrew as far as I was concerned. I could read chord charts, but I couldn't read notes.

Suddenly, everything stopped, and Costa said, "Glen, you've got the lead there."

Embarrassed, I told him what many of the players already knew.

"Mr. Costa, they should have told you. I don't read music."

He could have kicked me off the session, staffed by the finest musicians in California. Instead, he was the model of kindness.

"That's fine, Glen," he said. "You know the song, don't you?"

"Yes," I whispered.

"Well, all the part calls for is the lead," he said. "Just play the lead."

I instantly broke into the lead, and dressed it up with twin-stock harmony, on a song called "I Really Don't Want to Know." Steve Lawrence came in perfectly with the vocal part, and we did the song in one take.

Costa let me play by ear, the only way I could, on every session thereafter. Each time, he set out the sheet music and put my name and an arrow pointing to the songs' words where I was supposed to play. There was never again any reference to my not being able to read. We worked successfully together on many hit songs.

★★★

I think Bowen was pulling a joke on me when he asked me to sing live harmony with Dean Martin. I prided myself on being able to harmonize with anybody in a variety of parts. But Dean's lyrics were slurred and his delivery was minus a meter. I simply couldn't tell where he was going, and felt silly. One of the few times I ever insisted on overdubbing was in that session, but Bowen wouldn't hear of it. He pressed our songs into an album just as we recorded them.

People have asked me whether Dean was drunk or sober when I worked with him. I honestly don't know because he was always the same. That laid-back, slow personality prevailed, and he was always nice to me.

He just stood in front of the microphone and let his eyes wander around the studio as if he weren't paying attention. I don't know if his timing was bizarre because he couldn't follow the tempo or because he simply wasn't interested in what he was doing.

The guy was really detached, but he sure could croon.

In 1964, I got a call on a Thursday to come to Dallas on Saturday to play bass guitar and sing high harmony during a concert as a member of the Beach Boys. The legendary group's vital voice and bassist, Brian Wilson, had been ill. I was needed to pinch-hit for him.

I was asked because I had played on many of the Beach Boys' records. Studio musicians made many of the Beach Boys' recorded hits, which were later performed live in concert by the group's actual members. In the studio I had played on hits like "Help Me Rhonda," "Dance, Dance, Dance," and "Good Vibrations." This last song was from the band's famous *Pet Sounds* album. Brian Wilson put together most of that album in the studio. We did five separate sessions for "Good Vibrations," all the while singing the various parts and experimenting with the electronic manufacturing of sounds that had not been previously made.

My first show as a Beach Boy was the first time I had to play bass while singing high harmony. I must have made about a hundred mistakes during that show. But no one noticed.

The British Invasion of rock bands, led by the Beatles and with the Rolling Stones in tow, had not yet happened. The Beach Boys were the foremost rock 'n' roll band in America, and I was flattered, thrilled, humbled, and terrified at being asked to become a Beach Boy, particularly because I had so little advance notice. I toured with them for about a year.

I didn't really expect to be important to Beach Boys fans, because they knew I was a substitute. On my first date as a Beach Boy, I watched Mike Love, Dennis Wilson, Al Jardine, and Carl Wilson run to the limousine after the concert, escaping the enthralled teenagers. I had seen fan enthusiasm when I played with The Champs, but nothing like what happened with the Beach Boys. I could see rather than hear the audience screaming, because the music was played louder than any I'd ever played. Onstage, the volume was painful.

As I ambled to the car, my ears were ringing and my nerves were tingling from the sheer force of the music we had made.

"There he is," I heard someone scream as I left the concert hall. "He touched Dennis Wilson."

Suddenly, I was attacked by a posse of crazed women. My shirt was torn from my body, which was severely scratched, and my hair was pulled out by its roots. This wasn't adoration. This was pain. And it was frightening.

At the Boston Garden, Carl's arm was badly cut by a clawing woman who must have been wearing a sharp bracelet or ring, and he had to be treated at an area hospital. In Lexington, Kentucky, fans practically prevented us from leaving the arena. Dennis Wilson threw a bear hug around a policeman's waist, I did the same to Dennis, and a line of cops led the two of us through the teeming crowd.

I learned a lot about record production, and about the mob psychology that could be implemented through live performances of hit records. I'd seen fans get carried away and had been amused. The unbridled emotions at the Beach Boys' concerts made me realize how empty some peoples' lives were, and how they foolishly sought fulfillment from something that was intended to be no more than entertainment.

Working as a Beach Boy, I also benefitted in that my voice was raised in its range from singing all those high parts. I went from an A to being able to sing a C-sharp. Today, it's probably an A voice again.

The first half of the 1960s were among the most dramatically eventful days of my life. I had started the decade as an unheard-of pauper, and by its halfway point I was earning a six-figure annual income. I had also earned a good reputation among the best musicians in the nation.

My career had grown sweeter than I had ever fantasized it would. I asked Billie to quit work, bought a house, sold it for a profit, and moved into another.

My craft became a way of life. I worked and socialized with the same guys. We would finish a session, then head for the golf course and beer, and not necessarily in that order. I had played golf and did a little drinking back in Albuquerque, but I'd been recreational about both. I didn't take the game seriously, or get drunk, until the L.A. session days were in high gear.

Leasing a 1964 gold Cadillac was the only material thing I did for myself. The days of driving used cars that wouldn't start were gone forever. I liked that Cadillac a lot, even after I got in a wreck, and even after I got in another. I remember them both, but I don't remember the third. I was told I somehow hit a pole with my rear wheel.

Alcohol was waiting to ambush me. It would become, for years, as much a part of my life as my music.

Chapter 8

*F*ew studio musicians have careers as featured recording artists. I was fortunate that I had the extra income from playing on other artists' records while making my own.

I thought I was going to have a blockbuster when I recorded "Dreams of the Everyday Housewife," after having earlier hits with "Gentle on My Mind" and "By the Time I Get to Phoenix." Capitol put some promotion behind the record, and it took off, but Wayne Newton had also recorded the song and released his version of it.

I'd met Wayne earlier, when I played guitar for his recordings of "Red Roses for a Blue Lady" and "Danke Schöen." Wayne was and still is a major draw in Las Vegas. His "Dreams of the Everyday Housewife" took the sales steam from mine. My version got on the charts, and got significant airplay, but ultimately the versions canceled each other out.

I had gone out earlier on tour to promote "Turn Around, Look at Me." I was often an opening act for a celebrity—just my guitar and me. I didn't get paid for a lot of the shows because I thought I was supposed to do them strictly for their promotional value. All I collected was expenses. I was again victimized by my naïveté. On one of the rare shows for which I was paid, I was the opening act for The Doors. Jim Morrison was outrageous and frequently in trouble with the law for his onstage antics, including lewd behavior and obscene language.

I saw none of that on our show, but was curious about Morrison's clothes. He wore a leather suit on the plane to the show, wore the same suit in the concert, then returned to Los Angeles on the plane the next day in the same outfit. He sweated a lot during his show, and the absorbent leather needed a break. But he was Jim Morrison. He probably didn't care much about it, and probably cared less about what others thought.

I did extensive recording-studio work throughout the 1960s, until my own career as a soloist took off in 1967. I played guitar on some country sessions for a young singer from Bakersfield, California, about whom Capitol Records big shots were real excited. His name was Merle Haggard.

I didn't know Haggard had been in prison, and later decided that that was why he was so shy. I found out that he went to jail for trying to rob an all-night diner. He tried to break in through the back door. Trouble was, the place was still open for business. The proprietor heard the commotion in the back, opened the rear door, and asked the would-be burglars why they didn't come through the front entrance, like everyone else. He didn't talk long; the men fled, but not before the owner got a vehicle description and license-plate number.

Haggard turned twenty-one in prison, as one of his hit songs says, and was eventually given a pardon by then California Governor Ronald Reagan. He later returned to San Quentin prison to give a concert, and visited the cell in which he had been held. Haggard went on to record forty-one number-one country songs. He still performs, but doesn't have a recording contract.

That's a testament to the sad shape of country music today. A good-looking kid with an average voice can often get a record deal when a genuine legend cannot. The entertainment industry is like the athletic industry: Its youth will be served.

I landed a few motion-picture parts back then, not because of my celebrity, which was nonexistent in the mid-1960s, but because I played guitar. In *The Cool Ones,* with Phil Harris, Roddy McDowall, and Mrs. Miller, I played the guitar and had a speaking part. I did have a brief bit of dialogue and a fight scene with Steve McQueen in *Baby, the Rain Must Fall* in 1965. I got the role because the movie needed musicians for a band during a scene filmed inside a nightclub. I also did television shows with Dick Clark and appeared on *The FBI,* again as a singer.

Shindig was a popular network musical-variety show during the mid-1960s. It had a staff band that included David Gates and Leon Russell, both from Tulsa, Oklahoma, various other musicians who passed in and out of the group, and me. I backed artists who represented virtually every kind of popular music, and even did a solo myself on alternate editions of the weekly show. The producer, Jack Good, liked that I could play a wide variety of music, and he tried to make my solos somewhat off-the-wall.

I sang the popular songs of the day, and one week I was asked to sing Roger Miller's "Kansas City Star" while wearing a ridiculously large ten-gallon hat. (That scene is shown today during the videotaped introduction to my concerts. It always draws laughter.) I also sang what little country music there was on the song-and-dance show. I scheduled my recording-studio work around my *Shindig* filming.

Shindig was an important part of popular-music history, particularly rock 'n' roll. I'm proud to have been a part of it. It was a wonderful showcase for me because I got to play guitar behind artists as diversified as Tina Turner, Marvin Gaye, James Brown, Sam Cooke, and Diana Ross and the Supremes.

I was more impressed with Miss Ross than with anyone else on that show. She and the Supremes had a lot of hit records with the Motown sound, so popular among singers who came out of Detroit in the 1960s.

Working with her directly, especially during rehearsals, made me aware of her versatility. I knew that someday she would break out of the Motown mold, which she did, becoming a megastar of the 1970s and 1980s. A lot has been written about her temperament and the mood swings that supposedly make her a difficult person to work with, but I saw nothing like that. She was as gracious and charming as she was talented.

★★★

I met Donovan when he was a guest on *Shindig.* Between rehearsals, he played a song for me written by Buffy Sainte-Marie called "Universal Soldier." Donovan had done the song on an album. I asked him if he was going to release it as a single. He said no, so I cut it and it was a single for me. When Donovan's people saw how well my record was doing, they released his version as a single. His version killed mine.

During this period I was also a guest artist on *Hootenanny,* another network musical show. Its format was mostly folk music. A lot of people don't realize, I suspect, that I played guitar and banjo on some Kingston Trio recordings.

I continued to promote my own early records that I had made with Capitol. Nothing significant, however, was happening in my solo recording career. I was feeling the pressure again to come up with a hit for Capitol, and wondered how long the label would keep me if I didn't begin to sell records.

Driving to a recording session one day, I was listening to a Los Angeles country-music station and heard a low voice singing a song called "Gentle on My Mind," and it really stuck in my mind.

> It's knowing that your door is always open and
> Your path is free to walk
> That keeps my sleeping bag rolled up and stashed behind
> Your couch
> And it's knowing I'm not shackled by forgotten words

And bonds
And the ink stains that have dried upon some line
That keeps me on the back roads, by the rivers of my
Memory, and keeps you ever gentle on my mind.

The song had such a freshness of spirit, I thought. I loved the tune instantly. It was an essay on life as I viewed it then. I'm a big fan of titles, and I was knocked out by the words and images conveyed when I repeated to myself "Gentle on My Mind."

I bought the record and learned the song. At that time I had been with Capitol Records for five years. I had gone through five record producers, some of whom were really creative disasters. I got along well with most of them, but none of them were big-time producers, just nice guys.

I had recorded, upon the insistence of these producers, "Old White Mule of Mine" and other songs that were just not right for me. I hadn't wanted to record some of the songs, and did so only after being persuaded by the producers.

I decided that it was time for me to be in control and to select the songs that I wanted. When I suggested this idea to the Capitol executives, the announcement didn't meet with a lot of early enthusiasm. I can appreciate from firsthand experience what artists like Waylon Jennings and Willie Nelson went through to gain creative control over their recording projects. A lot of singers do their best when working for someone with a second set of ears, but I'm one of those people who feels he can gauge his greatest potential himself. Although I appreciate having a producer tell me if he thinks another take is necessary, and maybe why, I want to have significant, or total, say about what material I'm going to record and how it will be arranged.

Executive producer Voyle Gilmore heard my rendition of "Gentle on My Mind," and I think he released it only because he knew how serious I was about picking my own material. The irony is that while

I loved the song, I didn't especially like my version. This early rendition was only a work tape that I intended to revise. It was simply a recording wherein I sang a line, then talked to the musicians about how I wanted them to play and the "feel" I wanted them to maintain.

Gilmore took the tape, erased my spoken instructions, and released the song within that one week. Capitol previously had never shown this much enthusiasm for my work. What became my first big hit was intended to be no more than a demonstration tape from which the musicians would become sure of their parts for the master recording.

Because I didn't record the song in what I thought would be my final voice, I might, unintentionally, have incorporated a casualness that matched perfectly with the song's unusual arrangement. Also, it was uncommon in 1967 for a banjo part to be laced into a song recorded in that tempo.

Whatever the explanation, "Gentle on My Mind" burst out of the chute. The song changed my life in more ways than anything would until I became a summer replacement for the Smothers Brothers' TV show in 1968. I toured more than ever, trying to promote my new record, which, for all I knew, might be the biggest of my career. The ugly part about being a singer is that you have to work a record as hard as you can while you can, because there are plenty of other artists vying for your slot on the charts.

I became extremely busy as an opening act for Rick Nelson, Sonny James, the Righteous Brothers, and others. I performed on those shows with just a guitar. Later I hired a four-piece band and toured as an opening act with Bobbie Gentry. A few years later, she and I would have a platinum duet album containing two number-one records.

★★★

My life was fast becoming a marathon of music and miles. Once, in a rare moment of peace, standing in the old Western Studio Three in Los Angeles looking at record albums, I saw a Johnny Rivers album with a song whose title intrigued me. I didn't know if "By the Time I Get to Phoenix" was about the town or about the mythological bird coming out of the ashes.

After listening to the song, I told my producer at Capitol that just as I had found "Gentle," I had now found my follow-up release. In the wake of my first success, no one put any pressure on me to do things any way but my own. In fact, I discovered "Phoenix" about the same time that I found and recorded "Woman, Woman (Have You Got Cheating on Your Mind)." I recorded both tunes, and shortly after talked to producer Jerry Fuller, who was looking for a first song for Gary Puckett and the Union Gap. I was drawn toward "Woman, Woman," but felt just as optimistic about "Phoenix." Jerry didn't feel he had anything strong enough for an initial release for the Union Gap except "Woman," so I told him to take the song, and I would release "Phoenix."

I guess God smiled on my generosity. "Phoenix" was a hit single from my album *By the Time I Get to Phoenix,* which peaked at number one on the Billboard country charts in 1968.

I changed "Phoenix" somewhat, amending the chord progression at the end. It was the first of many Jimmy Webb songs that I have recorded. I changed almost all of these slightly, and Jimmy has always teased me that it's my obsession to tamper with his work, but something must be right about the alterations, in light of the Campbell-Webb track record.

Some people have said that I can "hear" a hit song, meaning that I can tell the first time a song is played for me if it has hit potential. I have been able to hear some of the hits that way, but I also can "feel" one. There is a special feeling that falls over a studio and its musicians when a hit is being created. I've heard actors talk about a similar feeling during the production of a motion picture. Although most movies are shot in segments and out of sequence, seasoned actors talk about the quiet but actual feeling that saturates a cast and crew when a true work of art is under way. That's the feeling I got during the recording of "Phoenix."

I had been in Los Angeles for seven years, during which time I had worked as hard as any studio player in town and earned a good living. My ultimate dream, to become a successful recording artist, was confirmed with "Phoenix."

If anyone thought my first hit recording was a fluke, those thoughts were erased with "Phoenix." I worked closely with producer Al de Lory, who produced all my big hits, from "Gentle" in 1967 through 1971.

I worked well with de Lory. I would record the vocal and instrumental tracks, and he would later apply his lush string arrangements. We had a good working relationship that ended as unexpectedly as it had started, so, for mutual benefit, we parted company.

The struggle to have my way regarding my music was over forever, I thought. Ten years later, I would find that this was not true. That's when the regime changed at Capitol Records. I found another great Jimmy Webb song called "Highwayman" and recorded it. It became the title song of an album, but Capitol refused to release it as a single record. These new executives said it wasn't commercial, and insisted that it would prompt neither sales nor airplay.

That "noncommercial" song eventually received a Grammy Award for Song of the Year as sung by a quartet comprised of Johnny Cash, Kris Kristofferson, Willie Nelson, and Waylon Jennings. Those guys built an entire tour around that song and called it "The Highwaymen." The tour is regularly revived to this day, and as recently as 1992 was responsible for a sold-out show at Madison Square Garden in New York City.

The song deals with reincarnation, and those country singers weren't certain as to what approach to take with the lyrics and arrangements. They asked me to help with the tune. I wound up arranging a hit for them that I should have had for myself. But I was glad to do it.

Somebody should have hit with that brilliant song, and besides, each of those four singers is an old friend.

After "Phoenix," my next two hits, both blockbusters, were "Wichita Lineman" and "Galveston." The great Jimmy Webb wrote both songs.

My faith in Webb in the wake of "Phoenix" was strong, so I had no reservations when he asked me to come to his house in Hollywood to hear some new tunes. I flipped over "Wichita" and we went into a studio to record it minutes after he first played it. I wanted the organ sound on my master that Webb had on his demonstration tape. I didn't think I could get it without his own instrument, so we carted his organ out of his house, onto a truck, across town, and into the studio. I hadn't done any manual labor in years, and Hammond organs are heavy, but I would have gone to any length to keep my recording success going.

The Hawaiian singer Don Ho had recorded "Galveston" before I ever heard the song. His version was too slow, set to the tempo of his big hit "Tiny Bubbles." He realized himself that his rendition wasn't in the groove and offered to give the song to me. I gladly accepted.

I again had that feeling that tells me I'm on to something when I decided to change the tempo of "Galveston" and recorded it much faster.

I had four major hit songs in little more than a year. I had other songs that were chart climbers on the country and pop charts, but these four held the number-one slot for weeks. My biggest dreams had come true, and at the end of 1968 I had four albums listed in the country and pop top ten. The previous year I had won four Grammy Awards. In 1969, I would sell more records than the Beatles.

Life was a perpetual party, and my friends and I saw fit to celebrate it. I achieved a first-name relationship with several Los Angeles bartenders, and often walked a crooked line into my house with feet that barely seemed to touch the ground.

My career just couldn't be any better, or so I thought. I soon found out that I was wrong, and was delighted to make the discovery.

Chapter 9

*I*t's odd how sometimes a person will remember only the insignificant details of an important event. About all I remember of an early 1968 appearance on the old *Joey Bishop* television show is that I wore a navy-blue suit with a baby-blue turtleneck sweater. That television appearance was one of the most crucial points of my career.

Tommy Smothers, a television producer and half of the legendary Smothers Brothers comedy team, called me after seeing that performance on the *Bishop* show.

"I didn't know you could sing," he said.

"You didn't ask," I replied.

I had recorded an album with the Smotherses, but they assumed I only played guitar.

"Can you read cue cards too?" Tommy asked.

"I can if the words ain't too big."

"Can you talk?"

"I'm talking to you, ain't I?"

That was about the full extent of the conversation, but it eventually would result in my own network prime-time television show. I would not have gotten *The Glen Campbell Goodtime Hour* in 1969 except for a guest appearance on *The Smothers Brothers Comedy Hour*. After that guest shot, Tommy asked me to become host of their summer replacement series, called *The Summer Brothers Smothers Show*.

It sometimes takes a long time for things to happen in show business. Then, once circumstances begin to change, they often change rapidly.

Two years earlier I was an anonymous Hollywood studio musician and struggling soloist known mostly by my peers. Then I recorded a few blockbuster records, and now I was hosting a network show. Things were happening too fast for me to think about what it all meant. People asked me how I contained my excitement, but the odd thing is I wasn't excited. I'm not the type that jumps up and down. If something good happens, fine. I appreciate it. I usually get more nervous than excited, and that was the case as I eased into network television.

I hosted six editions of the *Summer Brothers Smothers Show* and was paid fifteen hundred dollars for each. Going into the project I told Tommy that I wouldn't do anything controversial. The Smothers Brothers had a reputation for controversy, and their show would eventually be canceled by CBS because of their comments about Richard Nixon, the federal government, and the war in Vietnam, even though the program was high in the ratings.

Dickie Smothers was in New York City attending an automobile show when someone approached him and said, "Did you hear? You've been fired."

"That can't be," Dickie said. "Our option was just picked up."

A high-ranking official at CBS was seeking the ambassadorship to the Court of St. James. He was competing with other powerful men, all of whom were trying to impress Richard Nixon. The CBS executive impressed Nixon by firing the Smothers Brothers, thereby preventing them from using their show as an antiwar vehicle. The guy was rewarded with the ambassadorship.

The official reason for the dismissal was their alleged failure to deliver to CBS taped versions of the program by a deadline. The

Brothers deny that. Another reason, Tommy said, was an offensive comment made by David Steinberg on the program that aired around Easter.

Those reasons were no more than straws that broke the camel's back. Tommy and Dick were constantly in hot water with the network for their controversial scripts, which ultimately cost them their jobs.

I recall one skit in which I was supposed to refer to Ronald Reagan as a known heterosexual. I looked in the dictionary to be sure what the word meant. I wouldn't say it on television until I looked it up. I didn't want to bad-mouth the governor of California.

Another time I was asked to sing the old hymn "I Believe." I learned that Tommy Smothers intended to superimpose statistics about the war in Vietnam on the television screen while I sang, implying that the facts represented my convictions. I had no opinion about the war except that I supported the United States government and whatever its leaders decided to do. So I balked at the number.

The show was number one in the ratings, even when we went against the Democratic National Convention and the civil unrest that surrounded it.

Because of my no-controversy stance, I did little more than introduce the guest acts after performing my own numbers. I enjoyed the show mainly because it had a comedy format, and I love comedy. To this day, I incorporate jokes and one-liners into my stage show. I've often thought that if I hadn't become a musician, I would have liked to be either a stand-up comedian or a professional golfer.

The writers for *The Summer Brothers Smothers Show* comprised a "Who's Who of Comedy," including Steve Martin, Rob Reiner, Carl Gottlieb (who wrote the screenplay for *Jaws*), Mason Williams (who recorded the big instrumental hit "Classical Gas"), and McLean Stevenson, who became a star on *M*A*S*H.*

Reiner, at twenty-one, was the youngest writer on the staff. He was paid thirty thousand dollars a year and it was his first network job. He was overcome with excitement.

No one could have predicted then that Rob Reiner would one day star in one of the most successful situation comedies of all time, *All in the Family,* as the bright but misdirected "Meat Head," son-in-law of Archie Bunker, the Carroll O'Connor character who became the most famous satirical right-winger of the 1970s. *All in the Family* is still in rerun. Reiner also produced and directed one of the most clever romantic comedies ever committed to film, *When Harry Met Sally,* and was the brains behind the Jack Nicholson and Tom Cruise masterpiece *A Few Good Men.* In the spring of 1993 he began production on *North,* a motion picture starring Bruce Willis, Kathy Bates, and Reba McEntire that is scheduled for release in 1994.

In 1969 he was just an insecure and aspiring comedy writer who was in awe of his senior writers. He and Martin, because of their youth, had trouble getting their sketches on the air. They wrote a sketch titled "Renegade Nuns on Wheels," a spoof about Hollywood premieres.

Sketches were forever being canceled by censors on the eve of shooting. Head writer Allen Blye, panic-stricken, would assemble his writers in the wee hours of the morning to plead for someone to come up with a substitute sketch.

"We have something," Reiner and Martin would say. "We have the Hollywood premiere thing."

Steve Martin and Rob Reiner would act out the sketch in front of the other writers, who would howl with amusement. That happened two or three times, but their sketch was never aired.

Can you imagine a television producer today turning down a combined effort from those two legends of comedy?

"Basically, I think they just wanted Steve and me to perform for them," Reiner said in October 1992. "We were the [staff] jesters."

Reiner talked about the valuable apprenticeship that was his on the show. He said he learned a lot about his craft from Tommy Smothers, and ultimately saw in Smothers a man who relentlessly stood for his convictions.

"Tommy was fearless," Reiner said. "He really fought for what he believed. In those days of my youth, I thought Tommy was compromising his convictions. I learned later what he went through in fighting the networks. Tommy was trying to do cutting-edge television and they didn't want anything like that. They wanted problem-free fare."

Reiner said he realizes today how miscast many of the writers were for the family show that was desired by the network.

"At the time, all the writers were radical people," he said. "We were all against the war. We were all for civil rights and those things. We all smoked dope in those days and it was pretty wild."

The hardest problem I faced in my new role as a television host was timing. I didn't know how to deliver my lines. Later I discovered that I suffered, slightly, from dyslexia. I would simply get ahead of myself and read one word into another. I had to do several retakes of my scenes, and that became time-consuming and annoying to everyone involved, including me. I was a singer and a musician, not a public speaker. So I told Tommy Smothers to ask his writers to keep my lines as short and simple as possible. Tommy personally worked with me on reading from cue cards. By the time the videotaping began, I had committed many of them to memory. We found that worked better than the long, drawn-out setups.

Finally, I went on television not as anyone's replacement but as the host of my own show, on May 21, 1969. *The Glen Campbell Goodtime Hour* was a Smothers Brothers production, and I felt bad that the men who had brought me to big-league television and produced my show eventually lost their own because of politics. The Smotherses simply made one joke too many about Richard Nixon. Meanwhile, my salary was raised to fifteen thousand dollars per week.

My dad visited the program and sat patiently through a week of rehearsals before he was videotaped with my mother singing with me. He was polite and shy, and I could tell he was curious as to why anyone should be paid for clowning in front of a television camera.

My bass player on the *Goodtime Hour* was Bill Graham, who had been playing with me for years. My dad told Graham that he had a question to ask him, and he hemmed and hawed for an entire day before mustering up the courage.

"I'm really not trying to be nosy," my dad said to him, "and don't tell Glen I asked you, but shouldn't he be spending less time foolin' around here and a little more time out there trying to make a livin'?"

Bill explained that I was paid well to do the television show, but my dad wasn't satisfied.

"Well, just how much do you suppose that is?"

By that time, Bill was my stand-in during rehearsals, and he figured I spent only about three hours a week videotaping my part of the show. At any rate, he told my dad that I was paid five thousand dollars an hour to do the program.

"Oh *$%&⌐¬#(*," my dad yelled. "He ain't doing nothing but playing a guitar. No telling what they'd pay him if he did some work around here too."

He was serious. Bless his heart, he probably thought my salary would be raised if I did some "honest work," like help sweep up or something.

The first *Glen Campbell Goodtime Hour* was sponsored in part by McDonald's. A new sandwich called the Big Mac was introduced on that program.

I opened the show with Stevie Wonder's "For Once in My Life," then moved into "Little Green Apples" with Bobbie Gentry. The Smotherses were guests on the initial show. We did a skit in which they rode horses onto the set. Tommy's "horse," however, was a hippopotamus. The script called for me to insist that he wasn't riding a horse but some other kind of animal.

"I don't even think it can run," I said.

"Of course not," Tommy fumed. "It's a jumper."

The show was co-sponsored by Chevrolet, and I did a commercial for the company. In retrospect, I can't believe I was asked to sing and play for my own sponsor's commercials. You'll never see that today, but I thought nothing about it back then.

The list of eventual guest stars included Flip Wilson, Liberace,

Jonathan Winters, Carol Channing, Andy Griffith, Johnny Cash, Bobbie Gentry, Liza Minnelli, Roger Miller, Judy Collins, Joan Baez, Ray Charles, Jim Nabors, Kenny Rogers and the First Edition, Barbara Feldon, and many others.

I don't remember any singular show in its entirety, but instead recall skits or bits and pieces from the series, which lasted three years. My memory is foggy largely because I was busier then than at any other time in my life. Anyone who ever had his own network television show will tell you to do the show and nothing else.

The *Goodtime Hour* writers assembled at nine A.M. Monday through Friday. We would start rehearsing on Monday for the show we were going to shoot that Friday. Simultaneously, the writers were working on the following week's script. It could be confusing. We would shoot a dress rehearsal and an air version. We would shoot each in front of a different audience. We took a one-hour break between the dress and air rehearsals to fine-tune the script. On a few occasions, the show was actually rewritten during that time.

***

I had never been so busy, and didn't know how long it would last, so I tried to take on every engagement that was offered and nearly worked myself to death. I toured on weekends in live performances, and began collecting and recording enough songs to come up with two record albums annually for Capitol Records.

Meanwhile, in my spare time, I was trying to be a husband and father to a wife and three children. My visibility skyrocketed. I was on the covers of *TV Guide* and *Look* magazine. Reporters everywhere wanted interviews. I couldn't go out in public without being surrounded by well-meaning fans. I couldn't even go out of my house unless I was willing to stand for hours and sign autographs. I had become a prisoner of my fame, and that too was something to which I would have to adjust.

My entire family paid a price. My daughter, Kelli, once wanted me to take her to a father-daughter day at Dodger Stadium. I sincerely wanted to do it, but knew there was no way the fans in the stadium would have left me alone. I don't say any of this in an egotistical way, just as a matter of fact. Fans would act like that with anyone who had a number-one television show, and this time it just happened to be me. Kelli was heartbroken because we couldn't go, and so was I. They say that every adversity carries an equal blessing, and I sometimes think that blessings can carry adversities. Fame has its price, and the price is expensive.

In 1980, Naomi and Wynonna Judd were running around Nashville's Music Row trying to land a record deal. Naomi was working as a nurse in nearby Brentwood, Tennessee, and she and her daughter were friendly and familiar sights among the music-business crowd. After the duo attained superstardom, Naomi said that success wasn't always fun because she and Wynonna couldn't go out in public as they once did. Naomi would eventually take a bodyguard with her to church.

The success of the *Goodtime Hour* lay largely in the brilliant comedy writing. There was no drama on the program, just laughter and music. I did my hits and the hit songs of the day. My guests sang their popular records, and often I would accompany them in duets. The show was very informal, opening with me sitting on a seat in the middle of the audience. With his banjo, John Hartford would kick off the show's theme song, "Gentle on My Mind," which he wrote. I would rise from the audience and say, "Hi, I'm Glen Campbell." My voice registered high, but with a natural timbre and my own excitement. I became identified with this kind of a spoken introduction, almost like a whine, and I still use it today in my live shows.

The show offered up repeat performers, and the public became very fond of them. Comedian Pat Paulsen's popularity soared as it never had before because of the weekly exposure. Anne Murray, Jerry Reed, and Mel Tillis also became regulars who audiences loved.

Mel was an old friend who had been kicking around Nashville for about thirteen years. He had recorded some hit records, but I'd always thought that he was just as good a comedian as he was a singer. Mel stuttered and people laughed, but he didn't mind. I didn't think he was funny because he stuttered, but rather, his jokes and inflections made him funny. Nonetheless, he was known for that stutter, and the show's producers expected it from him. When he came to Hollywood to audition, he was nervous. He took a sedative before the audition and, relaxed, his speech improved. He didn't stutter at all during the audition, and that almost cost him the job.

I recall a hysterical skit involving Mel, Jerry Reed, Lily Tomlin, and me. The script called for Mel to come into a bar and tell Lily that her car was on fire. Mel's stutter prevented him from communicating, so Lily would try to second-guess what he was trying to tell her. Everything she said, of course, was wrong, and she never got the message that her car was burning. Mel kept trying to get her down from the barstool to go to her car, and she thought he wanted her to dance. He tried to steer her out the door, and she was trying to waltz with him across the floor. By the time she understood what Mel was trying to say, her car was a cinder.

One viewer thought I was patronizing Mel by letting people laugh at his speech impediment. She wrote to tell me that I was rude and that Mel shouldn't be on the show. I didn't agree. I didn't see why someone with genuine singing and comedy talent should be kept off the show just because he had a handicap. I said so on the air, and the studio audience burst into applause. That cemented Mel's position as a regular performer on the show.

The dry off-the-wall comedy of that series was ahead of its time. There was a certain degree of hipness in the scripts simply because the show was a Smothers Brothers production. *The Glen Campbell Goodtime Hour* was on the cutting edge. The show was innovative because it was not just another Hollywood variety show with predictable song-

and-dance numbers. It could entertain you while making you think. I liked that, as long as it didn't make you think about changing the channel.

Gun control was very much in the news in 1968. I remember a glib Pat Paulsen "commentary" about gun control that aired on *The Summer Brothers Smothers Show,* the format of which was largely interchangeable with the *Goodtime Hour*'s:

> A lot of people are shooting off their mouths about gun control. I believe the solution to this problem lies in adopting a uniform law giving everyone an equal chance. Either prohibit the posses-sion of firearms, or buy a gun for everyone and make them wear it. Let us not be guilty of oversimplification. If we outlaw all firearms, it will merely cause other problems. First, without guns, how can we shoot anybody? Second, what about children? Guns are great for kids to teethe on. Also, guns are not as harmful as poison to children, because no child can swallow a gun.
>
> Speaking of children, here is a little riddle for them:
>
> What did the mama bullet say to the papa bullet? "We're going to have a little BB."
>
> I get a bang out of that one!
>
> Let's face it, we need guns. You never can tell when you're walking down the street and you'll spot a moose.
>
> Suppose a man goes home early and finds another man with his wife. What's he supposed to do? Poison him?
>
> "Hey, fella, get up from there and have a little belt of arsenic."

⋆⋆⋆

Another odd and very funny skit was written by Steve Martin for Andy Williams and the Hollywood midget, Billy Barty. In it, Andy sang "Moon River," his biggest hit, to a crowd of people who all gradually walked away. A bewildered Andy looked at the people whose depar-ture he didn't understand in the face of such a popular song. Finally, no one remained on the set except a crooning Andy and little Billy. Billy looked up at Andy, then looked straight ahead to his kneecap and bit it. Then Billy walked off the set and left Andy hobbling alone. The skit was typically goofy, and successful.

Another attraction of the *Goodtime Hour* was the jam session at the end of each show with Hartford, me, and a guest artist or two. We would take our guitars and sit in the audience. It was extremely informal, and was the easiest and most enjoyable part of the program for me.

I tried to showcase country-music stars on the *Goodtime Hour,* but the network officials balked. I got a memo from the front office telling me to back off the country stars. I put together one show with Buck Owens, Merle Haggard, Johnny Cash, and me that really annoyed the network big shots. That week, however, we were again number one in the ratings. I began to feel that some of those guys sitting behind desks didn't know what was happening on the front lines of public taste. I also decided that they didn't care. They had to justify their decision-making jobs by making decisions, right or wrong. There will always be people, supposedly educated, who will have a hard time admitting that other folks know more about some things than they do.

At any rate, I had to compromise with the powers that be, and wound up singing duets with nice people who were fine actors but not professional vocalists. The network executives wanted big stars while I wanted good singers for a program whose format was largely music. All I wanted was talent, and I had Seals and Crofts, Willie Nelson, and Waylon Jennings on the show before they achieved national fame.

I capitalized on my desire to grab the brass ring by spending the summer after the first successful season of the *Goodtime Hour* in England, touring and doing six television shows for the British Broadcasting Corporation. I worked for Jeff Kruger, a concert promoter who had heard my records but had never met me. In 1967 Kruger had bought a five-year license from Capitol to release my records in England on his Ember record label. He took a chance on me just months before my career took off. I never forgot that. I have played England, Ireland, and Scotland just about every year since 1968, and I have always worked for Jeff Kruger. Professional loyalty is a way of life in which I was brought up.

Kruger's shows have taken me to every hamlet in the United Kingdom, and even to Belfast, Ireland, during times of militant civil unrest when you couldn't walk into the city's most prominent hotel without passing through sandbags, barbed wire, and armed soldiers. I played Belfast the night after Bobby Sands, the Irish Republican Army hero, died in prison. Tensions were high in the city, to say the absolute least, but the audience loved our show. It was as if our music was the diplomatic diffuser. I don't want to take credit where it isn't due, nor do I want to be overly dramatic, but who knows what kind of riot might or might not have transpired had our singing not soothed the city on that potentially explosive night?

To this day, my record sales and concert dates continue to flourish in that part of the world.

My early affiliation with Kruger provided a lesson about the wonderful by-products that can come from fame. It doesn't have to be merely an ego trip, as I suppose it is for some in the public eye. There truly is an up side. Kruger wanted me to do a charity concert, the proceeds of which were to be used to buy a bus for handicapped children. The GLEN CAMPBELL VARIETY CLUB SUNSHINE BUS is still in use today. Hundreds of less fortunate children have traveled thousands of miles in that vehicle. Helping to raise the money to buy that bus made me feel as though I was sharing some of the good things that had happened to me.

My popularity at the end of the 1960s was worldwide, and I was determined to do whatever I had to do to nurture it. My wife, Billie, eventually guided the construction of a new, 16,500-square-foot house befitting a network television star. I figured I had earned it, although the *Goodtime Hour* was off the air by the time the house was finally finished.

I had found a lot on top of a hill in Laurel Canyon. It had a view like I had never seen. I could stand on that hill and see the entire San Fernando Valley. I paid ninety-five thousand dollars for seven acres almost a quarter of a century ago. Billie and I could have moved to Beverly Hills more cheaply than we moved into the mansion we built in the canyon, but she felt it was important for our children to stay near their friends, and so we did.

The construction of the house was an exercise in sustained confusion. I turned over the responsibilities to Stan Schneider and Billie, and Billie had the dominant say, by far. She found an architect whose original floor plan called for an area of 19,500 square feet. I had stayed in smaller three-story hotels. Construction costs were projected at well over $1 million, and Stan, as my money manager, had a fit. So the floor plan was reduced to 16,500 square feet. Behind Billie's back, Stan insisted on taking me to Beverly Hills to show me what $500,000 would buy. Million-dollar houses, at least in Laurel Canyon, were nonexistent in 1973, when construction actually began on the modified lot. I built the first.

We hauled in several tons of dirt just to make the lot level enough to build against erosion. We made room for a putting green, a sunken tennis court, and a gazebo from which to watch the action.

Stan, who needed to be in his office, was nonetheless at the construction site at least every other day, supervising the construction and trying to watch Billie so as to prevent cost overrun. I was mostly on the road and left the two of them to play in the dirt.

Before we could get bulldozers to the lot, we had to build a road. The path up that mountain cost $50,000. Then Billie went berserk with accessories. I once took her with me to Europe, where she saw English Tudor–type mansion gates. She bought them for $8,500 each, then paid another $3,000 to have them shipped to the United States. I don't know what she paid to excavate enough native stone to line the gates.

Billie built an alcove into the bedroom. On the alcove walls, she had an artist paint our children's pictures in Old English attire. She then ordered the painting of cherubs on the ceiling.

She built an indoor atrium and spent a small fortune for carp to swim on the bottom of a wading pool. The fish were all poisoned by the paint that covered the bottom. Stan said we had thousands of dollars' worth of dead fish.

In those days, I was earning $50,000 to $60,000 a night. And we finally finished that house, a poor man's Hearst Castle, for $1.75 million. Stan was at the house in 1992 and said it looked exactly as it did when he had last been there, in 1976. Not one stone, not one matter of motif, had been changed.

I enjoyed that house, but it became one of my first lessons about the impossibility of finding personal peace from material things.

Shortly before I attained my career-making television exposure, I was performing at the Palomino Club in West Hollywood. John Van Horn, a talent agent, signed me to talent-agency representation with a company owned by Jerry Perenchio, who later became a production partner with Norman Lear, producer of many 1970s hit television series, including *All in the Family*. Van Horn, for some reason, later disappeared and I needed a new agent. Perenchio sent a new guy to meet me who was my opposite in almost every way. I was still a slow-talking country boy with a strong sense of family and conservative values. This guy was a fast-talking, finger-snapping hubba-hubba hustler. Stan Schneider called Perenchio and told him the situation wasn't going to be productive. Perenchio then sent another agent, Roger Adams. Roger and I had our obvious differences. I had not finished my secondary education, and he had graduated from Choate, a prep school attended by John F. Kennedy. Stan was again concerned about potential incompatibilities.

Roger and I hit it off instantly. He has been my agent from 1968 until today. For the first fifteen years of our affiliation, he never missed one Glen Campbell concert. He stopped coming around because he couldn't stand to observe my self-abuse, which I'll describe later. He cared about me too much to watch me self-destruct. He and I literally have done thousands of shows, performed after traveling millions of miles.

Roger is one of the most likeable men I've ever known. He was an agent whose delicate job was to collect the money after shows. He never leaned on the promoters, yet he always collected. He understood my priorities, and therefore wasn't overly curious when I was complaining one night about the pace caused by my new popularity. He and I were in a hotel room in Oklahoma City, where I had given a concert shortly after he became my agent.

"I miss my wife and family," I told him. "I don't know about this running all over the country and being in a different city every night. I want to go home."

"You do?" Roger replied. "Well, before you give up your career, let me show you something."

He picked up his briefcase, opened it, and turned the contents upside down onto the bed. The bedspread was covered with more than eighty thousand dollars in cash.

"That is how much you have earned the past few days," he said.

He began to throw it into the air, and I joined him. The room was raining money. I certainly had never seen so much cash, and realized that, in show business, there was no guarantee I would ever see it again. Careers can end just as rapidly as they begin in the entertainment industry.

I decided I would tour a while longer. That was almost twenty-five years ago and I'm still on the road.

Roger is also one of the most ingenious people I've ever known. Sometimes that proved to be both productive as well as amusing. A case in point has to do with the late Judd Strunk, a singer, songwriter, and banjo player who was my opening act on many occasions in the 1970s. Strunk was a comedian who had appeared on the late 1960s television hit *Laugh-In.* His easygoing humor went over well with audiences everywhere.

In 1973, Strunk and I were playing the Starlight Theater in Indianapolis, Indiana. He developed an interest in a hostess who worked at the restaurant on the top floor of our hotel. She was younger than Strunk, and that bothered him, so he would carefully situate his hairpiece, suck in his stomach, and swagger up to her as if he were a much younger man.

"Good morning, Louise," he always said. "Can I write you a song?"

He continuously asked her to come to our show, but she consistently declined.

One night, Strunk got drunk after a show, and he went to the swimming pool the next morning to ease his hangover. He got onto the elevator to return to his room drenched, not wearing a hairpiece, and with his stomach protruding noticeably over his swimsuit.

The elevator door closed, and he forgot to push the number that corresponded to his floor. Consequently, the elevator took him to the top floor. The door opened right in front of the woman he had been trying to hustle.

She shrieked, and said, "Oh, my God!"

Strunk returned to his room and called Roger.

"I think I've blown it," he said. "She saw me the way I really look. I'll never get a date with her now. Can you help me?"

Roger said he could.

He and I went to the elevator and rode it to the sky restaurant. Roger was all words as soon as we stepped into the lobby and faced the girl of Strunk's dreams.

"Say," he told the young woman, "we're looking for Judd Strunk's brother. Perhaps you have seen him. He's kinda fat and bald. He was down at the swimming pool a short while ago."

"Oh, yes," she sighed. "I've seen him. He was just up here on the elevator. But he didn't get off. He just looked at me strangely and then rode the elevator back down."

Bingo. The woman never knew she had seen the real Judd Strunk. He asked her again to come to our show, and she accepted. We were in Indianapolis for a few days, and they dated every night during the rest of our stay.

I had no time for drinking during those busy days in the wake of my popularity explosion. But I took the time anyhow. There were nights I would stay up with friends until very late, then have a hangover for the next day's trip to an out-of-town show. I always wanted to be a good host for my guests, especially the country stars, for whom drinking and partying was a way of life back then. We called it roaring.

Chemical-substance abuse was also very prevalent among some stars who had graced the *Goodtime Hour*. The entertainers took amphetamines for energy. Johnny Cash, Roger Miller, and others came forward years later to talk about the devastating effect of chemicals on their lives. Roger even spoke before the Oklahoma Legislature in an effort to make laws calling for tighter drug control. He testified that amphetamines had seriously damaged his career, and had nearly ruined his life. I respected the way he came forward.

For some wonderful reason, I escaped the trappings of uppers, whose nicknames in those days were "old yellers," "speckled birds," and "L.A. turnarounds." The yellers got their nickname among musicians because they were yellow. The speckled birds were so named because their exteriors were speckled. The L.A. turnarounds were so called because after you swallowed one, you supposedly could drive from Nashville to Los Angeles, turn around, and drive back without sleep.

About the time I went on network television, I played a show in Phoenix. I drove down from Los Angeles, and was told by a friend that the trip back would go better if I took an amphetamine. The pills were legally available, but only with a doctor's prescription. When you got them from buddies, as did most of the people in the music community, you might be taking a dosage that was way too much for your metabolism.

So I played the Phoenix date, popped the pill for the drive back to Los Angeles, and en route had a flat tire. The pills are notorious for making their users nervous, and the pill I took was no exception. I remember fumbling with the hubcap and jack, and shaking as I nervously tried to align the tire iron onto the lug nuts. It took me a long time to raise the car, change the tire, and put the car back down.

When I was through, I got into the car and drove away, leaving the jack, hubcap, tire iron, and fender skirt from a new Cadillac on the highway shoulder. I was so high, I forgot the tools at the side of the road. After that, I never took illegal pills again.

✰✰✰✰✰✰✰✰✰✰✰✰✰✰✰✰✰✰✰✰✰✰✰✰✰✰✰✰✰✰✰✰✰✰✰✰✰✰✰

Chapter 10

7 can remember where I was when I heard that Elvis died and I can remember what I was doing when I learned that I'd hit the top of the charts—my first number-one record. But I can't recall where I was or what I was doing when I was told that my television show had been canceled. My biggest springboard to stardom was gone, and I didn't even care.

I finished the final season without the guys who created the show, the Smothers Brothers. They had been fired by CBS. The show continued with another production company, but it wasn't the same. When the Smotherses left, so did their brilliant writers, including Steve Martin and Rob Reiner. The guys who replaced them just weren't as funny. The original producers had written a role for Glen Campbell. The new producers wrote a show and stuck Glen Campbell in it. I was at my best when I was allowed to be natural. The Smotherses let me be me. The new scripts seemed to make the show, and me, plastic. I hated the dumb things they asked me to do, and I told them exactly that. I would get angry and they would get resentful. From that kind of hostility creativity does not flow.

Doing a weekly show is always a marathon workload, but I had enjoyed it nonetheless. There had been days when I couldn't wait to get to the set because I knew I'd be working with a particular star, or because I knew I'd be acting in a skit written by a favorite writer. After the Smotherses were fired, going to work became an exercise in dread and frustration. However, the ratings didn't suffer. I think that had to do with my image at the time, and with the popular guests I fought to get on the program. But I knew the weekly shows were not my best. It isn't fulfilling to do good work when you know you can do better. The producers who were supposed to be helping me to bring out my best were, instead, suppressing it. For me, the glitter had left the gold.

The kind of show I wanted to do would have cost about $280,000 weekly. CBS could buy Sonny and Cher for $140,000, and so they did. Big companies always seem to look first at economics, and then, maybe, at the artistic content. These companies also have their own ways of doing things, and they don't want to change them, not even if it means success. Maybe it's because their "idea men" would look bad, and couldn't justify their salaries, if somebody told them how to improve what they do.

I've seen this happen so many times in the music business. An entertainer working clubs and auditoriums nightly, rubbing shoulders with the people, knows what they like to hear. Some big shot at a record company, who rarely gets up from behind his desk, nonetheless decides what kind of songs he will push for a certain artist. The songs don't sell, the singer is dropped from the label, and the big shot keeps his job, only to levy his mistakes on another artist.

Network television took a heavy toll on my creativity. It's so hard to compromise, week after week, when you know that what you're being asked to do is poor. It's unfortunate that artists have to be accountable to the bottom line. The absence of artistic integrity is what's wrong with modern television. Making money is the network's only objective, and so the programs are filled with guaranteed payoffs, such as violence, vulgarity, lame humor, and sex.

P. T. Barnum said that no man ever went broke underestimating the intelligence of the American public. He could also have said that no one ever went broke underestimating the public's standards of good taste.

If the networks got together and established criteria for quality programming, then obeyed them, the audiences would have no choice in what they watched. Give them a diet of good-taste fare and soon they'll acquire an appetite for it. But television is in love with reproducing itself. When one sex-oriented show becomes a hit, they immediately develop a batch of clones around it. It's a pity.

* * *

My life was a roller coaster during the *Goodtime Hour* as it had not been before or since. Everyone wanted me, or so it seemed. I often knew I was taking on too much work, but then I'd ask myself, "How do I know I'll get this work next year?" Memories of having been a nobody were still too vivid. I didn't want to have to work as hard as I was, but when opportunities came by, I seized them.

One such project was an ambitious album recorded live on July 4, 1969, at the Garden State Performing Arts Center in New Jersey.

As I look back on this album, I think it was the wrong thing to do at the time, despite its commercial success. It was an example, again, of my doing good work when I could have done better had I been allowed the time and money by the producers.

I took some of the finest studio musicians in Los Angeles with me to New Jersey for the album. We also used a symphony orchestra from New Jersey for the concert. At that time, symphonic players were unaccustomed to playing ballads and country songs, unlike what they routinely do today. More rehearsals would have made a better recording.

Don't get me wrong. I was pleased with the album. I just thought it could have been better. I've been accused of being a perfectionist to a fault, and perhaps there is something to that.

The record was kind of a "greatest hits" album set to applause, since it included many of my biggest hits. It did more to highlight my versatility than anything I had ever done. I even included such songs as "The Impossible Dream" and "The Lord's Prayer." The critics loved it, and it became a major milestone in my career.

The album came about at the urging of my manager at the time, a guy who I now suspect was interested only in getting his commission from the record company's advance. It was one of my first lessons in trusting the advice of people who stand to make money from their advice. They won't always be honest. They get the short-term profit by getting their way, and you get to live with the long-term consequences. Too many managers see their clients as commodities. They get what they can and go on to the next singer, whose coattails they can then ride. That isn't management, that's usury. Anybody can book a singer when he's got hit records and a hit television show. A manager in that situation has to do little more than answer the telephone. A real manager is the guy who can get you on television, get you a big record deal, or get you a premium booking, especially when your voice isn't all over the airwaves.

★★★

I once recorded a song that I didn't like and told the producer what I thought.

"This is a potential hit," he said. "Glen, you always said that if I found a song that I really believed could be a hit, you would trust me and record it."

I'd made that promise, so I kept my part of the bargain, but the more I rehearsed the song in the studio, the more I hated it. The song was released as a single and it flopped. I couldn't understand how a producer who knew so much about music could have been so wrong about that record. To my way of thinking, a deaf person could have heard the absence of quality.

Then I found out that the producer, who claimed to have had my recording career as his best interest, had been paid under the table by a publishing company to persuade me to record their song. I never worked with him again, but my string of hits had been broken, and the damage was done.

I don't like dealing with financial affairs, and prefer to have someone else handle them. Consequently, I've lost a lot of money trusting people.

The big exception is my accountant and current manager, Stan Schneider. He and I have been linked for thirty-two years, and his actions have been beyond reproach. In fact, he's been instrumental in pointing out the financial discrepancies heaped on me by others.

It is said that money changes people, but it also changes those who hang around the guy with the money. After my recording and television career exploded, I happily acquired what is commonly called sudden wealth. I had been so starved for financial dignity, I didn't care who knew I had finally achieved it. I bought Billie a six-carat diamond, rings for myself, a Rolex watch, big cars, that big house, and many other signs of conspicuous consumption. I felt we deserved it. Two years earlier, we couldn't afford to go to a supermarket. Now we could buy a chain of them.

★★★

My brothers, sisters, and parents turned out to be the best of everyone I knew in not allowing my new money to affect our relationships. They didn't treat me any differently than they had in the past. I remember going home to visit and seeing them struggle on stretched-out budgets and fixed incomes, as I had for years. I felt uneasy about my own prosperity in the face of their plights. But most of them acted as they always had, especially my dad, and I was tremendously relieved. I feared that some of them might think I had gotten too big for my Arkansas roots, and that the plain life I had once shared with them was now beneath me. I made it a point, and I still do, to visit with my family some time during the year. If I lost everything I have today, my brothers and sisters would be the first ones to take me in.

My new prosperity allowed me to help my family financially. I built a new house for my mom and dad, and loaned or gave money to many of my brothers and sisters to start their own businesses. Many paid me back and some are still paying, but not one has ever stiffed me. I can't say the same thing about people outside my family.

My brothers and sisters, of course, are grown, so now my nieces and nephews ask me for money. I've been asked for as much as fifty thousand dollars to start a business. I don't always feel I can do it, but so far I have always done it. I think God has blessed me for it too. To tell you the truth, I don't even remember who owes me how much.

My family supported me when, as a child, I had dreams of becoming a musician. No one ever said that I should acquire a trade and join a labor union for job security. When I was a teenager starving in New Mexico, my mother sent me what little money she could spare. And when major success at last raised its pretty head, my family and friends back in Arkansas were the first in line to celebrate with me.

July 13, 1968, was proclaimed "Glen Campbell Day" in the state of Arkansas by then Governor Winthrop Rockefeller. I got off the plane in Little Rock and there were scores of banners and streamers saying that the people of Arkansas loved their native son. I was so touched.

I played the Arkansas State Fair that night and had members of my family, including my parents, join me onstage. My dad played harmonica, and my brothers, sisters, mom, and I sang bloodline harmony. The audience loved it, and I felt warm all over.

My parents and I were invited to the governor's mansion for dinner. My parents hadn't been to many places that had central heat and air-conditioning, much less the velvet finery of the state's First Home. My farmer father wasn't intimidated a bit. I was proud of him for that.

We were served a succulent prime rib that oozed with au jus. Dad had a French roll that he thought was too hard, so he broke it with his hand, delivering a loud karate-type chop at the dinner table. The bread split like a wooden rail, and my dad used the pieces to sop up the au jus, just the way he sopped up his gravy with biscuits at home.

Dad sat next to the governor's wife, who was visibly horror-stricken at his manners, or what she thought was a lack of them. My dad had cut as much meat as he could from the bone of his entree, and the next thing I knew, he had picked up the bone with his hands. Here he was at an elegant, formal sit-down dinner with the governor and his wife, and he was eating with his hands.

The First Lady was not amused. She tried to be polite, and, blushing, she said, "Well, Mr. Campbell, make your dinner out," whatever that means.

"No, thanks," my dad said. "I've had so much now, I could stick my finger down my throat and play with it."

I fell down laughing. Mrs. Rockefeller never cracked a smile.

✶✶✶

My success took a different kind of toll on my own loved ones, including my wife, Billie. I hadn't anticipated it. I don't like the word *star*, but when you become one, you attract press coverage, and the coverage isn't always honest or accurate. During the last twenty-five years I've become extremely distrustful of many newspapers, especially the tabloids. They lie so much, they have to hire somebody to call their dogs.

I'd recorded two giant songs with Bobbie Gentry, "Let It Be Me" and "Dream." The tunes came from an album that had gone platinum in both the United States and England. We toured as a duet to promote the records, and the press quickly began publishing stories alleging that Bobbie and I were romantically involved. I was never in love with her, nor she with me. Nonetheless, I had a wife ten thousand miles away to whom life in the big time and fast lane was still relatively new. She had a family of her own and was embarrassed when the press reported that her husband was running around on her.

I came home, exhausted from those tours, to face Billie's jealous wrath. She was angry, but her anger was only the outward manifestation of her pain. She was embarrassed in front of our children as well.

Back in Billstown, my brothers and sisters were thinking that I had been seduced by the bright lights and show-business lifestyle. I learned recently that my preacher brother, Lindell, grieved and prayed about his little brother who was making scandalous news across the Atlantic Ocean. Lindell had never even seen the Mississippi River, and I seemed to be so far away and sinking so deeply into sin. The hearts of my family were breaking, and I felt pain for the trauma I was involuntarily inflicting on them. I hadn't thought much about the press until then. If you had asked, I would have said I believed in a free press, but not in a press that was free to lie.

There were times in my career when I would get bad press that was accurate. My drinking was at its breakneck worst during those days, and frankly it is very hard to remember things from the 1970s. There were times when I was too drunk to recall what I did or with whom I did it. I can live, unhappily, with the negative press that is accurate, even though I wonder why the press has the right to print that stuff. A person's private life should be private. And I'm also curious about the alcohol, drugs, and sexual habits of some of the reporters who delight in reporting on the morality of others. I've drunk a lot of whiskey with members of the press, and noticed that they didn't leave the room if someone else was supplying the narcotics.

So, I've taken my lumps from them. I just hate it, however, when people I love, and who have proven their love for me, have to swallow those same lumps for something they didn't do.

☆☆☆

Success breeds success, and it often attracts successful people. In the early 1970s I was pulled off the golf course one day by a former agent who said he wanted me to look at videotape of a comedian who he thought would be a good opening act for me. The guy's name was Lonnie Shorr, and we wound up working together off and on for fifteen years. When we met, he was a Las Vegas and major-talk-show regular. He eventually did *Merv Griffin, Mike Douglas,* and other big gab fests more than 150 times.

I was looking forward to our first packaging near Washington, D.C., at the Shady Grove Theater, a three-thousand-seat theater in the round. Shorr had been hyped hard to me. I was therefore sure that his lightning wit would have the crowd in the mood to be entertained when I came onstage. He was scheduled to do forty-five minutes, and I was to do ninety.

I wound up doing two hours and fifteen minutes with only my band. The comic who would work with me for one and a half decades failed to appear on opening night. Shorr was embarrassed about it, and I still love to tell the story about his absence.

He had gone with Kenny Rogers to Philadelphia to do *The Mike Douglas Show* on a Monday, when he assumed the theater would be closed, as most are on the first workday of the week. Not so with the Shady Grove.

Later that night, Kenny and Shorr were at Shorr's house in Maryland, where Kenny's telephone conversation was interrupted by an operator. The caller was Howard West, who was then Shorr's manager. (West is now the executive producer of *Seinfeld*.) He got Shorr on the line and wanted to know if he had recovered from his car wreck.

"What car wreck?" Shorr asked.

"The one that made you stand up Glen Campbell and miss your opening!" West fumed.

"No, dummy," Shorr said he told West. "That's tomorrow night!"

"No, dummy," West fired. "It's tonight!"

Shorr's mistake was explained to him, and he decided to take a train to Baltimore, rent a car, and arrive in plenty of time for Tuesday night's show. He rode the train as far as Wilmington, Delaware, where, without explanation, it stopped.

"It just stayed there, it just stayed there," he later told me. "They'll never believe this. They'll never believe I missed two nights in a row. Negotiations had gone on for so long for me to get the job, which was such a big step up for me, and here I am going to miss the second night."

The train had undergone mechanical failure, and at last began to move. When he arrived in Baltimore, Shorr made a mad dash for a rental car and his destination. He ran to the back of the hall, where no provisions had been made for his dressing room. Perhaps because he was a no-show the first night, organizers thought he was no longer a part of the program. He was thrust into a giant room reserved for the chorus, except that there was no chorus line on that program. I accidentally opened the door and saw Lonnie Shorr in person for the first time in my life. He looked like a lost and lonely pea in a giant pod. He later told me he expected me to explode, but I had no such inclination. I took one look at him and somehow knew that his absence had been accidental. He said I merely smiled at him, and I remember him smiling at me. We never spoke a single word at that introductory moment.

He went onstage and was still breathing heavily from his sprint to the hall. He told some outrageously funny jokes and had the crowd in a jovial mood that is every headliner's fantasy.

Lonnie eventually would become one of my closest confidants. We became friends, and for a somewhat unusual reason: He always appreciated my friendship with him.

He did an interview once in which he told of an incident that I, frankly, had forgotten. He prefaced the story by saying that I had opened doors for him in his career. Gratitude is always appreciated and usually is rare in show business. Then Shorr recalled our playing the Riviera Hotel in Las Vegas, where singer-dancer Pia Zadora was married to the hotel owner. The owner wanted Shorr to carve fifteen minutes off his act and share the remaining time with Pia, who eventually became a polished performer but left a little to be desired in those days. Later, she decided she wanted to do more time onstage, and wanted Shorr to do less.

I knew how hard he had worked on his act. Also, I knew how he had gotten his job, and knew why she had hers. So I put my foot down and backed up Shorr. I said I wanted him to have his full time onstage.

Years later I read the interview in which Shorr thanked me for backing him up, saying that the Riviera engagement had generated additional work for him—work he felt he would not have gotten had it not been for me. I don't know if that's true, but I do know he didn't have to say that. And that's what makes me appreciate him.

Chapter 11

★★

*I*n 1969 I was performing on a weekly television show, making records, and touring. A friend joked that the only thing missing was a starring role in a major motion picture: Who did I think I was, John Wayne?

So, to make the hysterical circle complete, I was offered a starring role in a movie with John Wayne. It was truly one of the most memorable experiences of my life.

I'd sat as a boy in a Delight, Arkansas, movie theater and peered, open-mouthed, from the front row at the larger-than-life Wayne on the screen. My brothers and I would scrimp all week to see his movies. He represented both the real and fictional parts of Americana, like a combination of Babe Ruth and Superman. He stood for everything that was fair and decent, and practiced immediate justice with one swing of his awesome fist. A lot of little boys shared that perception of Wayne during the 1940s.

I had been in a few films before, but speaking parts had been limited, and my stage experience was nonexistent. I was cast simply because my music career was hot and they thought "Glen Campbell" would sell tickets. I didn't care how or why I got the role. I simply intended to give it 110 percent. *True Grit* was the film, which also starred Kim Darby, Wilford Brimley, and Robert Duvall.

I had been raised around horses on a farm, but I wanted to sharpen my riding skills to impress Wayne on the first day of shooting. Two or three times a week I took time I couldn't spare to drive to rural Los Angeles County and ride the horse I was supposed to ride in the film. I wanted that nag to be familiar with me so I could come off as a valid Western horseman.

On the first day of filming, it was apparent that my little horse could not keep up with Wayne's bigger steed.

"Duke, you're going to have to slow down," I panted between takes. "My little horse can't match yours and I'm falling out of the shots."

I had to keep kicking my mount while struggling to say my lines without the appearance of a struggle. Then the director, Henry Hathaway, decided that my small horse was nonetheless too big, and the contrast to Wayne's horse wasn't stark enough. He wanted Duke's horse to look huge, so my horse kept shrinking.

Another problem arose: Duke's horse bit my horse on the neck. My horse now feared the bigger one. He wouldn't walk beside Duke's without walking sideways.

"Cut, cut," Hathaway yelled. "Glen, can't you hold your horse straight?"

"No," I said. "He's afraid."

The wranglers on the set in charge of the livestock grew weary of Duke's aggressive horse, so one of them hit it over the head with a two-by-four. Duke's horse never bit mine again. If you ever see a rerun of *True Grit,* watch Duke's horse pull its head away from my horse whenever the two walk together. He's got a terrific headache.

I did every conceivable thing I could think of to prepare for my performance with Wayne. Weeks before the project went into preproduction, I started learning my lines. Then I learned Wayne's. Then Duvall's. I memorized the entire script. I had never been so nervous about anything.

It is said that one always gets what he fears the most. I had a phobia of making mistakes, and so, of course, I made one.

Wayne's character, Rooster Cogburn, was a one-eyed sheriff who wore a patch where his eye used to be. The patch, naturally, gave Wayne a blind side. Hathaway directed me, in one scene, to approach Wayne from the left, apparently forgetting that Wayne's eye patch would prohibit him from seeing me come at him. I walked up, spoke my line, and Wayne sort of jumped, as if startled. A reaction like that wouldn't do for a character who was supposed to be a two-fisted hero.

"I don't think this is going to work, Duke," I said timidly.

"Hell no, it ain't gonna work, 'cause you're on my blind side!" he yelled in front of the entire cast and crew. "What the hell is the matter with you? Ain't you got enough sense to know this is my blind side?"

I wilted. I was a nervous wreck, wanting to please the man, and now I had gotten him angry. But I surprised myself by coming to my own defense. No one else on the set had the guts to, even though I had only made the mistake of following directions.

"Walk up to me on my other side," Duke thundered.

"I can't," I said. "This is my first time, and Hathaway told me to do it this way."

Then, as if I were absorbing some of Duke's own courageousness, I actually stood up to him.

"Now, if this is wrong, you tell Hathaway, or I will," I said, "but don't chew me out when I'm only doing what I'm told."

There was a long silence, and then Wayne's craggy face relaxed.

"You know, kid," he said, "you're right. It ain't your fault you don't know what you're doing. I'm sorry I yelled at you."

John Wayne apologized to Glen Campbell in front of the entire cast and crew.

✭✭✭

I didn't know that motion pictures aren't shot in the sequence of their story lines. On the first day, I showed up prepared to begin at the beginning, and learned that we were about to do a scene that was midway through the story. My memory of that scene wasn't vivid, so I had to undergo a crash refresher course. I was on the set from daybreak until past dark, and then I sat up in my trailer squinting over the next day's lines. I developed an incredible respect for how hard people work in the motion-picture industry.

✭✭✭

My involvement in *True Grit* aroused my curiosity more than any other aspect of my career, and most of it had to do with John Wayne. Duke had a mystique that intrigued me. He was the same offscreen as he was on. I've heard people say that Wayne didn't act, but just got in front of the camera and played himself. It was hard to separate reality from fantasy when you were around him. Being in his presence was no different than being in a movie with him. After *True Grit,* I used to visit Duke at his house in Newport Beach, California. We'd sit in the living room having a drink, and it was as if cameras were rolling. I kept catching myself waiting for the director to holler, "Cut."

John Wayne's days of hard living were largely behind him by the time our paths crossed. He had been famous for his smoking, cursing, drinking, and womanizing, but I saw none of that. He had lost one lung to cancer, and smoked nothing but cigars when I met him. He was physically, for him, weak, but even so, he was still stronger than most men. And he was always a gentleman to the women connected with the film.

There was one incident that gave me an idea of how he must have drunk in his prime. We were having lunch in an authentic and beautiful cowboy bar in Telluride, Colorado. I had a glass of beer and Duke asked for a glass of whiskey. The waitress brought him a shot.

"I said I wanted a glass of whiskey." He handed her his water glass, about the size of a small Mason jar. "Fill this up," he snapped.

She poured straight bourbon whiskey into the glass until it was about three-quarters full. Duke swallowed it calmly and rhythmically as if it were iced tea. He never coughed or gasped.

Duke was always playing pranks on people associated with the film. For example, there was a big chase scene in which a dozen cowboys had to mount their horses hurriedly and storm down a trail. The actors leaped into their saddles, and the saddles slid to the ground because Duke had loosened the straps around the horses' bellies. Everything came to a stop while the saddles were put back in place. It was a waste of time that translated into a waste of money, but who was going to complain to John Wayne?

Hathaway, in fact, was visibly intimidated by Duke. Although the director was supposed to be in charge, he would regularly ask Duke how he wanted a camera angle or how he wanted to set up a shot. There was a very concerted effort to keep Duke happy.

The final scene in the movie, for example, shows Duke jumping a four-rail fence on horseback. The scene had to be shot early in production, and Hathaway thought that letting Duke ride his own horse in that shot would be dangerous and financially risky to the project. If Duke were injured during the stunt, it could mean the postponement of filming and falling behind in production, which is financial suicide in the motion-picture industry.

But Duke insisted that he do his own jump.

"I ain't having no one jump for me," he shouted at Hathaway. "I'll do my own stunts, thank you. Besides, I can jump a four-rail fence without a horse."

So, John Wayne, referred to as a "one-eyed fat man" by his movie enemy, rolled in the saddle as his nag ran at a gallop in the snow toward the chest-high fence. The horse stretched, Duke rose, and the two cleared the fence with plenty of room to spare.

We shot the film in the fall, and faced heavy Colorado snow on more than one occasion. We even had to strike the entire set and move it several hundred miles south just to get around the weather and finish the picture.

While the move was being made, I decided to take a break and go to Carson City, Nevada. I just wanted to drink and play blackjack and forget about motion pictures for a day. It had been a year since *The Summer Brothers Smothers Show,* and I thought I could wear a disguise and pull it off. I donned a cowboy hat and sunglasses, but to no avail. Well-meaning fans wouldn't leave me alone, and I returned to the new set without the relief of having been away from show business for a moment.

I was once again naïve, but this time about the film industry. At the end of each workday, the actors and actresses watched dailies—rough cuts of their performances from two or three days earlier. Each day I would hear someone say he was going to the dailies, always held after dinner. I didn't know what dailies were.

"Okay, go on to the dailies," I would say. "I'm going to bed."

So, I never got a chance to evaluate my own performance until I was about one third of the way through filming. By that time, my character was firmly set and I couldn't change anything.

There is a lot I would do differently if Duke were alive today and I were doing a film with him. For one thing, I would try to maintain better contact with the other actors and actresses in the picture. Making a movie is such a curious thing. You eat, sleep, work, and worry with a group of people, and you all are pulling for the same thing. Then the production ends, and you go your separate ways, as if you had never known each other at all.

Robert Duvall was a tremendous help to me when I was in *True Grit.* He was a star at the time, but went on to become a megastar in *The Godfather.* I think often of Wilford Brimley and Duvall and run into them occasionally. They sure are nice people.

Not long after *True Grit* was wrapped, I got involved in another film project, *Norwood,* starring Kim Darby, Dom DeLuise, and Joe Namath. The film was based on a novel by Charles Portis, who had written *True Grit.* Hal Wallis, the executive producer, was forced to do the film in order to get *True Grit.* There is no other reason to have produced such a corny movie. It was a ridiculous story that set back the cause of country music and perpetuated every stereotype of country musicians as hicks.

Namath used to throw a football to me during breaks in filming. He once hit me so hard, I was spun around in midair solely from the force of the ball. My shoulder was black and blue for days. It wasn't smart to try to catch Joe Namath passes without pads, but I had never played with a pro, and had no idea how hard those quarterbacks throw.

In this movie I played Norwood Pratt, a dumb old country boy. Pratt was a hayseed whose big dream was to get on the *Louisiana Hayride* with a pet chicken standing on his guitar. In rehearsals, the chicken kept defecating on my arm.

Had it not been for working with John Wayne, I wouldn't have enjoyed working on *True Grit.* Since Wayne wasn't around for *Norwood,* I liked nothing about making that film.

I can't see the fun of doing something exactly as it's written on a script. Making music, with the ability to be spontaneous, is much more fun. And it paid more. Making those movies actually cost me hundreds of thousands of dollars in time away from the concert stage.

I had three movies left to do on my contract. I walked away. I haven't been in a motion picture since, although there have been offers. I didn't particularly like my performances. I may have acting talent, but most of my talent lies in music. My manager at the time wanted me to take acting lessons and pursue a rounded career of music and theater, including Broadway. I didn't know which was less, my interest or my aptitude.

★★★

The United States Congress gave John Wayne a special gold medal to commemorate his service to the nation. The award was given on May 26, 1979, on his seventy-second birthday, at the University of California Medical Center in Los Angeles. Sixteen days later, Duke died in the same facility. A man lay at rest who had made two hundred motion pictures over half a century. He was the biggest male box-office draw in history.

John Wayne was among those few Hollywood actors who let their political views be known, no matter how expensive to his career. He was an archconservative and anticommunist who supported the United States involvement in Vietnam. His convictions set him up for a lot of criticism.

Wayne responded by making *The Green Berets,* a film that unequivocally supported the war. The movie was a hit in 1968 even when American voters unseated a president because of his involvement with the war.

Wayne was frequently the target of criticism from left-wing political and academic groups. No doubt the intellectuals at Harvard University thought they would intimidate him by asking him to speak at the Ivy League school in 1974, the year of the end of United States involvement in Vietnam. Wayne not only accepted the invitation, he arrived at Harvard in an armored personnel carrier.

The man was unconquerable. Only death could still him, and not without a fight. He lost his lung to cancer in 1964, bragged that he had whipped "the big 'C,'" then survived open-heart and gallbladder surgery in 1978. In 1979, he began the year by having most of his stomach removed. Four months later, he appeared on television at the annual Oscar awards.

I have seen *True Grit* perhaps twenty times. I run clips from the film in my live concerts, and the audiences love it. The theme song was the only country song ever nominated for an Academy Award. Even after all these years, the video is very popular. Americans never get enough of seeing a one-eyed John Wayne with reins in his teeth and a rifle in each hand, confronting the bad guys. It was one of the most exciting film shoot-outs ever.

I take it personally whenever anyone says anything bad about that film, Duke, or my performance.

The film critic Gene Shalit wrote, "Glen Campbell has never acted in films before and his record is still clean."

I always say that I made John Wayne look so good in *True Grit* that he won his only Oscar.

I may be wrong but I've never understood why somebody who doesn't sing is qualified to write reviews about my singing, or why someone who doesn't play a guitar is qualified to write a critique of my instrumental skills. They're giving opinions about something that they don't do themselves. I say that straightforward and heartfelt—as John Wayne would have.

Chapter 12

*I*n 1971 I was invited by Queen Elizabeth II of England to the Royal Palace to sing. It was a command performance. There was a little flap in the press about a country singer sought by royalty. The combination, I guess, was unprecedented.

Not long afterward, I was summoned for a second performance, this time for the queen mother. The royal family's interest in my music did wonders for my popularity in the United Kingdom, which was already soaring because of the exposure I had on the BBC while I was doing the *Goodtime Hour.* I was getting almost as much television exposure in England as I had in the United States. My records sell well in the United Kingdom to this day, where I tour almost annually.

Since my life was so busy in 1972, I didn't really appreciate the significance of a command performance. There had never been much discussion about protocol in my life as a studio musician, recording artist, television host, or touring musician. I associated the term "command performance" with classical musicians.

Everyone around me told me how flattered I ought to be because I was sought by Britain's royal family, so I accepted. I took a rhythm section from Los Angeles to accompany me, with British horns and brass, and when I played before the queen mother, I had an English symphony orchestra behind me.

I recall how intricate the rehearsals were, and how everyone but me seemed to be uptight. The English musicians were very concerned about their posture and profiles. Those of us from the States weren't quite as worried. I was appreciative of having been invited, and respectful of royalty, but I was also confident that I could perform. A concert's just a concert, after all.

Everything went well during the rehearsals. I did the first show for the queen at the London Palladium and the second for the queen mother at another hall. I wore a tuxedo for each show, and the crowds were incredibly formal and stuffy, barely patting their hands when they applauded. Everyone from Britain affiliated with the show was walking on eggshells in fear that something might go wrong. And it did.

I was introduced, walked to center stage, and the hall fell quiet as the remote-controlled microphone rose from the floor. It was supposed to rise to my mouth, but instead stopped short of my belt. In order to sing, I would have had to drop to my knees, and I had been told not to bow before Her Majesty until after the performance, when I would meet her in a receiving line. So, there I stood, the microphone at my fly and the audience hushed with discomfort.

I've seen entertainers lose control when something goes wrong onstage, and I was determined not to let that happen here. I've always tried to turn a mishap into a positive experience, and take advantage of it for the audience's sake. That's what I did that night.

I broke into a guitar instrumental selection, playing it directly into the half-mast microphone. The queen mother knew I was improvising, because the list of "Selections to be performed by Mr. Campbell" was on the program.

"You are a most inventive young man," she told me after the show. I liked her, and felt she liked me.

Going through the receiving line at each command performance was more complicated than the show itself. I had been coached about the procedure by Buckingham Palace officials.

At the first palace reception, I stood with Petula Clark, Tom Jones, and Engelbert Humperdinck, waiting to meet Queen Elizabeth II and Prince Charles. We were put together, I guess, because we were all entertainers. A valet carried vintage wine from guest to guest on a silver tray. An orchestra played lush, magnificent arrangements. I was stunned by all the incredible art that lined the palace walls. Palace guards were everywhere, starched and rigid.

Petula Clark was the first of us to meet the queen and she was visibly nervous. It seemed very important to her to approach at the right time and in the right gait. She had rehearsed her curtsy and was consumed with doing the proper thing and making the right impression. At last she was motioned to approach Her Majesty, and she cautiously stepped forward. She took two steps and was stopped dead in her tracks. By me.

I unknowingly stood on the train of her dress.

Smiling and blushing, she frantically struggled to lunge forward, hoping to break the hold my foot had on her gown. I still didn't notice. She kept pulling while I looked around the room. Finally I noticed her glaring at me and thought that if looks could kill, I would be a dead country boy, but I couldn't imagine what her problem was. She finally took a couple of steps backward and shook me.

"You're standing on my dress," she whispered.

"What?" I said, not sure I understood.

"You're standing on my dress," she said again, with more volume.

By this time others were looking, including the queen. She must have thought her musical guests were a bunch of bumpkins. I think that's what Petula thought of me. I couldn't believe she was getting so upset over a little footprint on a dress. And why would anyone wear a dress that dragged on the floor three feet?

Playing for British audiences is a tough test of one's ability to entertain, because the English are reserved audiences. These crowds will let you know right away whether they enjoy what you're doing. American audiences will always applaud to some degree, just because it's appropriate. Not the English. I've occasionally seen every member in an auditorium sit silently, motionless, at the end of a singer's biggest number, leaving him to force a smile and mutter unnecessary thank-yous before pressing on to another song that might not go over either. I'm glad that has never happened to me.

The year 1973 marked the only time I ever canceled an entire tour, missing eleven dates in New Zealand. I had just done fourteen dates in Australia, and was looking ahead to the eleven shows, all of which were sold out.

I came down with acute laryngitis. I walked onstage at an outdoor show and told six thousand people in my strongest whisper that I could not sing, but that I would be glad to provide an instrumental show. The audience was less than satisfied.

Stuart McPhearson, the tour promoter, had tears in his eyes when he told Stan Schneider that I was going to miss every date on a sold-out tour in which he had invested heavily in advertising and in the cost of transporting my band, crew, and me from Los Angeles to New Zealand by way of Australia. The money for every show was refunded to perhaps a hundred thousand people, as some of the venues were quite large.

I told McPhearson that I would return and play the tour again. I did, and all dates were again sold out.

In the meantime, I had been ordered by my doctor not to talk for two months. What he meant was that I shouldn't emit sounds through my throat. I have the ability, however, to talk like Donald Duck without straining my vocal cords. So, for more than sixty days, I put my quacks to syllables. That's the only way I communicated.

★★★

My passions in life are my Lord, family, music, and golf. I took up the game at twenty-four, while living in New Mexico. Obviously golf wasn't a game played in Delight when I was a boy, and my friends weren't interested in it when I was a younger man. We all had roots in "country," where golf was thought to be a sissy's game.

At the time of my command performances in England, I was a near-scratch golfer and won the Duke of Edinburgh Tournament. This competition was made up of European celebrities playing against American entertainers.

I think I have a natural feeling and aptitude for golf because of my Scottish ancestry, Scotland being the birthplace of the game. I became consumed with the game shortly after taking it up, and to this day I love to play it, always trying to improve.

Golf is a no-bluff game. You can't rely on teammates or padding. There is no referee to influence the game. In golf, the guy who plays the best wins the round. I love the honesty.

Show business, on the other hand, is filled with bluff and hype. A singer can sell records and wind up with top billing simply because a publicist or record company generates publicity for him or her. Some of the greatest singer-musicians I know are among the least famous, and some of the most famous are among the least talented. This unfairness doesn't exist in the world of golf.

In 1971, the Los Angeles Open golf tournament was having trouble getting name golfers to participate in the tournament and in getting celebrities to play in their Pro-Am tournament. So they asked me to attach my name to the tournament as a marketing aid. It was an attempt to duplicate the success of the Bob Hope and Bing Crosby tournaments.

From the very first year, my Pro-Am always drew at least fifty celebrities and massive crowds. At my suggestion, the tournament was subsequently moved to the world-famous Riviera Country Club, where I was a member. This enabled the committee to attract great golfers such as Jack Nicklaus and Sam Sneed, among others.

After twelve years, I gave up the Glen Campbell Los Angeles Open because I moved to Phoenix and because it was becoming too much work for me. Though it was incredibly time-consuming because of the scores of details I had to attend to, I often miss it.

Some of my fondest and funniest memories are wound around golf. I was awestruck when I joined the Lakeside Country Club in Los Angeles and ran into Walter Brennan, Jim Davis, Gene Autry, Forrest Tucker, and other legendary movie stars in the locker room. These were actors I'd seen as a kid in the movies in Delight, and now I was rubbing shoulders with my boyhood idols.

I used to run into Dean Martin at the Riviera Country Club. I always liked Dean because of his lack of hypocrisy. People accuse him of drinking a little and he tells them they're wrong, he drinks a lot. His car has a license plate whose inscription reads, DRUNK. He made a fortune acting drunk on his network show in the 1960s, and many in the cast said he wasn't acting at all. While I don't envy his drinking, I can't fault his honesty about it.

Like most folks', Dean's drinking, and mine too back when I drank, caused mood swings. One day he was at the club, I was told, toting an expensive set of golf clubs over his shoulder, when an official with the club asked to talk to him. He told him that he was bringing too many guests to the club. Dean reportedly got very insulted and angry. This was evident by the way he hurled his golf bag through the pro shop's plate-glass window. Glass, clubs, balls, and accessories went flying in every direction. People said the crash was deafening. I guess Dean thought those clubs were expensive enough to pay for anyone he had brought to the course, because he never picked them up. He walked away instead, and never returned.

I always thought Dean was wrong, but the club was also wrong to jump on him. The mere fact that Dean belonged there added to the club's prestige. A lot of folks wanted to join just so they could be around the big stars. Dean commanded fortunes for commercial endorsements back then. And there he was, unofficially endorsing Riviera, and they complained because he brought guests.

My country-boy naïveté came into full flush on the golf course. I didn't understand the rules of gambling on the links. It was no secret that I was making a pretty good living, so I was hustled by golfers who tried to take advantage of me.

Once, I was playing with a bunch of Dean's friends and someone suggested we play for a dollar Nassau. I said fine. I didn't know that, in their parlance, a dollar meant a hundred. I lost nineteen hundred dollars in one round. I didn't gamble long. I had enough vice in my life as it was with the drinking that went on before, during, and after some rounds. I will say, though, that playing for money made me play more seriously, and was probably responsible for improving my game.

I once played in a Country Music Association Pro-Am tournament in Nashville where the pro golfer Don January and Mel Tillis also played. This was Tillis's first time on a course, and he was proof positive regarding naïve country stars and golf. January had the second shot on the first hole on a par four. He hit the ball onto the green, and marked it with a dime. Mel needed ten or twelve shots to get to the green, where he saw January's dime.

Now it was January's turn to putt, and he couldn't find his ball marker.

"Where is my marker?" January said.

Other players looked around the green for his marker.

"Now, what could have happened to my dime?" January said, interrupting play.

"Was that a ball marker?" Mel said. "I thought I'd found a coin and put it in my pocket."

One day, Buddy Rogers, who was then eighty-seven, and I were playing in the Bob Hope Classic at Palm Springs, California. Buddy wasn't in my group, but we both had early tee-off times and the weather was unusually cold. So was the water in the ponds on the fairways.

We were each given twelve balls for tournament play. That should have been enough for anyone, but early into play Buddy knocked a ball into the water. Why he didn't use another ball I'll never know. The ball was visible beneath the water, a short distance from the bank, but it was just out of reach of Buddy's club. He told his caddy to reach for it while he held his hand. The caddy stretched more and more over the water, and Buddy, still clutching his hand, eased closer and closer to the water's edge. The caddy's weight became too much for Buddy, and the caddy started to pull Buddy into the water. I don't know why the caddy didn't let go of Buddy's hand and simply take the plunge himself. Buddy Rogers, decked out in a cashmere sweater, was pulled into the muddied water. He emerged, a cussing, wet, and muddy wreck. The tournament was carried over network television, and the announcers had a field day joking over the incident.

Another time, Jack Lemmon was hitting balls off the first hole at the Bing Crosby Open into the ocean for practice. It was raining, his grip became slippery, and the next thing he knew his club was airborne. He offered his caddy money to wade into the ocean during a thunderstorm to find that club. The caddy wouldn't go. Lemmon kept raising the bounty, but the caddy refused and the club was never found.

✳✳✳

Bob Hope and Bing Crosby were among the best show-business golfers I ever knew. Crosby was a scratch player and Bob at one time was down to a two or three handicap.

The worst show-business golfer I ever played with was Jackie Gleason. He never took the game seriously, and never stopped being Jackie Gleason. At a Jack Nicklaus tournament he did little more than follow Hope around. Each time Hope tried to putt, Gleason coughed or loudly cleared his throat. He would holler, "And away we go!" as Hope lined up for a drive. Gleason got a lot of laughs, Hope got a terrible score, and the gallery got a good show.

✳✳✳

Jim Garner is one of show business's most avid golfers. He is a down-to-earth guy who gets very animated when he's frustrated. One day he missed a putt and angrily threw his putter into a tree. It just hung there and wouldn't fall down. That only added to Garner's frustration, so he proceeded to climb the tree to retrieve his club. The star of *The Rockford Files* and *Maverick,* one of the biggest television celebrities, was grunting and straining his way up into a treetop. He was high up in the branches and stretching to his limit when he tore a new pair of $250 pants. Those who hadn't noticed him up there at that point now heard him. He was cussing and having a fit.

"Jim, you ain't good enough to get that mad," someone told him. That made him angrier.

He worked his way down to the ground, scratched, his underwear showing through his torn pants, and left the putter in the treetop. For all I know it's still there.

✶✶✶

I played in the first Music City Celebrity Golf Tournament at Harpeth Hills in Nashville. Faron Young, who has been known to speak his mind very candidly, was paired with the professional golfer Lionel Hebert. They approached the first green and Hebert was lining up to putt.

Suddenly, a ball rolled toward the cup, and then another. Faron was practicing his putting while Hebert was concentrating on his shot.

The gallery was packed with spectators, and Hebert turned to Faron and said, "I don't want any balls on the green while I'm putting."

Faron began to cuss at Hebert loudly.

"You $#@!*&%," he said. "I make a lot more money with my #$%&*! guitar than you do with that @#!$%&* golf club."

A hush fell over the crowded gallery.

"You know," Hebert said, "I suppose you do."

Play resumed, and Faron practiced his putting at every hole without another word of dissent from Hebert.

✶✶✶

Talk of drinking and golf reminds me of my friend Buck Trent, a *Hee-Haw* star who was an instrumental partner for seven years with Roy Clark after working for eleven years as a banjo player and lead guitarist for Porter Wagoner. He was the first person to play electric guitar for RCA Records behind Dolly Parton.

Buck has an obsession with golf that he says has often been unhealthy. He knows a lot about unhealthy addictions because he is a recovering alcoholic who has been sober for more than ten years. The way he has changed his life has been an inspiration to many people, including me. I remember how he used to annoy me with talk of sobriety when I was still drinking. I'm glad, however, that he persisted in sharing the joy of an alcohol-free life.

Trent used to see his golf game seriously impaired by booze. I've seen him play with a horrendous hangover, and I've seen him play, or try to, while dog-drunk. He was a Scotch drinker, and he says his driving and putting used to be affected by his "Cutty Sark" jerk.

Whenever Buck would play Las Vegas with Clark, he would play a round of golf with the men who managed or owned the hotel in which he was working. On this particular day he was playing with Sam Hogan, manager of the Frontier Hotel.

Buck was winning the match. The pressure on him was increasing as the pain of his hangover was intensifying. He posed over the ball to tee off at the sixth hole. He steadied, put himself in alignment, swung, kept his head down, followed through, and completely missed the ball.

Trent's embarrassment was about the same as that of a major-league outfielder who misses a lazy fly ball. His humiliation, mixed with the booze pulsating through his veins, overcame him. He threw his driver backward into the air. It sailed about half as far as his ball should have. The club went over a fence and crossed six lanes of traffic.

Golf is a gentlemen's game, and the gentlemen with whom Trent was playing were not amused. While they waited, Trent scaled the fence, then danced through half a dozen crowded lanes of traffic, fetched the driver, and weaved his way back. He was wearing golf shoes, which have little traction on concrete. He slipped and nearly fell in front of the honking cars. He could have been killed. He walked back onto the fairway, where Hogan told him never to do that again.

"The next time you swing and miss, just drop the club until your sanity returns," Hogan said.

Buck is the only golfer I know who became frustrated because he got a hole in one. He topped the ball, and was cussing as it rolled into the hole.

"I don't want to be rewarded for anything I do wrong," he said.

As a golfer, I can understand that. Golf can possess you, prompting you to play better and better, but never to your satisfaction. I have analyzed my game and changed it hundreds of times. There are days I can't do anything successfully because I'm consumed with doing everything correctly. Golfers call that paralysis by analysis.

✵✵✵

You can tell a lot about a man's character when you play golf with him. I've seen guys swing at the ball, miss, and look around to see if anyone was watching, and if they thought no one was, they didn't count the stroke. I've seen players use their foot to nudge their ball slightly to get a better angle.

Golf is a game that requires simultaneous relaxation and concentration. A guy who can't control his emotions will never be a good golfer, and a guy who can't leave his problems in the clubhouse and focus on his game won't ever be any good.

I love the way the game forces me to think about it and nothing else. No one can think about two things at once. It's not only a hobby, it's therapy.

In a strange way, I sometimes feel closer to God on a golf course. The trees and rolling hills make up part of the wonders of His creation. The manicured grass shows how He has entrusted man to care about what He created. It's a simple observation, but inspirational to me.

I come alive on a golf course these days, unlike the times when my senses were dimmed by alcohol. I'm more stimulated by life in general now, because I'm sober. I celebrated my sixth year of sobriety in August 1993. That too had a lot to do with God.

✩ ✩

Chapter 13

*G*arth Brooks earned forty-four million dollars in 1991 after recording only four albums. He said he may soon retire from show business. I wouldn't blame him if he did. His life is a confusing marathon of demands by people pulling on him from all directions. Only someone who has been there can appreciate the full-scale insanity that engulfs an entertainer with runaway popularity.

In the late 1960s and early 1970s, I didn't have a career. My career had me. I lived under the dictates of airplane schedules, managers, booking agents, concert promoters, disc jockeys, talk-show hosts, and the millions of fans who were buying my records and tickets.

One risk connected to that much travel is the danger factor. The odds of accidents occurring increase with the number of miles traveled. A terrifying ordeal in the early 1970s gripped Billie, Stan Schneider, his wife, Mady, and me.

The four of us had gone to Europe, hopping from country to country. On our last takeoff on the way back to the United States, we left Paris during a foggy and violent rainstorm. The flight attendants were still in their seats when suddenly we heard a deafening crashing sound, the aircraft reeled, and a blue flame shot down the center aisle for the length of the cabin. The plane had been struck by lightning.

"We all intellectualize it now, but the reaction from everybody was, 'Did you see that lightning? It came right down the middle of the plane!' " Stan later said.

I felt I had witnessed a sign from God, for whatever reason. I remember asking Stan if he had seen God shoot through the airplane. There's no telling what he thought.

It seemed like an hour before the pilot's voice came over the loudspeaker, although it was probably no more than thirty seconds.

"We have just defused some electrical current off the plane, and there is nothing to worry about," he said.

I felt as if his big words were just false comfort to the passengers. He probably had been as terrified as the rest of us.

About ten years ago I was flying from Prescott, Arizona, to Phoenix in a private aircraft. The tower waved us off as we approached the landing strip, so the pilot circled the field. He retracted the plane's wheels, then forgot to put them back down. The plane was a turbo propeller jet. We landed without wheels, and the plane went immediately onto its belly. The whirling propellers dug into the concrete, and sparks flew seemingly fifty yards into the air.

"Oh, God," I heard the pilot say, realizing his mistake.

I was sitting right next to him, and I remember that I was reading the Bible. I'm glad now that I was. It proved to be very reassuring.

Fire engines chased the plane down the runway, and by the time the aircraft stopped, smoke had begun to emerge. The rear of the airplane was on fire. I had been to a golf tournament and was still wearing my golf shoes. I told the other passengers to beware as soon as the plane stopped.

"If you all ain't out of the way, I'll leave my cleat marks in your back," I yelled above the noise of the propellers on the concrete and the steel sliding on the runway.

There was more than $300,000 worth of damage, and my tournament partner's golf clubs were lost in the fire. He didn't really need them anyhow, as he didn't play well enough to require a set that expensive.

Some people take one extended trip annually and worry about safety. Touring musicians take extended trips daily and have to take safety for granted. Yet many entertainers, myself included, have realized that it could have been them in the aircraft that killed Buddy Holly and the Big Bopper, or riding on the Jim Reeves plane that fell out of the sky during a thunderstorm in 1964, or on the plane that flew into the side of a mountain a year earlier while carrying Patsy Cline, Hawkshaw Hawkins, Cowboy Copas, and Randy Hughes.

The entire nation reeled in March 1991, when seven members of Reba McEntire's band and her road manager died instantly in a fiery crash only seconds after takeoff near San Diego. The pilot was instrument-rated and was flying a jet, but he was a human being, and human beings make errors. His was that he flew too close to the ground, the plane's wing touched the earth, and the aircraft spun into a cartwheel. Singer Kathy Mattea said that crash represented every contemporary singer's worst nightmare.

A tornado ravaged Tulsa, Oklahoma, in April 1993. Seven people were killed. A network news reporter interviewed a survivor who had been inside a van that was picked up and hurled fifty yards through the air. He said that he didn't know why God had spared his life while allowing the taking of the lives of others, but that he was so appreciative, he was going to begin living "right." I believe there is such a thing as having the fear of God thrown into you. I've had harrowing experiences after which I couldn't help but thank God that I walked out alive. Those two aviation incidents that I mentioned above are among them.

Although I still travel extensively, I don't travel as much or as hurriedly as I did twenty years ago. For sheer safety reasons alone, that pleases me.

⋆⋆⋆

During my popularity prime, I employed eighteen people on the road, including a sound-and-light crew. We hired a twenty- or thirty-piece orchestra in every major city we played, and I often traveled on Bill Lear's personal jet. I had met Bill while playing in Reno, Nevada, and he leased his jet to me for $1.82 per mile, a lot of money back then.

My dad was overwhelmed when he learned about the flying rates, which he thought were outrageously high.

"Is that your plane?" he asked.

"No, Dad," I said. "I just leased it to come down here."

"You mean you paid a dollar and eighty-two cents a mile to come here?" he asked.

"Yes," I said.

"But ain't it about two thousand miles from California?" he went on.

"Yeah, Dad, it is," I replied.

"Well, I'll declare," Dad said. "No wonder Jesus walked everywhere he went."

There is no way you can be at your best when you're setting up equipment, playing it, tearing it down, and moving it to another town a thousand miles away, day after day. The routine is impossible for a sober man, which I wasn't. Add it to the outrageous demands that the toll of daily and nightly drinking has on you, and the whole thing becomes a formula for insanity.

I had fame, wealth, a wife, and children. But I didn't have a life. One of the reasons I'm so adamant about guarding my family time today is because I was so neglectful of it during my first two marriages. I was not a good husband, and probably an even worse father, but it wasn't because I didn't love my family. It was because I was physically and mentally gone all the time.

Absentee love has its limitations. Children would rather feel love in person than hear the word over a long-distance telephone call. My three kids with Billie—Kelli, Travis, and Kane—often didn't know when I was going to call, or from where. I would fly from one town to

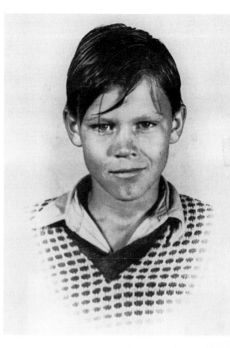

Glen Travis
Campbell—age eight.

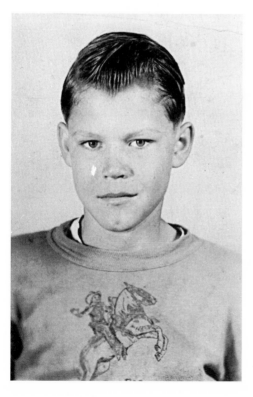

A school photograph
at age thirteen.

Albuquerque's Club Chesterfield with the Dick Bills Band in 1958. Players, from right, are Jimmy Walker, me, Dick Bills, Buzz Burnham, Red Rembert, and Johnny Toswell.

This was my Western Wranglers Band, formed shortly after I moved to Albuquerque. I was about eighteen years old. From left are Donny Cotton, Jerry Smith, and Johnny Arvin. I'm seated in front.

My eldest daughter, Debby, was two years old when this was taken in 1954. I had gotten married at seventeen to Diane, who was fifteen.

Here I am at J.D.'s Club in Scottsdale, Arizona, before trying for the big time in Hollywood. (*Photograph by Johnny Franklin*)

The Champs. From right are Jimmy Seals, me, Dash Crofts, and Bob Morris.

My first publicity photograph for Crest Records, about 1962.

Someone snapped this shot of Elvis and me backstage in Las Vegas about 1970.

Bobbie Gentry and I collected an armload of Grammy awards early in my Capitol career. (*Photograph by Jasper Dailey*)

I was joined by Tommy, left, and Dickie Smothers when I became host of the *Summer Brothers Smothers Show* in 1968.

Here are my first four children posing with my second wife, Billie. From left are Debby, Kelli, Travis, and Kane.

Lonnie Shorr, left, at Lake Tahoe, Nevada, with Roger Miller and me after my 1977 wedding to Sarah.

I put this cast together one week for a highly rated *Glen Campbell Goodtime Hour.* Despite an enormous viewing audience, the show's producers thought it was "too country." From left are Johnny Cash, Merle Haggard, Buck Owens, and me.

My parents, Wes and Carrie Campbell, joined me on my television show in 1968.

Jerry Reed and Anne Murray were on the *Goodtime Hour* before Reed became host of its summer replacement show.

Steve Martin, who wrote comedy for the *Glen Campbell Goodtime Hour*, joins me on stage in 1978 for an impromptu number.

Here I am on the set of *True Grit* in 1969 with John Wayne.

Here are the ten Campbell children and their parents at a family reunion in 1971.
Standing from the left are my dad and mom, Wes and Carrie, and their sons, Gerald,
Wayne, me, Lindell, Ronald, and Wayne. Seated from the left are Billie, Jane, Barbara,
and Sandy. I performed that night at the Houston Astrodome, and everyone here
joined me on stage.

In 1972 I began closing my show by
singing—and then playing bagpipes on—
"Amazing Grace."

Here I am with the late Roy Orbison.

Here I am with Jerry Reed and Minnie Pearl on the *Goodtime Hour* in 1970.

Here I am at the Grammy awards show in 1974, when I won, along with Loretta Lynn and Charlie Rich.

I used Bill Harrah's private jet to fly to Lake Tahoe, where this lady became my third wife, Mrs. Glen (Sarah) Campbell, in 1977.

From left, Roger and Joanne Adams, me, and Mady and Stan Schneider at my wedding to Sarah.

Johnny Cash and I sing one during a television taping in the early 1980s.

Lee Trevino and I start a round in the early 1980s. (*Photograph by Lester Nehamkin*)

This picture of Tanya Tucker and me appeared on the cover of *People* next to a headline that read: "The wildest love affair in showbiz today: Campbell, 44, and Tucker, 21." (*Photograph © Harry Benson 1993*)

Linda Ronstadt joined me on the *Goodtime Hour* in 1969.

Neil Diamond, Peggy Lee, and me during a *Goodtime Hour* television taping.

Willie Nelson, left, shares a laugh with Robert Duvall and me about 1983.

My son Cal was only a year old when he was photographed in 1983 with songwriting legend Kris Kristofferson, left, Ray Charles, and me.

Here I am in 1985 with sons, from left, Cal, Travis, Dillon, and Shannon. The bear is unrelated.

My publishing company did very well with the songs of Alan Jackson. Here we are on *Hee Haw* in 1990.

Kim was a dancer at Radio City Music Hall when I met her in 1981.

My parents
join Kim and me
at our wedding
in 1982.

At home in Phoenix.
Ashley is seated. From
right are my wife, Kim,
sons Cal and Shannon,
and me.

Kim and me in 1993 inside our Phoenix home. God used her to save my life.

My collaborator, Tom Carter, joins me backstage at the Grand Palace in Branson, Missouri, to write my life story.

another and then hurry to a pay telephone. By the time I phoned home, the kids were sometimes asleep.

"Well, tell them their daddy called," was all I could say.

It's very difficult for a marriage to survive that kind of stress. People can remain legally bound, but a legal marriage and a spiritual one are two different things.

I've never been all that interested in one-night stands, but there have been exceptions. Many entertainers take advantage of the road life— the easy women who hang around celebrities. The general public has no idea about it.

I was a man in the prime of my life who had no spiritual convictions, nothing to prohibit me from straying. I knew a single night with a woman wouldn't make up for several without one, but at times the miles and monotony bred a loneliness that was too much. I didn't care if what I did was wrong. I was ready to do anything if it meant not having to spend another night by myself. And so I occasionally strayed.

Most people don't understand the confusion of being two thousand miles away from your loved ones and standing in front of twenty thousand people who are cheering your name. The music stops, the show ends, and you go to a hotel room. The crowd was entertained while you were working. Those people go home to houses with each other. You go to a strange room in a strange city to face loneliness, which is no stranger at all.

On the road, days become interchangeable. It usually doesn't matter whether you are in an exotic place if you have to perform that night. You don't have time to sightsee. You have to get to the sound check, dress for the show, perform the show, then either go back to the room to rest for the next day's journey or leave that very night.

I've done twenty-city tours and seen nothing but the airports, hotels, stages, backstages, and all the traffic in between. I couldn't count the times I've looked for a telephone book or a book of hotel matches just to remind myself where I was.

Given my chaotic life, I don't wonder why my marriage to Billie Jean failed. I sometimes wonder why it didn't fail sooner.

About this same time, I began to alter my brain further with something that soon became my personal demon—cocaine. The first time I ever tried cocaine was with Billie Jean. She had accompanied me to Palm Springs, California, where I played in a celebrity tennis tournament for charity. One of my partners was Bill Cosby, who kept complaining that I was the worst tennis player he had ever seen.

I thought I would use the break from Los Angeles to snatch a bit of rest and relaxation with my wife. Back in our hotel room after the game, I was fast getting drunk. Fatigue from the day's tennis combined with the relaxing effect of the whiskey were making me too weary too fast. Billie said she had something that would perk me up and prolong the evening.

I, of course, had heard about cocaine because it was extremely prevalent in show business, and much of society, in 1975. Years later, I would struggle to quit cocaine, and lose the battle because of alcohol. I could never say no to cocaine when my resistance was lowered by booze.

My first attempt at snorting cocaine was awkward, and I probably missed some of the powder. To inhale it took only a couple of seconds per nostril, but those seconds changed my life for the worse for several years. I not only wish I had never done cocaine, I regret the day I ever heard the word.

I had smoked marijuana, but with little success. It always made me sleepy and I didn't care if I ever did it again. Cocaine, however, was different. The first time I didn't feel much. A lot of people have said the same thing about their first experience. But your system soon becomes accustomed to it. You stop looking for that big high and learn to appreciate the subtle high. You have the illusion of new energy and refreshment. You think you're alert and you become optimistic and happy, but this feeling lasts only ten or fifteen minutes. The cocaine that made you a new man then leaves you wanting the same old drug. So, you have more snorts. The addiction is psychological. You get to a place after a few days where you think the only time you can feel rested and happy is when you're using cocaine. It's a vicious circle that quickly becomes a nightmare.

When cocaine's high wears off, its other effects don't. It keeps you awake when you're ready to sleep. A depression grips you that is more intense than the high was. You want to sleep to find peace, but the cocaine is still in your body, which is fighting hard to metabolize it. There were times when I couldn't stand "coming down," so I would get up and inhale more cocaine. That would postpone, but not eliminate, the inevitable crash.

Bob Felts, my drummer, and I had worked together in Albuquerque as far back as 1957. Felts moved to Los Angeles at my request, was a part of the Smothers Brothers productions, and went around the world with me three times. His daughter was hit by a car on the Pacific Coast Highway and I was able to float his medical expenses without his asking, and he paid me back without my asking. We were friends as close as brothers. He was known as "Lurch."

"Lurch," I said, "you know what your trouble is? You're like a frog on a lily pad. You ought to be down here in the mire."

He told me that I was killing my career and that ultimately I was going to kill myself. I resented his warnings, and got to the point where I unfairly found fault with things he did. I was lashing out at him because he was stronger and wiser than the rest of us. He stood steadfast, but I made it so rough on him that he finally quit. We had played together off and on for twenty-one years, and I abandoned loyalty like that for cocaine.

Ultimately, however, that Godless drug would cost me a great deal more. It was the final weight thrown upon a crumbling marriage.

As I look back now, I realize that I should have been aware that Billie was losing interest when she stopped traveling with me. She would go on an occasional show date or two, but didn't want to be with me all the time, as she had when my career first took hold. Yet she had no aversion to going to England, or staying for days at a time with an interior decorator who was doing our house. I wondered later about their relationship.

Then, about a year before our divorce, Billie began to hang out with a faster crowd. I would call home and she wouldn't be there. That's worrisome to the mind when you're tired, the hour is late, and you know it's late back at your home in Los Angeles.

I told Stan Schneider that Billie was becoming obsessed by our wealth. She seemed to be consumed with being the boss of the hill. She craved power.

While I was filming *True Grit* I kept my band in Los Angeles on full salary. Billie called Bob Felts one day and told him that our pool-pump house needed painting, and that since he was drawing a wage, she expected him to do it. He called me in Colorado to tell me that he was a musician, not a house painter, and I agreed. I told him to forget the paint job, and told Billie to leave him alone. She resented both Felts and me.

I wasn't that interested in the mansion Billie was then building. It was nice, to say the least, but all I've ever cared about is being comfortable. I didn't need all the fancy architecture and expensive decorations. And I don't care to this day how fashionable something is if it isn't comfortable. Living in that minicastle was like living in a museum. It was impersonal, a place built for people who want to get away from each other. I thought the house had ten thousand square feet too many. "When that house is finally built," I once told Stan, "I'll be gone."

Billie and I argued all the time. Looking at the situation in hindsight, I know why. She was doing the very things she was accusing me of, and vice-versa.

I had an expensive wardrobe of show clothes made by the designers Harvey Krantz and Tom Stasinis. Billie, without explanation, gave away most of it. Then she held a garage sale to sell more clothes while I was gone and gave the proceeds to the school my kids attended.

When you've lived with someone for sixteen years, you get to know every facet of the relationship, including how it will end. I could see, but not prevent, that part.

The highlight of that period was discovering "Rhinestone Cowboy," my biggest hit of the 1970s, and the biggest hit I ever had in some countries. I had heard the song on the radio a year earlier. It was sung by Larry Weiss, the writer, and I bought a cassette copy. I listened to it during a tour of one-nighters in Australia. When I got back, I met with Al Coury, the vice-president of promotions and artists and repertories at Capitol Records.

"I've got to do this song I found—period," I said. "I won't take no for an answer."

He replied that he would listen to the tune if I would first hear a song he had found for me. I told him he was the boss, and agreed to listen.

He played "Rhinestone Cowboy." We had both found the same tune without even knowing it. That was a sign that the song had to be right for me. It eventually wound up number one on country, pop, and adult contemporary charts.

I cut the song in Los Angeles, determined that the lyrics call attention to themselves. This was the first time I had ever made a record in which the words needed to shine above my singing. I recorded the vocal melody, then electronically overdubbed my voice harmonizing with myself. I thought the duet would compel listeners to focus on the words.

> I've been walking these streets so long
> Singing the same old song
> I know every crack in these dirty sidewalks of Broadway
> Where hustle's the name of the game
> And nice guys get washed away
> Like the snow and the rain
> There's been a load of compromising
> On the road to my horizon
> But I'm gonna be where the lights are shining on me

I loved the line confessing compromising in the first verse. I thought it was my autobiography set to song. A song like this can do immeasurable things for a singer's career. In the entertainment industry, in fact, it is called a "career record." I've been lucky to have more than one career record.

I couldn't wait to play it for Billie. In the past, she had celebrated with me whenever I found a song like "By the Time I Get to Phoenix" or "Galveston." I was standing in our den, fumbling with the recorder, eager to get her reaction to my version of the song. But before the first note sounded, she said she hoped I wasn't going to play that dumb old cowboy song.

I was deflated. I had been looking for five years for a giant record like those that came before and during my television show. "Rhinestone Cowboy" was literally the culmination of my search. I couldn't understand how Billie wouldn't like the song if our minds were at all in tune. I could no longer deny what I hadn't been willing to admit— that this woman and I had grown as far apart mentally as we had physically. After the record went on sale, a few million buyers agreed that my musical judgment was still intact. I wished my wife had been among them.

We argued some more about the song, and Billie ended the discussion by saying that she wanted a trial separation. I told her I'd give it a try.

Lonnie Shorr was staying with us at the time, and I went to his room. I awakened him and told him that I thought he and I were going to have to go to a hotel. Billie was right on my heels.

"You don't have to go," she said to Shorr.

"Well, I won't stay if he can't," he said. I think Billie was surprised at his reply.

He and I walked out. I never went back. Lonnie and I stayed for five days at the Beverly Hilton Hotel, then resumed our schedule of one-night shows. Then it was back to Los Angeles.

Billie called me one night, later on, and confirmed my worst suspicions. She said she had been seeing another man.

"I figured you had a boyfriend, or you wouldn't have been accusing me of going out on you," I said.

Her announcement didn't even make me mad, or jealous, because I knew the marriage was hopeless.

On September 25, 1975, Billie filed for divorce in Los Angeles Superior Court. She claimed irreconcilable differences and asked for custody of our daughter and our two sons. She also wanted "reasonable support payments." The filing was only five days after our sixteenth wedding anniversary. I had endured poverty, gained wealth and stardom, reveled in the births of our children, and experienced much more with Billie Jean Campbell, but I would not go to court against her. I didn't even meet the judge who granted Billie's decree.

She got the house she loved so much, and $5 million in cash and assets. Later, she was offered $10 million for the house, but she declined to sell. She thought it was worth $16 million. After her death, her estate sold it for $3 million, although, as of this writing, the sale has not been finalized. (There was a $2-million loan against it.)

I moved into a hotel apartment in downtown Beverly Hills, but mostly I lived on the road. Compared to the spaciousness from which I had come, it was no more than a glorified closet. I could have gotten a bigger place, but I wasn't interested. I wanted to be alone, and found myself booking personal appearances just to be out of town—to be working—to be doing anything except thinking about my life. I went to places I really didn't want to see, just to keep from going home.

I had limited time with my kids. When I wanted to take them for a weekend, I was told they were busy. She knew I had few free days, but it was as if she were trying to pit the children against me. That hurts me to this day.

I couldn't always control my thoughts, and found myself remembering hundreds of little things that Billie and I had done through more than one and a half decades together. I found myself yearning for the innocence of Albuquerque, where Billie and I had been kids embarking on an incredible journey. I wondered how we could have been so happy while poor, and so miserable when prosperous. When one misses someone, he thinks only about that person's good qualities. I remembered plenty of good things about Billie. Mostly, however, I just thought about not thinking, and sought out people, anyone to keep from being with myself. But solitude eventually became inevitable, along with the taking of mental inventory that comes with it. I found myself in the psychological red.

I was drinking and drugging now to ease the pain. The abuse was fuel to the flame of my life, which was burning hopelessly out of control.

Chapter 14

★★

*A*bout a year before Billie and I divorced we gave a party. I remember the occasion because I had decided to have my hair curled about the same time. I had grown weary of its length, fashionable in those days, and decided to change my image for the first time since my career began. In another period of my life I had received a lot of mail merely because I had changed the part in my hair from the side to the middle.

If my fans had seen me with curls, there is no telling how they would have reacted. But they didn't get the chance. I felt very uncomfortable with my new image, sort of like one of the Marx Brothers. So, by myself, I bought a bottle of Afro-Sheen hair straightener and combed the inexpensive stuff into my hair, straightening out the perm that I had paid over a hundred dollars for the previous day in a Hollywood salon. My hair felt like straw for a month.

Another reason I remember the party is that it was the first time I met Sarah Davis, the wife of an old friend, Mac Davis, whose songs I had recorded. Mac, in fact, wrote most of the songs I sang in *Norwood*. I'm sure I had met Sarah earlier, but I don't recall it. I only remember thinking she looked cute and incredibly young that night, and I didn't see her again until after my separation from Billie in 1975.

I had gone to Texas to play in the Pro-Am at the Colonial Invitational, and spent several days drinking and partying with my old friend Roy Clark. I vividly recall a woman there, whom I'd never met, promising to attack me on the eighteenth green. "Rhinestone Cowboy" was the number-one song in the world at that time, and a hit that big often draws a few crazy people to the star who recorded it.

Tournament officials took the woman seriously and beefed up security. I had just stepped onto the eighteenth green when a screaming woman burst from the gallery and charged me. She was grabbed by two officers, who had trouble restraining her. The three wrestled and fell headlong into a sand trap before rising to fall into another. The woman, who scratched, kicked, and cussed the whole time, was wearing very little clothing, and appeared to have on no underpants. As she struggled, one breast fell out of her halter top.

The sight of large cops struggling with a tiny and nearly naked woman was more than the crowd could stand, and they burst into laughter. Someone emerged with a shirt, and it was thrown around her. Handcuffed, she was led away. I had never seen her before, and I haven't seen her since. I've always wondered who the pitiful woman was.

I was on my way back to California when Mac called. He was working in one of the major Las Vegas hotels and asked that I stop by on my way home, to play a little golf. He thought the recreation would be good therapy for me, as he knew I was facing a breakup with my wife after sixteen years.

In Las Vegas, I joined Sarah and Mac for dinner in a house they had rented. He insisted I attend his show that night and sit with Sarah, her sister, and her brother-in-law. Mac sang "In the Ghetto," "Baby Don't Get Hooked on Me," and his other hits, including "I Believe in Music." One of the lyrics of the last song is, "I believe in music, / I believe in love." Mac told the crowd to shout the word *love* at the appropriate time. He sang his line, the music stopped, and he shoved the microphone toward the audience as it bellowed, "Love!" The shout faded, the musicians kicked into the chorus, and Mac began to bow his way offstage. I thought it was a clever way to end the show, and the audience loved it.

After the show, the four of us went to Caesars Palace to see another late show. Mac had to stay behind to do a second show and wasn't able to join our party for the rest of the night. My interaction with the Davis family was still innocent, though there were reports afterward that I played golf with Mac on that Vegas trip and faked illness on the course so that I could go off with his wife. There were also stories going around that Mac was going to get a pistol and shoot me for trifling with his wife. None of this was true.

On that Vegas trip, Mac did surprise me by telling me that he and Sarah were having marital trouble. I had had no idea. I hurt for him. My own separation showed me how painful breaking up could be.

I've heard of the blind leading the blind, but this was a case of the wounded trying to comfort the wounded. Mac and I had been buddies for years, and I had done a guest appearance on his network television show in the early 1970s. I wanted to say something, anything, that might make him feel better. I was concerned for Sarah too, although I didn't know her well. I told her that I knew she and Mac were having problems. She said that they hadn't been getting along, and that it was curtains for the marriage. I told her that divorce really hurt.

If neither had told me the marriage was in trouble, I would have known anyway. It was obvious. They rarely spoke, and when they did, they bit each other's heads off. I didn't have to be a marriage counselor to know that their marriage was over. Divorce was just a formality.

Sarah came to my hotel room the next day and we talked for a long time. I called her a few times, knowing she was still married but also knowing the marriage was in trouble. I'm telling this straight from the heart, exactly as it happened. We talked about how unhappy we were in our separate marriages, and how happy we might be able to make each other.

I returned to California and lived briefly in a hotel, alone. It was a nice place, but a far cry from my mansion on the hill with Billie. I was busy with my touring schedule and consequently spent a lot of time away. I spent little time at my temporary home, but any time was too much. Idle hands are the devil's hands, and an idle mind is a devil's mind, particularly when it's reeling with pain and confusion.

I guess misery really does love company, because I called my friend Mac, who I knew would have some understanding as to what I was going through, and vice-versa. Sarah answered the telephone. I asked for Mac and she said he had gone to Nashville for the Country Music Association Awards. She told me that she and Mac were splitting, and I could hear her hurt. I felt sorry for her, and I felt sorry for me.

"Well," I said, "do you want to talk about it?"

She said yes.

"Well," I said, "why don't we just go out and see what the world thinks about it?"

At that point, my separation from Billie had not been publicly announced. Mac and Sarah were among the few people who knew.

Sarah agreed to go out with me.

Jimmy Bowen and his wife were going to have dinner that night at the Bat Rack restaurant, and Sarah and I joined them.

When we walked into the Santa Monica steak house, Bowen flipped out. His mouth actually opened, seeing two people who were married to two others carelessly walk into a public place together. All he could say was that he didn't know what to say.

Alone, later that night, we talked a long time about our misery and marriages. My divorce was granted a few days later, and Sarah and I seemed to be together all the time afterward. Eventually, separated but still married to Mac, she moved in with me.

Soon I began to hear that Mac was furious with me. I understand his anger now. I would never do anything like that today—live with a woman, married or single, unless she was my wife. In fact, I wouldn't even try to be a close friend to a distressed woman if she was separated. I would leave that to another woman.

I'm not making excuses for what I did, but my judgment and values were distorted because of the alcohol and cocaine. Medical people say three days are required for the average human body to flush itself of cocaine. If that's the case, my system was rarely without the drug.

Tragically, Sarah and I centered our life around cocaine. Sometimes we did it day and night, at home or on the road. We would get so high for so long that we thought we couldn't get any higher. Then we would get strung out, exhausted but unable to sleep because the cocaine was activating that part of the brain that allows sleep.

Lonnie Shorr had been away from me for about six weeks when he returned for our engagement at the Riviera Hotel in Las Vegas. He said he couldn't believe how thin I had become.

"Glen looked like he weighed about one hundred pounds," Shorr said in 1993. "Sarah looked like she weighed fifty. That might have been at the height of his cocaine addiction."

The reasons not to do drugs are too numerous to mention here. They comprise an entire book unto themselves. But one of the many characteristics of a chronic cocaine user is that he lies about his use, and I was no exception.

Friends, including Stan Schneider, occasionally mustered their courage to tell me I was killing my career and myself. I, however, insisted I wasn't using the drug, and became angry at them for accusing me. I never did the drug in front of many nonusers, but my paranoid and erratic behavior tipped them off that I was using nonetheless. When their accusations told me I didn't have them fooled, I became angrier, and told them to mind their own business. I lashed out at people who were trying to save my life.

I owe an apology to the people to whom I lied, including veteran comedian Foster Brooks. Brooks reportedly told people I was using cocaine, and if he believed that, I wish he had said it to my face, not to others. But I was wrong to dress him down and call him a liar in front of others when his accusations were correct.

Stan tells stories today about my incredibly rude behavior while I was using cocaine. They make me cringe. I've worked hard at forgiving myself for the sins for which I've been forgiven by God. When Stan suggested I consider medical treatment, I let him have it, insisting I didn't need to be treated for something I wasn't doing. Stan said I became routinely nasty to waitresses and flight attendants while under cocaine's influence. In restaurants I would make frequent trips to the men's room to snort, and I would go in and out of an airplane's bathroom to get high. I'm sure enlightened passengers knew what I was doing. I wasn't fooling as many people as I thought.

"The one thing that you can say about Glen Campbell is that he is an incredibly nice guy," Stan said in the spring of 1993. "So I knew he was using cocaine when he would become mean to total strangers for no reason. I remember flying on a United Airlines plane once when he became so rotten to the stewardess that Roger Adams and I got up and hid in the back of the plane. We just couldn't stand to be with him."

Stan said I became loud and profane, attracting the attention of other passengers. I hope those passengers read this book to know that I'm sorry, and that I haven't lived that way in years.

Sarah and I, in the meantime, were trying, foolishly, to form a real relationship while undergoing synthetic highs. We thought we always had to have cocaine, and panicked when we thought we were going to run out.

Buck Trent told me a story about Sarah and me that I have no memory of, but I don't doubt its truthfulness. I played a show in the late 1970s at Oral Roberts University to benefit the Children's Medical Center in Tulsa, Oklahoma. Bob Hope was often a guest on that annual show, with Jerry Lewis, Fred MacMurray, the Oak Ridge Boys, and Roy Clark as the host. Buck said I approached him right outside Oral Roberts's dressing room with Sarah and asked if he had any cocaine.

He handed me a bottle containing two grams and said that Sarah and I snorted half the contents right there outside the Reverend Roberts's quarters. I'm ashamed.

Sarah and I were married not long after her divorce from Mac. The ceremony was held at the home of Bill Harrah at Lake Tahoe. None of my family was there. I felt guilty about the circumstances surrounding my courtship with Sarah. Most of the people on hand were Sarah's friends or relatives. My friends were, among others, Lonnie Shorr, Stan and Mady Schneider, Roger and Joanne Adams, John Davidson, Roger Miller, and Kenny Rogers, who photographed the wedding. Kenny was in dire financial straits in those days, and told me that the photographs were his wedding gift to us.

Shorr remembered that Roger Miller got up just in time for the afternoon ceremony, held at three P.M. He remembered that Roger walked outside and saw the sunlight reflecting on beautiful Lake Tahoe.

"Bill sure has a good exterior decorator," was all Roger said.

The reception banquet included wedding cake, punch, and booze, and a great deal of cocaine had been brought by the guests. Bill Harrah probably had no idea that cocaine was being used at his party.

Sarah and I moved into Barbi Benton's old apartment shortly before our wedding. Afterward, I rented a house for six thousand dollars a month across the street from Wayne Rogers on Beverly Drive, in Beverly Hills.

The Beverly Drive place was actually a small estate with a tennis court. Kenny Rogers was an avid tennis player and regularly played on our court. He and I had been friends since I was a Los Angeles studio player in the 1960s. I had played lead guitar on a song he had recorded with the First Edition—"Just Dropped in to See What Condition My Condition Is In."

Shortly afterward, Sarah found a house she liked on Delfern Drive in the Holmby Hills section of Bel Air and I bought it for $925,000. If big, fancy houses could make a man happy, I would be a master of bliss.

But no matter how lavish my external circumstances were, I was never happy during my drug and alcohol days. Or should I say *daze?*

I was living with allegations that I had stolen Mac's wife. I didn't steal his wife. She jumped over and got into my pocket. I do think that Sarah loved me, and I know I loved her. I still love her, although I'm not in love with her. However, we fought constantly, as our conflicts were drug-induced. Stan Schneider contends that we would argue about anything.

"One would say, 'Isn't this a pretty green carpet?' " Stan recalled. "The other would say, 'The carpet is beige.' " Voices would raise, and tempers would flare. We would have a verbal free-for-all over something as stupid as the color of the carpet. It was the drugs.

Bill Maclay, who has been my road manager for fifteen years, said he developed an instinct for when to leave the room. He said he could sense a fight building before we could, and he would conveniently avoid our presence. But that didn't prevent him from hearing us down the hall, he said.

Perhaps the most curious thing about my addictions is that they never lessened my spiritual appetite. God was on my mind a great deal. I realize now that God's emissary, the Holy Spirit, was dealing with me. I could run but I couldn't hide from a God who wanted to bless me and assure eternal salvation whether I wanted it or not.

When people are high, they are uninhibited, say whatever is on their mind. Since God was mostly on mine, I used to get high and talk about spiritual things. If people didn't want to discuss those things, I would preach to them. Imagine! I was wasted out of my mind and trying to tell others what was wrong with their lives and how they could find a better life through Jesus Christ. That turned off a lot of people who still haven't forgiven me. My mental health was in worse shape than I realized.

Yet I never escaped the psychological thirst for information about spiritual things. I would get high on cocaine, then start to crash. You can do cocaine to prolong staying awake, but you can't prolong the high. When I was awake but not alert—strung out, in other words—I would go to my bedroom with my cocaine to scan the TV channels for religious programming.

One day I came across a curious man whose face filled the television screen. He looked into the camera through bifocal glasses while smoking a cigar. And he quoted from the Bible. Dr. Gene Scott's program became my favorite while I lived in Los Angeles. He's a fine teacher. His knowledge is insightful, his delivery hypnotic. At the time, much of it, unfortunately, was wasted on me. I sat like a zombie, watching Scott speak. I thought about the things he said and tried to apply them to my own life. I often wound up feeling guilty and wanting to change, but I didn't. I soon grew to hate life with cocaine, but I feared life without it. So whenever I wasn't on the road, I would go to my bedroom to take in the drug and the religious programming.

I read the Bible almost incessantly. My eyes would go over the words, but my mind was unable to absorb the text. I was struggling to get to God when I should have relaxed and let Him come to me.

Sarah went with me everywhere during those days and did almost everything I did, except play music. I had had another big record, "Southern Nights," in 1977, and my income was fine. My career had undergone ups and downs, but essentially I had been riding high for about eight years. I did guest shots on major television shows, played the main Las Vegas show rooms, and made records under a strong contract with Capitol Records.

All the outward signs of happiness were present. My public image had suffered a blow with the tabloid press because of Mrs. Mac Davis and me, but a lot of folks didn't take the tabloids seriously in those days, and with good reason. Most of the stories contained only a grain of truth inside a bushel of lies.

So, my overall image was still pretty much intact. Millions of people would have traded places with me, but not one of them could ease the loneliness I felt inside. They had no idea how hard it was being Glen Campbell, living in mental and spiritual bankruptcy.

Sarah and I fought not only because our minds were always impaired but also because I resented the nearly constant presence of her mother, who often lived with us. The woman seemed to have enormous influence over Sarah. I told Sarah and her mother that the situation was impossible, which her mother resisted.

Because of the experiences in my prior two marriages, I was determined that we would be faithful to each other. Sarah and I vowed that we would not cheat, and that we would be honest with each other. We renewed that promise frequently, and I trusted her.

I came home one day to find her crying. She told me that she had lied to me, and that she had had an affair while married to Mac. Our pact of honesty applied to the past as well as the present, and Sarah had sworn to me that she had never cheated on Mac, and therefore wouldn't cheat on me. Then she said things that made me think she was still seeing the guy. I accused her, and she denied it. It was hard for me to believe in someone who had confessed to having lied. I was never again able to put aside the distrust I developed, and things were never good between us again.

Today, I have a pretty good idea about Sarah's alleged loyalty to me. I was more brokenhearted about the dishonesty than I was about the past adultery.

We almost saved things when Sarah told me she was pregnant. Children can sometimes save relationships that adults cannot, and I was extremely excited about the baby. With the child on the way, I struggled to make a new life. I fought, unsuccessfully, against the cocaine. I could go a few days without it, then weaken, and wind up going on a three-day binge. Sarah and I promised we would help each other get off it, but wound up hiding the drug from each other and lying. We decorated a nursery, and the thought of getting the chance to be a good father thrilled me.

Our friction continued to mount, however, in the face of Sarah's mother's nearly constant presence. I felt I had bent over backward to be nice to that woman. I even bought her a new Cadillac and allowed her to live in our beautiful home as our guest. But the upcoming baby was the only person I wanted permanently in our shaky household, so I asked Sarah's mother to leave.

"If I go, I'll take my daughter with me," she said.

"Well," I replied, "give it your best shot."

A week or so after my son was born, Sarah left with her mother and our baby. My heart was as empty as the nursery. I cried for a week. I could not find Mrs. Glen Campbell, our child, or her mother. I searched frantically everywhere, wild with rage and a broken heart. I even considered hiring a private detective. Sarah or her mother had sworn her friends to secrecy about her location.

Looking back, I realize now that a lot of folks didn't want to divulge her whereabouts to a crazed cocaine addict. Perhaps they were afraid I would do something awful if I found them. Later I learned that Stan Schneider had known all along where they were, but wouldn't tell.

Finally, someone told me they were at the Beverly Hilton Hotel, and I went there with Stan. I walked into the room. Sarah looked awful. She had lost weight and her face was red and swollen from crying. I kept looking at my new son. I melted at his beauty, struggling to hold back the tears.

"Well, kid," I said, "it looks like one of us has got to go, and it looks like it's gonna be me."

Sarah leaned into me, and we hugged. It was the last time we ever embraced. I patted her back, then said, "I'll see you, kid," and walked out. I've never been back.

My son Dillon is now thirteen years old and is a beautiful young man. I occasionally get to see him, but not as much as I should. Sarah has done a good job as a single mother raising a young son. She has let it be known that she might write her own book some-day, and implied that it would cast an unfavorable light on me. She is welcome to say whatever she wants. I mean that just as sincerely as I mean that I'm sorry for my part of the wrongs in our relationship.

Sarah sued me for divorce, and got a portion of the house I had bought for her. We sold it, and her settlement for her three years with me amounted to about two million dollars.

The thing that hurt me most was knowing that my son would grow up without me. I really wanted to be a normal father inside a normal home.

After my third divorce, I was as low as the sky is high. The drinking and drugging intensified. I didn't kid myself. I wasn't drinking and drugging to enjoy life, but to escape it. I was trying to numb myself.

By now the Bible reading and cocaine use had reached marathon proportions. I would stay up for as long as three days, furiously snorting the coke while devouring the Holy Scriptures. My impaired mind struggled to understand what I was reading. I came out of my room occasionally to eat. The hyperactive effect of the drug kept me pacing the floor like a man in a cell.

When I went on the road, members of my band and others didn't want to be around me. They hated the sight of a man who was out of his mind on illegal drugs preaching the word of God. God put up with a lot from me.

Curiously, fan mail began to arrive as it hadn't in years. Strangers wrote that they cared about me and were praying for me. Many had guessed that my life was in shambles from what they had been reading in the press. They were wrong. My life was not in shambles. It was totally out of control.

I realize now that I was the beneficiary of the "unified prayer" of which the Bible speaks. The prayers of people I had never met perhaps saved my life. A fatal overdose was entirely possible for someone drinking and drugging as heavily as I was.

On one quietly hysterical day, a day like all the others, the telephone rang.

"Glen," a woman's voice said, "I've been hearing that you're going to get a divorce."

"Yes," I said, "it's true."

"I want to help you, Glen," she said. "You could use a friend."

"Sure," I said, "I could use a friend."

I hung up the telephone, and waited for Tanya Tucker.

Chapter 15

★★

I had known Tanya Tucker over the years because she and I had been booked on some of the same concerts and television shows. I enjoyed her music, and thought she was one of the best singers in the business. I initially met her backstage at the Grand Ole Opry when she was twelve. We eventually became acquaintances, but not close friends. The first time we ever had an extended conversation was years later in 1977, when Elvis Presley died.

Tanya idolized the man. She had even been accused by many critics of impersonating Elvis onstage, and she never resented the accusation. She drew freely from his act, and didn't care who knew it, because she could think of no entertainer more worthy of emulation. She took his death as hard as she would that of a member of her own family. She knew that Elvis and I had worked together, and perhaps that's why she wanted to talk to me about the death of the most popular entertainer of our time. Years later she told me that our conversations had been a source of comfort for her.

I saw Tanya at least twice during my separation from Sarah while I still lived in the house on Delfern. I had dinner with Tanya and her mother, and saw her another time in my house when she was with Buddy Killen, who was then the president of Tree Music, the world's largest country-music publisher. She, Killen, and others sat around in my den, talking and singing songs. Those visits took place in the spring of 1980.

Tanya had a reputation for personal recklessness. I surprised myself by pursuing her romantically, and many friends strongly advised me against it. They told me she was an incurable party girl who was incapable of faithfulness. Eventually I decided they were right. Nonetheless, I began dating and sleeping with Tanya before my divorce from Sarah was final. There is no fool like an old fool, and thirteen years ago, at forty-four, my foolishness could have competed with anyone's at any age. I had been through two divorces in five years, had broken countless hearts of friends and family, and had been the whipping boy of the tabloids and sometimes the mainstream press for my devil-may-care behavior. But then I discovered that I hadn't really known what bad press was.

During the fifteen months I dated Tanya, I got as much press as I had during my entire thirteen-year career, a career that had generated the sale of more than thirty million records. I learned to endure or ignore the stories, though my anger could no longer be restrained when one of the rags ran a story that implied that my parents were about to disown me because of my fast lifestyle. My parents would never have turned me away. Like the prodigal son, I could have gone home at any time and they would have taken me back. Of course I would never have considered that. However, the prodigal son was repentant, and in 1980 I was not.

I hated that tabloid story because of the unflattering light it shed on my good-hearted folks. I wanted to sue the newspaper, but was advised against it. I was told that I would lose the lawsuit because of the newspaper's First Amendment rights, and that my lawsuit would only generate more publicity that would keep the story alive.

Besides landing regularly on the front pages of the tabloids, our antics were the too-frequent subject of stories in daily newspapers, the Associated Press, and *People* magazine. We appeared on the cover of that magazine on June 30, 1980, four months after we had begun dating. Richard Pryor's fight for life after a freebase-cocaine explosion was also covered in that issue, as was a Kennedy family wedding. Those stories seemed more interesting to me than reading about an affair between two singers, but the magazine opted to put Tanya and me on the cover. The headline proclaimed, THE WILDEST LOVE AFFAIR IN SHOWBIZ TODAY.

I don't understand the priorities behind editorial judgment. The content and overplay of those articles is embarrassing to me to this day. I'm equally ashamed of the first sentence in the article, a quote from me: "I gave God a prayer . . . and He gave me Tanya." I even posed on my back with Tanya lying partially on top of me on a mountain outside Las Vegas. The photograph was blown up to a two-page spread. Man, was my thinking messed up!

The following May 4, Tanya and I were back on a *People* cover next to a headline that read, TANYA VERSUS GLEN, IT'S KAPUT FOR THE RHINESTONE COUPLE AND A SPURNED TUCKER TELLS WHY. It's all so ridiculous. Much of the article was inaccurate.

The articles and the affair that prompted them accelerated Tanya's popularity. She was a woman who never hesitated to get on the pages of the tabloids. She enjoyed publicity, good or bad, and she used to do things intentionally, just to get attention from the press. I don't think she would have dated me had I not been a successful entertainer with access to a lot of press. She appeared to enjoy having her name publicly associated with mine. It's been suggested that she dated me to further her own stardom.

Tanya was consumed with becoming a big star. She once wanted me to be her opening act in Las Vegas while she took top billing. Stan Schneider was furious.

Each of us looks back at things we did in our lives and wonders why.

As a child on the farm, I thought nothing of wading through waist-high weeds to a filthy swimming hole, never considering the poisonous snakes lurking in the underbrush. I was two miles from home and getting bitten would have meant death before I could have gotten medical attention, but I didn't think about the danger at the time. That analogy fits my affair with Tanya.

After the divorces, financial losses, emotional depletions, and overall mental depletion that I suffered at the hands of cocaine, my main priority in 1980 was to try to rid myself forever of the demon drug. And so I began to date Tanya. Back then, dating Tanya to escape cocaine was like jumping into a lake to avoid getting wet.

Tanya once addressed her problem at a recovery center. I respect her efforts to recover, but have wondered if they worked. She was one of the heaviest cocaine users I had ever met. She and her friends always seemed to have plenty.

Once, a friend of Tanya's came into our room soon after we had taken a vow of cocaine abstinence. I could tell by the way Tanya was acting that the woman had brought cocaine.

When neither of them was looking, I peeked inside the woman's purse, and saw that it was filled with gram and half-gram packets of the drug.

Tanya and I were terrible for each other as far as drugs were concerned. We promised we were going to help each other get clean. Our promises were the equivalent of a drowning man tossing another a boulder. Tanya and I were drowning in a sea of white powder.

Lonnie Shorr said in 1993 what no one would say in 1980–81—that my shows suffered as a result of the drug. He said that my singing was fine, but that I would mindlessly ramble between songs. He said he saw members of the audience look at each other and ask, "What did he say?" "What did he mean by that?" Many times he stood in the wings and cringed about the spoken senselessness I was exhibiting onstage, he said.

The trained eye could tell I was using drugs. I had lost substantial weight, my color was bad, and my mood swings were drastic. I would snap at the band for no reason.

On July 14, 1980, Tanya and I sang the national anthem at the Republican National Convention. I have often wondered what members of the Grand Old Party would have thought had they known that their opening-day singers had recently been higher than the notes they were singing.

During the 1992 Republican National Convention, whose platform included family values, Dan Quayle lashed out at the fictional Murphy Brown for having a child out of marriage. I wondered if he knew that the real-life Tanya, who had performed at the convention, had had two children out of wedlock. A few newscasters raised the same question. The man in charge of booking entertainment for the 1992 convention reportedly was fired because he had hired Tanya.

Tanya, in a way, was good for me in the first week of our relationship. She was understanding about my grief over Sarah and Dillon. She spoke with compassion. I've since wondered if she wasn't simply taking advantage of a wounded man.

It doesn't take a genius to know that a man with a broken heart and a drug-altered mind makes poor decisions, as I did when one day I asked Tanya what she was doing with the rest of her life. I wanted her to do it with me.

I sang background on some of her records, and we did a duet called "Dream Lover." I think the song would have been a big hit if it hadn't come out in the midst of all the bad publicity. We had a good stage show, and we talked privately about a Valentine's Day wedding, and even planned to go into business together. I spent $115,000 on a Beverly Hills boutique that was to have been called Rhinestone Cowgirl. I had intended to invest as much as $350,000 and ride a white horse into the store as part of the grand opening. Tanya had begun to assemble inventory before we broke up. Later she wore the thousand-dollar dresses we were supposed to have sold, while I wore egg on my face. The store was just one more disaster that sprang from our relationship.

Tanya seemed to have two personalities. At times, all she cared for was herself. When she was sober, she was nice. She charmed my parents when I took her to Arkansas. She could be so humble, and the impression she made on many members of my down-to-earth rural family was lasting. She told one of my brothers that she wanted to put horses on his land. Ten years after our breakup, he asked someone who knew me if Tanya was ever going to deliver those horses. The acquaintance said he doubted it because Tanya and I were long since broken up.

"Well," he said, "I don't see what that's got to do with her running a few horses down here."

She really did win the hearts of my kinfolks.

When Tanya was drinking and drugging, she was a crazy woman. She became verbally abusive and physically aggressive. Although she was small, she was strong. The woman had the nerve and strength to fight a chain saw. Too often, she viewed me as the saw.

In our sick slavery to things of the flesh, we were either having sex or fighting much of the time. We even fought during sex once or twice.

We once tore the drapes off the walls at the Plaza Hotel in New York. I had to pay twelve hundred dollars for damages on top of the room fee. Stan Schneider checked us out of the hotel, and was told by management that they preferred that we never return. Stan remembered in 1993 how Tanya and I were cussing and throwing things at each other, and obscenely swearing that we never wanted to see each other again. By the time he got us out of the hotel and into the limousine, we were smooching, he said. How warped I was back then.

He also reminded me about a golf tournament and private party in Texas. Stan was sleeping at one end of a condominium; Tanya and I at the other. Except that we didn't sleep. We fought all night, and Stan says I threw and broke a lot of things. He could hear us down the distance of the hall through two closed doors.

At daybreak, still high, I went onto the golf course (which was right outside the bedroom) in my underwear as golfers were approaching. Stan felt an obligation to get me out of public sight, but was afraid to approach me because I was so verbally violent and destructive. So Stan approached the war zone yelling that one of us was going to kill the other. He said he was also afraid I might turn on him.

"Glen's not physical," Stan said in 1993. "I didn't think he would ever hit me, but he got so violent when he got high that it was scary. Up here he is very strong," he said, patting his chest. "You know, I thought, 'There could always be the first time,' but he never did."

And I never would have, not even in my reckless days.

Just the memory of all that mayhem and confusion makes me want to thank God for delivering me.

Not long after we began dating, Tanya and I went to Phoenix to visit her sister. We returned frequently, and I fell in love with the city. I eventually bought a house there and I still live in it today. That was one of the few positive things that emerged from our association.

I made news on March 11, 1981, for a "mysterious" admission to a hospital in Donelson, Tennessee, for "emergency" treatment. The hospital refused to tell the press the nature of my illness, but by then my reputation for clashing with Tanya was fueling rumors all over Nashville. Mike Borchetta, a record promoter, had heard that I had been hospitalized because Tanya hit me with an iron skillet shortly after she and I had videotaped scenes for *Country Comes Home,* a CBS special. This wasn't true. I had done the scenes with Tanya, but missed the taping of my solo the next day because I was in the hospital. The truth is that Tanya and I had had a giant cocaine-laced argument after our videotaping session, and I had had all I could stand. The fighting had been going on for a year, during which I had become an emotional wreck. I don't remember who called an ambulance for me, but I really thought I had gone off the deep end.

I remember lying in that bed looking at the ceiling and thinking how pitiful it was that things had gotten so far out of control. I stayed in the hospital, sedated, for four days. I was in the one place where no one could find me, and where I couldn't get illegal drugs. The recuperation was wonderful. I just lay there reflecting on what had been the most tumultuous year of my life.

There were several false starts on my ending with Tanya. I couldn't get her out of my life as rapidly as I wanted because I was a weak creature of habit and manipulation.

I remember one breakup, for example, that almost ended in reunion when Tanya showed up unexpectedly at the Sands Hotel in Las Vegas in 1981. My defenses toward her, and the rest of life's pressures, were low because of cocaine. When I heard she was in town, I became physically ill.

"Don't go back to her," admonished Lonnie Shorr. "Just ignore her. Hang out with me if you want to."

Shorr said in 1993 that he remembered coming backstage at the Sands at ten-fifteen P.M. to get ready for our eleven o'clock show. He passed me in a corridor, where I told him I wasn't going to do the show because I was sick. I canceled, and ticket holders were given refunds.

"This [show] is your organization," Shorr had snapped at me. "I'm not a part of the daily organization, so I don't have to be your 'yes' man."

Then he told my band and me what he thought about my allowing myself to be so affected by Tanya's return. He was right, but he was sober. Lonnie doesn't smoke or use drugs, and never has. Drugs and alcohol were keeping me beaten down and eliminating my resistance to the slightest weakness. It was as if Tanya were an addiction. In other words, I dreaded the very thing I wanted, the way some alcoholics dread getting drunk. But in my Godless existence I couldn't seem to get away from her cleanly.

Lonnie has never hit a woman in his life, but he almost belted Tanya. I did my show the next night, and Tanya came backstage while I was still performing. She approached Shorr, who had never met her. She put her hand on his, and simply said, " 'Come on, man, give it up,' " he told me.

"Give up what?" he asked her, suspecting that she thought he had drugs. He told her he didn't know what she was talking about, and ordered her to stop touching him. "If you don't let go of my hand, something's going to happen to you right now," Shorr said he told her. Pressed about what he meant, Shorr said he was "very close" to hitting her.

"I never had a good time with her," Shorr said, "because it was very obvious to me what she was. She seemed to be opportunistic and pushy at the time, and whether she was or not, I just didn't like what was happening to Glen. I didn't like seeing him like that."

Several months later, after our breakup in May, I was playing in Dallas, about a forty-five-minute flight from Shreveport, Louisiana, which was near where Tanya was playing at a Bossier City hotel. I don't know what prompted me to fly out to see her, but it was like old times. We got into the booze, the cocaine, and arguments after the show. She locked me out of her hotel room, but my coat was inside. I began to curse and kick on the door, wanting my coat. She didn't respond. Hotel security was called, and then the police came and threatened to arrest me if I didn't settle down. About five A.M., I was told that I could either go away from Tanya's door or go to jail. I left, and never got my coat, but I did get a lot of publicity. Although I was not arrested, a story that I had been jailed was reported in a Shreveport newspaper and picked up by the Associated Press. It appeared in newspapers throughout the world.

Tanya, even when sober, was a spitfire and a daredevil. She couldn't stand to be outdone. We were rafting the Lava Falls in the Grand Canyon, and she kept daring me to go through the right side of the falls, the roughest part of the rapids. With her, everything was reduced to competition. It was like, "My dog is better than your dog and I'll bet you." All this was annoying to me, as I subscribed to Roger Miller's laid-back approach to competition.

Roger said he made a list of the men he could whip, and showed it to a guy whose name was on top.

"You can't whip me," the man said.

"Okay," Roger said, "I'll take your name off the list."

This kind of willingness to let Tanya have her way didn't always work. She kept on daring and goading until she got a reaction out of me. And she often did.

Tanya and I got into a fight one night in Las Vegas and she proceeded to break many of the fixtures in my room. She kept trying to hit me, and I kept trying to hold her off. She stormed out of my room and into another next door. I stood there looking at the shambles and wondering how much I would have to pay for the damages. After a while, things became disturbingly quiet in her room. I knocked on her door. She didn't answer. I had gotten to know my temperamental girlfriend thoroughly, and my instincts told me something was wrong. I knocked on the door again. Nothing. I kicked it open and my heart leaped at the sight of Tanya, sobbing quietly in the half-dark. There were tears on her face and a knife in her hand. She was sawing at her wrist. She had begun to bleed, and might have died had it not been for the small size of the knife and its dullness. I had used it to clean my golf shoes, and its edge was badly worn.

I kicked the knife out of her hand and tried to calm her down. Then I called a doctor who was a friend. He sewed up her wound and consoled her. He talked about how close she had come to doing a terrible thing and she was visibly shaken.

I, however, was soon back into the cocaine, and someone in my band had called Stan Schneider in Los Angeles, where it was not yet daylight.

"You'd better get up here. They're going to kill each other this time," Stan was told.

His wife didn't want him to get out of bed and fly out of state to attend to Tanya and me. Understandably, she had had it with Stan's being a referee during my drug-laced fights with women. But being the true friend that he is, Stan nonetheless flew to Vegas on the first available flight.

He walked into my room and it was a shambles. By then, the sun was high, and so, still, was I.

Stan called a doctor, who administered a syringe filled with tranquilizers. Stan recalled that when I received the injection, I was so out of it on cocaine, I couldn't talk. I had often been so high, I would lose my motor skills. Watching me shake and hearing me mumble mindlessly, he feared I had finally gone too far and had overdosed. And this episode wasn't even the worst.

The most terrifying moment of my life came later, also under the grip of cocaine. I was convinced I was going to die and enter eternity begging God for life. Tanya was with me. It happened during the only time I ever smoked freebase cocaine. Freebase is similar to crack in that both are lighted and smoked through a pipe. Freebase, however, involves igniting highly explosive ether. Do it right, and the burning ether and cocaine will make you high. Do it wrong, and the ether can explode and set you on fire.

Someone already high on cocaine held in his shaking hand the flame to light the ether. I was placing my life in the hands of someone who was obliterated. But I was so high from having snorted cocaine, I didn't think about the risk.

Tanya had taken me to the Las Vegas house where the freebase was being cooked. I took my first drag and could have been bathed in flames, as Richard Pryor had been. I pulled the cloudy smoke into my lungs, and felt my head leave my shoulders. I had never experienced such an immediate and intense high. Then my heart started to pound. And pound. And pound. With my hand I could feel my heart beating inside my chest. I thought that it was going to explode, literally, and that I was going to die right there of internal bleeding.

My high turned into hysteria. I flopped onto a couch where I lay facedown, begging God to let me live. I could feel my heart pounding against the cushion. People around me kept smoking more freebase.

"Please, God," I pleaded, "don't let me die. If you'll spare my life, I'll never smoke cocaine again."

The pounding and pleading went on for six hours. When it was over, I could barely stand, and tottered from the house to a car that took me back to our hotel.

I have no trouble understanding how the basketball star Len Bias died at twenty-two after he took his first snort of cocaine, which became his last. He was the number-one draft choice of the Boston Celtics, and would have played with Larry Bird. To celebrate being picked, he tried cocaine and his heart exploded.

I think only someone who uses cocaine is dumb enough to use cocaine. I can't believe I was so desperate for the drug that I was willing to snort it on a regular basis and risk my life. God has given me many good things. But if He had never given me anything but deliverance from cocaine, that alone would make me thankful forever.

Tanya might have died during another cocaine-induced accident. We were at the home of a friend and had gotten into the powder. She went outside and could have reentered through the door, but instead, a deafening crash filled the room as Tanya, high, walked through a large plate-glass window, barefoot. The glass was thick and could easily have punctured her throat or an artery. She was lucky that it broke in such a way that it cut only her feet. She was bleeding all over the place and should have been taken to the hospital, but I was too high to drive. I don't remember what we did to stop the bleeding. I just remember blood on the floor.

There is no point in itemizing further our hellish behavior. You get the idea that our relationship was one of runaway madness. Besides, I can't remember many of those days because I was wasted, and because fighting and hell-raising weren't memorable. They were routine.

I threw a lavish twenty-second birthday party for Tanya in October 1980 that cost $57,000 at the Bistro, a chic Beverly Hills restaurant. I told her I would buy her a giant diamond, but Tanya settled for $4,500 worth of earrings and a ring. Her dad later wanted a Caterpillar tractor for his business. I gave him $25,000, but I don't think he used the money for that purpose.

When we broke up, I felt as if I had been taken to the cleaners again by a woman, and couldn't help wondering if money had been her incentive all along.

Once, when Tanya and I were in New York City's lavish Plaza Hotel, I noticed an expensive dress in her closet. I recognized it as one that was supposed to be a part of the inventory of the Rhinestone Cowgirl store. I was annoyed that Tanya had worn it. My annoyance was compounded when I discovered that the dress had been torn in front. When I demanded an explanation, Tanya said she had torn the dress on an object. She finally told me that the dress had been torn while she was with a famous television producer. Tanya had gone to his house behind my back. I had never trusted her, and trusted her less after discovering her charade. I had no idea whether he had torn it off her, or what they did after if he had. There were more lies before she confessed. I called the producer and told him that I had thought he was my friend, and that I didn't appreciate him secretly entertaining my girlfriend. He said their time together had been innocent, but I wondered why, if it was so innocent, I hadn't been invited.

That was the final straw for Tanya and me.

An article appeared in May 1981 saying I had dumped Tanya because she had gone to L.A.'s Le Dome restaurant without me after I had asked her not to go. I did ask her not to go, but I didn't break up with her because she went anyhow, then lied about it. A limousine chauffeur told me the truth, and Tanya again owned up to her dishonesty.

The torn dress, and the unfaithfulness that it implied, was the finale in a series of maddening ordeals with Tanya.

Having made up my mind that it was over, I went to The Nugget casino in Reno, where Tanya was playing, to say good-bye. Her mother, father, sister, and brother were there. Those people always seemed to be around her, and as a result, Tanya and I didn't spend a lot of healthy time alone.

"I'll see you later," I told Tanya. "There are no hard feelings."

It was that brief. I had gotten good at good-byes.

I was more hurt than I let on to anyone. I wanted company, and sought out my old friend Loretta Lynn, who was also playing Reno, at Harrah's. I called her and asked if she would talk to me.

Loretta and a friend shared a room, and the three of us sat there visiting in the wee hours. Loretta said she was going to tell me how to get over Tanya and my broken heart. I prepared myself for some deeply philosophical advice.

"Did you ever see a mule eat saw brier?" she asked. "He eats it like this," she said, and then she forced a wide grin while chewing slowly. The mule "grinned" to prevent the jagged saw brier from hurting the sides of his mouth. "Well, that's what you have to do, Glen Campbell," Loretta said. "You just force yourself to grin and bear it."

It was homespun advice from perhaps the most practical person with whom I'd talked in a long time. And I took it.

Less than a week later, I was off on a tour of Europe without Tanya.

I never run into Tanya anymore. Her career is going well and I congratulate her. In 1991, she was the Country Music Association's Female Vocalist of the Year, a title formerly bestowed upon, among others, Loretta Lynn, Tammy Wynette, Dolly Parton, Reba McEntire, Barbara Mandrell, and Emmylou Harris. Tanya's singing rightfully puts her in that company. She's been singing since she was twelve, and deserves the success that has come to her.

Recalling these stories of our time together has been difficult. I want to tell the truth about myself, but don't want to incriminate anyone else. That, obviously, has been impossible to avoid with Tanya.

I also have an ethical obligation to set the record straight about one of the most publicized times of my life. My collaborator, Tom Carter, told me that the most frequently asked question he heard as he and I wrote this book was, "Is Glen going to tell it right about Tanya?" Some people's priorities for gossip are regrettable. But at this point in my life, I have nothing to hide, and much for which to be thankful. I can't undo some of the things I've done. I can just say I'll never do them, or anything like them, again, Lord willing. I don't think folks would have much respect for me or my credibility if I hadn't addressed my insanity with Tanya.

I don't remember when I last saw her, except occasionally on television. When I do, I'm inclined to pray for the woman with whom I shared a poisoned relationship. I have since found another love that offers not the threat of death but the promise of eternal life. I pray that Tanya might find that too.

Chapter 16

★★★

*B*y the middle of 1981, I had enjoyed as much romance as I could stand. I had no romantic interest in anyone and didn't want any. Women came around after my shows, as they always had, but I was virtually indifferent. Three divorces and a broken engagement will have that effect on a man.

Instead, I dived headlong into my music. Interest in country music had been revived in 1980 almost solely because of the motion picture *Urban Cowboy* with John Travolta. The movie was about a manual laborer who enjoyed dressing like a cowboy and dancing to country music.

The country lifestyle in the film caught on. Americans suddenly were back listening to country music as they hadn't in years. Because of the country thrust, hit songs began to pour out of Nashville, and I decided to record more there and less in Los Angeles. I made most of my 1980s records in Nashville.

I also focused on live performing. From 1981 through 1983, I performed two shows nightly, seven nights a week, approximately twelve weeks a year, in Las Vegas. When I wasn't working Las Vegas,

I was on the circuit of one-night engagements. Someone working that much doesn't have a lot of time to think about his personal life, or the lack of one.

The road can be a grind, but it can also be an escape. The songwriter Billie Joe Shaver wrote that "moving is the closest thing to being free." When I'm constantly in motion, I develop the illusion of outrunning my problems—and thoughts. At the end of a whirlwind thousand-mile tour playing to thousands of people, I return to the quiet of a lonely room, where my thoughts ambush me. But not for long. Soon I have the crutch of having to move again. The forced travel becomes therapy defined by distance.

As I look back, I realize I was doing no more than running from my problems, and using my career as an excuse.

One of the questions that I have been most frequently asked is how I handle the monotony of the miles. Generally, I take the trips, but there have been times when they've taken me—when the pace and pandemonium have been too much. During these moments, humor is a release. Some people think that musicians are overgrown children because they're given to mischief. There have been times in my life and career when humor was more than just amusement. It was a mental pressure valve. I thank God for the gift of laughter, and that I knew it before and after my conversion to Christianity.

One of the many negative effects of the drugs I'd been taking was that they caused me to say exactly what I was thinking. I was forever letting my mouth overcome my common sense in those drug-and-whiskey days. Some of the stunts may have been funny then, but now I realize that they could have carried serious consequences.

In 1981 I was flying to Indonesia. An official of the Indonesian government was in first class, where I also was sitting. Members of my band were flying coach. I don't know if they were using cocaine, but they were particularly restless. They wouldn't stay in their seats, and kept coming up to the first-class section to talk to me.

The bodyguard for the Indonesian official didn't appreciate that.

He told them to return to their seats, and that made me angry. It probably seemed like discrimination to me at the time. Then he came over to my seat and told me to keep my friends in their place. I was drunk, and thought he was out of place, and told him so. Then I said I was going to call my friend Ronald Reagan and ask him to bomb Indonesia.

That really offended the guy, who told his boss, who told the flight attendant. I could have started an international incident at thirty thousand feet. The band members had long hair, and the flight attendant might have thought they were terrorists. One of the guys in the band said that every time he looked at the stewardess she was already looking at him, and making a lot of notes too.

All the while, unbeknownst to us, the flight crew had called ahead to report our rowdy behavior.

We were met by Indonesian officials when we landed, and they were not amused. My road manager, Bill Maclay, hurried me through customs to a waiting car. I was rushed to my hotel by a driver who I tipped one hundred dollars. I later found out that the money represented a month's wages for him.

Meanwhile, my band members and Stan Schneider were still being held at the airport by angry customs officials. My people were questioned and harassed about our in-flight behavior for ninety minutes. Stan told me later that he was scared. He didn't know if members of my group would be allowed to enter the country, be deported on the spot, or be whisked to prison, where they would never be heard from again. He kept thinking about the motion picture *Midnight Express,* a film about an American arrested in Turkey, where police put him in a filthy prison and tortured him for drug possession. American diplomats were unable to get the guy released for a long time, during which he was savagely beaten and raped.

My drinking and the behavior it induced had caused all the trouble. My banjo player, Carl Jackson, wasn't drinking at all. He became smart with Indonesian officials.

"You can't hold us here at this airport," he began to shout. "We're Americans!"

He wouldn't shut up. Stan was sure that Jackson was going to get everybody arrested. So Stan, almost always in control of his emotions, physically grabbed Jackson. He later told me that he grasped Jackson's mouth in an effort to force it closed.

"Shut up or I'll break your face," he said he told Jackson.

The group finally was loaded into cars, and everybody rode to the hotel in virtual silence. Indonesian officials were leery of my entourage and me throughout our brief stay. They were afraid that my show might contain something offensive or something that might start civil unrest. So I was forced to audition for a panel of military generals before I could give my live concert. Some of Indonesia's top brass sat motionless in the front row of an otherwise empty auditorium. I played, sang, told jokes, and did all the rest that comprise my show.

No applause. No smiles. No response. They just glared at me. When the last note was sounded, they huddled and whispered, and I was given the go-ahead to do my show for the public later that night.

✮✮✮

The funniest things that have happened to me in my career have been accidental. I have always been very aware of public relations and pretty willing to do whatever anyone asked if it would help my career.

I was asked to do a commercial shortly after the release of "Gentle on My Mind."

Mike Borchetta said I should do it for Leo Pearlstein, a Southern California entertainment mogul, although I don't know why. I'm sure Mike had his reasons, and thought that my helping Pearlstein would indirectly help me. Finding such schemes was a big part of Borchetta's job, and he was the best.

I showed up at the radio station to tape the commercial and paid no attention to the script until I was doing the commercial live over the air.

I waited for the director to cue me. He pointed, and I began, thoughtlessly, to speak aloud what was on the page.

"Hi," I said, "I'm Glen Campbell, and whenever I need a lift, I simply pop a prune . . . I do what?!"

I wasn't a big fan of prunes, and was amazed by what I had just said. My astonishment was heard across Southern California.

I guess the disc jockey made a joke about my candid remark, and that probably sold more prunes for them than would have been sold had I done it right. But I was never asked to advertise prunes again.

✴ ✴ ✴

After "Gentle on My Mind" hit, I was able to hire musicians of quality to tour with me. Like most people who are good at something, they were ambitious, and wanted to better themselves. The bass player, Bill Graham, reminded me recently of an incident involving Dennis McCarthy, the keyboard player we had then who is now one of the top television music arrangers and composers in Hollywood today. When he started with us, however, he had not yet learned to arrange music. But he had a burning desire to learn. We would see him reading books with titles such as *How to Arrange Music* on the airplane between shows. The rest of us would be sleeping, or cutting up, but Dennis was doing homework, advancing his craft.

We once played a club in California. Having arrived late, we had no time for a rehearsal with the orchestra. Since my early songs had been recorded with orchestras, we hired new ones in every town to reproduce the sounds on my records.

Our would-be arranger debuted his new skills on that California show. He hurriedly distributed sheet music to the various orchestra members, and they placed it on their music stands.

I was introduced, the banjo introduction to "Gentle on My Mind" kicked off, the curtain rose, and the other musicians fell in. The band, of course, knew the song, and needed no charts. Dennis had written the arrangements perfectly, except for one thing: The sheet music was in the wrong time signature. In other words, my band was playing at one tempo, the orchestra at another.

It sounded like a Chinese fire drill.

Dennis should have quit right there and tried again on the second show. Instead, he began to run nervously around the stage with an eraser. He tried to erase the time signature and write a new one on every piece of sheet music while the show was under way. Some people in the audience thought it was a comedy act. I didn't know what to think.

The orchestra players, who were in black tie, were dumbfounded at this guy trotting around in front of them. The band was laughing too hard to play and some of the orchestra members quit too. We stopped the program altogether until all the charts could be amended.

I wonder if Dennis remembers this inauspicious beginning to what has become a distinguished career.

✴✴✴

For every "star" in show business there are a hundred people behind the scenes. Many of the folks behind the curtain are as important or more important than the celebrity out front, but the anonymous workers are often unrecognized by the famous. The most comical example of that kind of thing came one night in the 1970s when I played Las Vegas at a hotel in which Elvis had closed the previous night. Elvis stayed in town a day longer to see my show, and I was flattered. I introduced him to the audience, and he stood up at a table but didn't come onstage.

Bill Graham was always the first member of my band to get to the dressing room after a concert. He hated neckties, and almost ran to the dressing room to get out of his. He did the same thing that night in Vegas, then eased behind the wet bar to fix himself a cocktail.

The second person to enter the room was Elvis. When Graham saw him, he attempted to be hospitable.

"Mr. Presley," he said, "may I fix you a drink?"

Elvis told Graham what he wanted.

Before Graham could get out from behind the bar, another person came into the room, then another, and soon the room was full. Graham, who knew everyone there, asked each person if he or she wanted a drink, and fixed it because he happened to be at the bar.

I sat down on a couch with a vacant space beside me. Graham finally fixed himself a drink and sat down beside me, directly across from Elvis, who had a funny look on his face.

Someone giggled and I said, "Elvis, have you met my bass player, Bill Graham?"

"I thought he was the bartender," Elvis said.

At that point, Elvis knew he had made a mistake, and he knew everybody knew it. The room exploded with laughter. Elvis never asked Graham to serve him another drink.

★★★

When you're in charge of six or eight musicians, and an occasional orchestra, you can't always know what each player is doing. I learned recently about a couple of pranks that I'm not sure I would have thought were amusing at the time, and I certainly don't now. Life on the road can drive grown men to do things they would never do at home.

The Royal Scots—the Royal Regiment for Scotland—that nation's premiere group of bagpipe players, played Las Vegas for a few weeks with me. They were my opening act, and were terrific at getting the crowd in a festive mood. They were incredibly theatrical, playing, some thirty strong, in the casino first, then marching into the show room and onto the stage. The sound of that many bagpipes set to marching feet is deafening. The crowds often became excited and received the players with a standing ovation.

The men were in full Scottish regalia, and performed native dances and folk songs. They were serious men who took what they did seriously. They were, in fact, forbidden to smile during their performance by official order of their government.

The impish boys in my band couldn't stand it. They were determined to break up those players. They stood where the crowd couldn't see them and made faces at the bagpipers. They pulled on their trousers as if they were kilts, and pranced around like little girls, but nothing they did penetrated the discipline of the trained and commissioned players. That is, until my musicians papered the floor of the bagpipe players' platforms with photographs from *Playboy* magazine.

Bagpipe players must look down. This night, when they did, the platforms on which they stood were covered with the centerfold photographs. One of my musicians said he could see the men shifting their feet, trying in vain not to stand on the photographs. The men couldn't contain themselves, and laughter swept through the marchers. Because they couldn't play while laughing, many had to "set out" a song or two. The crowd had no idea what was happening.

My players had been disrespectful to men who take family values and their craft very seriously. I can only apologize in hindsight because I didn't find out about it until recently.

★★★

I was on a diet in 1978 while playing an engagement at Lake Tahoe, Nevada, with Lonnie Shorr. He and I were staying in a two-story suite provided by the hotel we were performing in.

Twenty-four-hour food service was provided by two live-in chefs. One agreed to fix Shorr and me a "Southern" dinner, complete with fried vegetables and hefty steaks. Neither the chef nor Shorr knew that I was on a weight-reduction program that I had read about involving light-heavyweight boxer Archie Moore.

When Moore was training for a fight and wanted to lose weight, he would chew but not swallow his food. In this way he would derive all the vitamins and minerals from the food, but none of the bulk. I decided to try it.

I chewed my beef, then discreetly placed the chewed portions on another plate, visible only to me. Soon, a pile of chewed meat was on the table.

Then I began hurriedly passing food to Shorr.

"Have some okra," I said, and almost shoved the plate in his face. "Have some beans, have some sliced tomatoes, have some grits," I continued. He became caught up in the momentum of taking food off the passed plates. "Have some of these," I said, and thrust the platter of chewed nuggets into his hand.

Perhaps he thought they were chicken gizzards, a common entree at Southern tables. He began to scoop the meat onto his plate. I could see him wondering whether he was supposed to eat the colorless stuff with his fork or his hands. Perhaps he didn't want to insult the cook by asking what sat before him. As he raised a piece of chewed meat to his mouth, he looked at my plate and noticed my steak was missing.

He instantly "snapped" to what I had done to him. I wouldn't have let him eat the meat, and after that incident, he didn't want to finish his meal anyhow.

✴ ✴ ✴

Musicians are representatives of the bandleader or star (a word I hate) for whom they play. Most musicians are relatively unknown by the public at large. So, if my bass player misbehaves, for example, it's noted that "Glen Campbell's bass player did so and so," while the offender himself is never mentioned by name.

I'm much more concerned that my players meet certain behavioral standards now than I once was. If I had always made the same demands on my musicians that I make today, I would have fired a lot of players through the years.

For twelve years, I stayed at London's elegant Carlton Towers Hotel whenever I played in the vicinity. Each time the band and I returned, we were called by name and given royal treatment. The staff couldn't have been nicer about making us feel at home.

Hotel management strongly hinted that I stop staying there after two members of my band got into a free-for-all inside the dignified surroundings. One guy was small in stature, and the other deemed himself a macho man. It started out as friendly shoving, then evolved into a fistfight that took the fighters over and behind a bar. Glasses were broken, ashtrays were upended, and alcohol and other waste covered the floor.

I didn't know about any of this at the time. Nor did I know that some members of the band had been carousing and harassing female members of the hotel staff for days.

On the last day of what became my last stay, the macho man I mentioned above, for no apparent reason, threw an ashtray through the lavish hotel's two-story mirror at the bottom of a staircase that looked like something out of *Gone With the Wind.* I had to pay for the damage, and the guy was fired when we returned to the United States. Stan Schneider had to give the guy his notice, and told me he feared the fellow's explosive temper. Stan even told some of the women in my Los Angeles office to listen outside his door while he fired the guy. "Come and see about me if you hear loud noises," he told them.

"You know what?" he told the macho man. "It's just not going to work out."

"Okay," the guy said brightly. "Thanks for all of your support. I'll see you down the road."

He left without incident.

I wish he had been that well behaved when he worked for me. He might still have his job.

Bill Maclay was forever having trouble with that same musician, as the fellow overslept constantly. The entire band and crew would be packed and ready to leave for the airport, and Bill would have to go to his room to shake him awake.

One day we had a five A.M. departure call. Bill had warned the guy that he had better not carouse all night because he was tired of having to shake him from a drunken sleep. He told him that he was on his own, and that he would leave him in the hotel before he would again wrestle him awake.

So the guy packed his bags the night before and set them by the door, as is the custom in some European hotels.

The next morning, as Bill was rubbing the sleep from his own eyes, he heard the hotel maids giggling and tittering outside the macho man's door. He had left the door open. Inside, he was passed out on top of his bed. He apparently had fallen asleep before he could turn down the sheets, and lay sprawled out on the bedspread. He wore nothing but cowboy boots and a vest. Anyone who walked by his room could see him through the open door.

I think I would have fired him had I known about that incident.

The guy was forever missing planes and the rest of the group would leave without him. That happened before we played Oklahoma City, and the band went onstage without the absent player. The crew had set up his equipment, but no one expected him to make the show.

Just as we were walking onto the stage, Bill was called on his two-way radio by someone else in my organization.

"You're not going to believe this," the caller said. "Look to your right."

The offending musician had rented a car and was driving it across a furrowed field. Its front end went up and down like the gag car on television's *Dukes of Hazzard*. It looked like a Marx Brothers routine. The kicker is that another car was with him and it too was bouncing across the plowed rows. It belonged to a police officer! My mischievous musician had gotten a late flight after oversleeping. He landed in Oklahoma City, rented a car, and told the cops who-knows-what in order to get a private police escort to the show.

This guy was always renting cars at his own expense to get him to a show for which his transportation had been prepaid. He once rented a car in Minneapolis and Bill reminded him to turn it in. He did—two months later. The guy forgot to return the vehicle for more than sixty days, and had to pay the rental fee for all that time.

✭✭✭

There was a great deal of drug abuse among many of my musicians in the late seventies and early eighties. Stan wanted to fire anyone for doing drugs, but realized the obvious conflict of interest, considering I was doing them myself. Besides, I frequently did drugs with my players, so that made Stan's antidrug stance even harder to assume.

One time when we were returning from Canada, my band and I were given routine searches by customs agents. I had a guitar player who tried to hide marijuana inside his guitar case. He simply laid the drug on top of his instrument, so that it was in plain sight when the agent opened the case. The hiding job was so terrible, I assume the musician was high when he hid his dope.

When the marijuana was discovered, the agent became angry. He searched musicians, and their instruments, who had previously been cleared. That time, he found a single marijuana seed in the bottom of a piano case. Ironically, the pianist had stopped using marijuana about a year earlier, and the seed was an unwanted leftover from his previous days.

The next time my band and I went through customs, each musician was meticulously searched, as it was recorded in official documents that Glen Campbell's band had tried to smuggle dope into the United States. One band member was even strip-searched.

I had musicians who cut holes in the foam rubber inside their instrument cases. They filled the holes with dope, then used glue to attach foam rubber over the hole. The trouble was that the glue smelled. A customs agent smelling new glue on old equipment becomes suspicious.

Bill Maclay has been a real diplomat in talking agents out of arresting many of my men. He was sometimes unsuccessful, however, in preventing their detainment, during which the offending guys were scared to death.

I had one player who once taped marijuana inside his mandolin under the strings. It was totally invisible to anyone holding the instrument. But the agents who searched us on our way back from Hawaii found it.

I'm ashamed of some of the behavior that my players and I exhibited. You haven't seen fear until you've seen a musician ten thousand miles from home who's been detained or arrested for a narcotics violation. Agents usually make him wait for hours before telling him whether he's free to go or if he's going to go to jail in a strange land. It's hard for me now to understand why anyone would want anything badly enough to risk his liberty for it, but that's the way of the regular drug user.

I can't thank Stan, Bill, and Roger Adams enough for the patience they've exhibited in their jobs, which have often been reduced to that of glorified baby-sitters for my musicians and me. Telling these stories reminds me of others, and I see no reason to dwell on our decadence. Yet I have to thank Stan specifically for the night he went above and beyond the call of duty after I got into an argument with one of my musicians after a night of heavy drinking. We were again in a swanky hotel, and the musician grabbed an elegant, heavy antique cabinet filled with rare dishes. He hurled the cabinet downward onto a table, shattering the cabinet's front glass and breaking its dishes. From three A.M. until eight A.M., Stan labored on his hands and knees, picking up small slivers of glass from the hotel carpet and cleaning up the mess. He had been sleeping soundly, but jumped from his bed at the sound of the crash. He said he honestly had thought he was experiencing an earthquake.

Needless to say, the argument that had initiated the furniture breaking was alcohol-induced. I've said many times that I'm thankful for my delivery from drugs and alcohol, but I've never said it enough.

When I at last became drug-free, I "retired" for eight months, disbanding my drug-using band. When I went back to touring, I hired a group that was drug-free, to the best of my knowledge.

☆☆☆

In 1987 I hired the Jeff Dayton Band, the backup musicians who tour with me to this day. The group consists of six musicians who play as a unit. The players strive to blend rather than stand out by themselves. I like that.

Our first engagement was private, performed for John Deere Company, the agricultural- and industrial-implement company in Moline, Illinois. Deere sent a private jet to Phoenix and transported us the approximately twenty-six hundred round-trip miles to Moline. My new players loved the lavish treatment, and thought they had landed the best job in the world. I didn't bother telling them that we wouldn't always go in such style.

Playing private corporate galas has become an integral part of my career. The engagements usually pay well with a minimum of hassle. One doesn't have to deal with the crowds and confusion that go with public venues. There is actually a circuit of corporate shows, and if you do well on one, word usually spreads to other corporate promoters. So, it was important to the band and me to make a good impression. We did, but only through a miracle.

We were crammed onto a tiny stage with barely enough room for the players and equipment. The banjo introduction to "Gentle on My Mind" was kicked off, and Bill Maclay signaled for the curtain to be raised. Then he noticed that the switch that controlled the curtain was on the other side of the stage. Bill had no choice other than to run around the outside of the building to the side of the stage containing the control panel. Meanwhile, the band continued to play the song's introduction.

John Deere is the world's leading company of its kind. It is to farm and industrial machinery what Boeing is to jet manufacturing. It represents the Rolls-Royce of agricultural and industrial machinery. Three hundred of its top executives were sitting restlessly, listening to the same banjo riff over and over, wondering why the curtain didn't rise.

Bill finally found the appropriate switch in the dark, the curtain went up, and the applause began. The audience couldn't see me, sitting inside a massive John Deere four-wheel-drive tractor. I was supposed to leap from the contraption during an entry tailor-made for the Deere group. I tried, but the door was locked. I was trapped inside the tractor onstage. Because I wasn't wearing a microphone, no one could hear me. Bill later said he wondered if I had fallen asleep inside the tractor waiting for him to raise the curtain. Neither he, the band, nor the audience could understand why I didn't come out. I just kept rattling the tractor's door, while the band kept playing the song's introduction.

Finally, the door popped open, and I jumped to the floor of the stage. And stood there. My coat had caught on the door handle. I struggled to free myself, and the band continued to play the song's introduction. By now, the introduction had lasted twice as long as the entire rest of the song would.

I waded among the instruments, amplifiers, and machinery, and the show went ahead. Paul Knedler, the Deere public-relations spokesperson, said the audience loved the program, and invited us back. He had no idea I had been trapped inside the tractor. I heard that he later said we should shorten our show's introduction.

✻ ✻ ✻

As you have no doubt surmised, some of the most memorable and therapeutic comic relief that occurs on the road is unplanned, and not funny at the time. Such was the case about ten years ago as I endeavored to put a serious and provocative ending on my show through the performance of the most time-honored hymn in the world, "Amazing Grace." You will recall that I do that number vocally, then end the song while playing its melody on the bagpipes.

I was playing a fair in San Diego, California, to thousands of wonderfully receptive people. The outdoor stage was perhaps fifteen feet high, so that I could be seen by the back row of the sprawling crowd that lay before me. When I play before an audience that large, a spotlight is almost always beamed directly into my face. For this particular show, I think overhead screens were utilized so that everyone could see my slightest facial gesture.

I was most of the way through "Amazing Grace," a reverent hush fell over the crowd, and I slowly raised the bagpipes to my lips.

And knocked out my front tooth.

I had a gaping hole in the middle of my smile. I looked like Alfred E. Neuman in *Mad* magazine. I figured everyone could see, judging by the gasps that swept the audience.

Now here is the kicker. Members of the audience moved forward to the grass in front of the stage. There, many dropped to their hands and knees and began looking for my tooth!

And someone found it!

Soon, my front tooth, wrapped in tissue, was hurled onto the stage. It was actually a porcelain crown. I didn't know what to do, so I stuck it back on the root and finished the show.

But something was taken from the spell of "Amazing Grace."

✶ ✶ ✶

I have been guilty of playing a practical joke or two myself, particularly if I thought the end results would be harmless. I played one on McLean Stevenson one night that was not only harmless but also productive.

He was opening for me in 1975 at the Hilton International in Las Vegas. Stevenson is a hilarious guy, but he wasn't going over well with the crowd. Roger Adams said that Stevenson was always funnier in somebody's living room than he was onstage.

Roger's thirteen-year-old daughter was a gymnast at the time. Stevenson was standing at the front of the deep stage, and probably could not have clearly seen the back of the stage, where it was somewhat darker, especially with the spotlight in his eyes. So Roger persuaded his daughter to do cartwheels across the back of the stage during Stevenson's act. The crowd began to laugh loudly. Stevenson thought they were roaring at his jokes.

The next night, the child did the same thing, and I joined her. I think he was truly disappointed when he discovered that it was our antics, and not his comedy, that was prompting the laughter.

I did something similar one night at a show with John Davidson, whose act included a satire about contemporary television commercials. He did a takeoff on Doublemint chewing gum in which he used an enormous mock package of the gum as a prop.

I got ahold of the giant stick, which was perhaps six feet long. I was wearing a swimsuit and nothing else when I held the gum package horizontally by my waist and walked unexpectedly behind Davidson during his act. To the crowd, it looked as if I were wearing nothing except the gum package. They fell out laughing. Davidson, for a short while, wondered what all the laughter was about, and then he saw me.

A month later, I was playing Reno, Nevada, and Davidson came to my show, unbeknownst to me. He brought his big gum package and wore his underwear as he walked across the stage behind me in the middle of my show. Again, to the crowd, it looked as if he were shielded by nothing but the gum package.

Turnabout is fair play.

✭ ✭ ✭

Nothing can disarm a performer more than having something go wrong just before he goes onstage. Roy Clark told me that his cronies used to turn the knob affecting the high E string on his guitar without his knowledge. He would step before ten thousand people, strike a chord, and it would be a discord.

People play practical jokes only on those they like, and I had a tremendous fondness for Judd Strunk, as did most people who knew him. Strunk dressed in casual attire, and would have worn about anything before wearing a flashy gold lamé suit. So the wardrobe man at the Hilton International made one for Strunk as a joke. The thing was hung in his closet and that's where it stayed.

I went to dinner one night in the mid-1970s with my former wife

Billie, Roger Adams and his wife, and Judd Strunk. The wardrobe man and Roger and I concocted a plan. Roger and I would keep Strunk at the table until only a few minutes before he was to go onstage to open our show. Meanwhile, the wardrobe man would go to Strunk's dressing room and hide all his clothes except for that obnoxious gold lamé suit.

In Las Vegas, a performer doesn't go onstage late—not if he wants to continue working there. Strunk was frantic when he could find no clothes other than those glorified pajamas, and that's what he had to wear onstage.

He used to open his show by saying, "Hi, I'm Judd Strunk from Farmington, Maine."

"I'll just bet you are," someone in the audience yelled out that time.

★★★

Some of the funniest men I've ever known have been able to think on their feet. The late Paul Lynde was that way.

I was playing Las Vegas one night and my parents were in the house. My mom and dad sang "Silver-haired Daddy of Mine" with me, and the audience ate it up. Then they walked offstage and I continued the show.

I knew Lynde was in the audience, and I thought the crowd would get a kick out of meeting him, as he was a popular attraction at the time on television's *Hollywood Squares.*

I introduced him, the people applauded, and then I approached him with a handheld microphone. I spoke to him about the same time the applause faded for my parents.

"I think it would be wonderful if Paul Lynde played Las Vegas," I said. The people applauded. "Paul, what do you think about playing Vegas?" I asked, and pushed the microphone into his face.

"I can't," he said.

"Why not?" I asked.

"Because my parents are dead."

* * *

Remember Jerry Fuller, with whom I stayed when I first went to California from New Mexico? I see him occasionally today in Nashville, where he and I have mutual song-publishing interests. We lost contact for years during my crazy days, but that didn't stop him from playing a practical joke.

When Fuller and I were young, we used to go hunting. I was with him one day in the wilderness and felt the call of nature. I responded, and Fuller sneaked up to take a photograph of me with tissue in hand. It was a highly embarrassing shot that he later hung in his den. I was at his house years later with my second wife and other mixed company. Lo and behold, I, in all my splendor, became the conversation piece. I told him to take the picture down.

He did.

Thirty-one years later, Fuller talked to Tom Carter without my knowledge. He asked Carter if he could send him that photograph and surprise me by having it published in this book.

* * *

There have been a lot of extremely talented players who have worked for me through the years. Many were as funny as they were talented.

But fun is not the long and short of my life as it once was. The word *fun* does not appear in the Bible. My craving for fun has been replaced by an appreciation for peace, and for joy. I still have fun, but never at someone else's expense.

The peace I have passes all understanding. It's frequently amusing, and always satisfying. I'll take that over fun any day.

✯✯

Chapter 17

*C*arl Jackson, my friend and former banjo player, met Lynn Wilford, a former Miss North Carolina, in 1981. Shortly afterward, we played New York City, and Lynn came to see him. Carl, Lynn, and I were going to a James Taylor concert on our night off, and I wanted a date.

Lynn said she had a friend, a dancer at Radio City Music Hall. My parents were my guests at the Waldorf-Astoria Hotel, and Carl and Lynn came by with her friend. They were all waiting for me in the suite's sitting room. I'd had a few glasses of wine, and decided before I met her that I would break the ice that always exists on blind dates.

"Like a Rhinestone Cowboy," I sang out, and busted into the room with my guitar, as if I were a singing cowboy minus his horse. Then my eyes fell on those of Kimberly Woollen.

That was twelve years and three children ago. We celebrated eleven years of marriage on October 25, 1993. I am a man richly blessed, despite myself. God has been merciful to me even when I've been mean to myself. But of all He's given me, there is nothing for which I'm more thankful than Kim.

She says it was love at first sight, but confesses that happiness was a little longer in coming. At first, our life was a rocky road over stones of alcoholism and drug abuse. I was holding out against the will of God. I'm sorry that I ran from God, and thankful that I couldn't outrun him.

I've asked my wife to describe for this book some of the details of our stormy courtship and the early part of our marriage. Some of the events are funny now, but only because they happened to another man who once inhabited my body. Some of my strongest resistance to things good and Godly came in my final days of living purely for carnal pleasure. I continued to ignore the teachings of Christ after accepting Him as my personal savior. I wore the garment of salvation, but not the cloak of righteousness. I was a carnal Christian.

I eventually lowered my guard and opened my heart. He changed me in ways in which I would have never changed myself. Kim was praying toward that end the whole time. Her prayers just might have saved my life. Here is her version of our courtship and marriage:

"Boy, you didn't tell me she was going to be so pretty."

Those were the first words I heard Glen speak. He entered the hotel room where I waited, nervously, to meet him for our first date. I didn't realize he was forty-five years old because he looked about thirty. He was tan, trim, and gorgeous. I had thought he was attractive on television. In real life, he was so handsome.

I had looked forward to the date, but hadn't taken it seriously. I knew absolutely nothing about his personal life, including whether he had ever been married or if he had children. I had read nothing about Tanya Tucker and him, and had heard none of the stories of his former wives, who claimed he drank heavily and lived recklessly. It's not that I was isolated, but just that I was uninterested in that kind of journalism. I'm glad I was. I had no preconceptions about Glen and was able to form my own opinions. Had I read some of the accounts of his former lifestyle, I might have been afraid to go out with him. That would have been a tragedy.

I also think my knowing so little about Glen made our first date fun for him. He seemed to enjoy meeting someone who was meeting the person, not the personality.

We all went downstairs to the Japanese restaurant in the Waldorf-Astoria. I liked his parents instantly. They were salt-of-the-earth country people who reminded me of some of the people around whom I had grown up in North Carolina. Carl was from Nashville, so I was comfortable with him too.

We were seated and Glen ordered a beer. He might have had two or three before the food was served, and then he bowed his head and said the blessing. I was very impressed.

"Are you a Christian?" I asked.

"Yes," he said firmly.

"I am too!" I said.

I noticed that Glen drank a lot of wine during and after dinner.

We went to the Taylor concert and went backstage afterward. James Taylor's mother, who is from North Carolina, was there, and I told her I was too. She didn't seem impressed.

Glen, whom I'd known for perhaps four hours, there, in the hubbub of backstage, kissed me. It was unexpected, perhaps forward, and wonderful. As the expression goes, "The earth moved."

But the evening quickly began to sour. We got into a limousine and returned to the Waldorf, where we rode the elevator with strangers. By now, Glen was in his cups. He struck up a conversation with the unknown guests, and they were obviously impressed to be talking to Glen Campbell. The elevator stopped on their floor, they got off, and Glen got off with them. His parents, Carl, Lynn, and I followed him as he followed the strangers to their suite. He just walked inside and became obnoxious. His behavior turned me off, and the fact that it was alcohol-induced turned me off more.

We persuaded Glen to return to his room, and we all went inside. Glen continued to drink. Then his parents went to their room. Carl and Lynn weren't there, and Glen told me he wanted to "jump my bones," meaning he wanted to take me to bed. His remark came as he lay listlessly on the couch, almost passed out from the alcohol. I thought that he wouldn't have made the remark had he been sober.

This is not turning out like I thought, I said to myself.

"Well, you know, I don't want to do that," I said to him. "It's getting late and I'm going to go home."

"If you walk through that door," he said, "you'll never see me again."

"Well, it was nice to meet you."

I would have walked out that instant, but I had no money. So, after resisting his advances, I had to ask him for cab fare. He handed me some money, and I went directly home, the words about never seeing him again echoing in my mind.

He called the instant I walked through my door and said he wanted to make sure I got home all right. He called again the next day and asked me to come with him for his show in Philadelphia.

I was a dancer at Radio City Music Hall and had lied to my dance captain by calling in sick so that I could accept a blind date with Glen Campbell. I lied a second time about my illness in order to go with him to Philadelphia.

Trouble is, someone with the press spotted Glen, and took his photograph holding hands with me. The *New York Post* ran the picture above a caption that identified Glen and called me a "mystery beauty."

I was no mystery to the Radio City Music Hall dance captain, who saw the picture. He wondered how I could be well enough to go out with Glen Campbell while too sick to come to work. I could have been fired, and I really needed that job.

When Glen asked me to go to Philadelphia, I accepted, but with a stipulation. "I'd love to come and see your show and I'd love to be with you," I said. "But I'm not going to come and have you expect me to sleep with you."

But I did.

The sleep, however, was innocent. I stayed in his room, I lay in his arms, but there was no sex.

After I returned to New York City, Glen got a few days off and came to visit me. By now, I was really falling for him.

I was twenty-two years old and living from hand to mouth in the most expensive city in the world. I ate a lot of tuna fish, and walked everywhere to stretch pennies. I actually saved ten thousand dollars my first year in New York, and that was a fortune to me.

Suddenly, I was dating an international star who was sending limousines to pick me up at Radio City Music Hall. The other dancers were buzzing.

"Kim, it's him, it's him," the girls would giggle as they pressed their faces against doors and around corners to see what was happening.

I suddenly believed in Cinderella, and believed I was she.

By then, Glen and I were having sex. I had been reared in a Christian household, but was not obedient to the biblical teachings about fornication. In fact, I didn't even know what the word meant.

I had lived in New York for two years, and I was homesick. I began to pray for God to send me a Southern gentleman who would take me away from it all. I prayed regularly, privately, and sometimes publicly. I even prayed while walking down the street with the three girls who were my roommates. The Bible talks about praying without ceasing, and that, in essence, is what I did. I believe that Glen is the answer to my prayers.

But that doesn't mean the relationship was without travails. I found out that Satan can tamper with what God sends.

I had dated Glen for about a month, and then he didn't call me for three. I was devastated. I had trusted and given myself to the man who I believed was Heaven-sent, only to have him disappear.

The Bible says, "All things work together for them who love God," and I'm proof positive of that promise. Glen's absence from my life gave me time to take some serious spiritual inventory. I realized that I was trying to manipulate my whole life, through God, to get what I wanted.

So I changed the tone of my prayers. "God," I said, "I thought you sent him, and now I don't know if I'll ever see him again. But you know what's best for me, and if I never see him again, that's probably for my best interest, so I'm going to entrust the whole thing to you."

Glen called the next day. He wanted me to join him in Lake Tahoe.

To my surprise, I didn't jump at the chance. I had two reasons.

First, Glen was incredibly and understandably sad over the death of Judd Strunk, a musician friend whom he had last seen three months earlier with me at a party at the home of Jimmy Webb. Webb, in fact, had told Strunk that the little plane he flew was dangerous, and had even given Strunk a parachute. The plane crashed and Strunk died along with a friend of his.

Glen was crying when he called. I wondered how much he wanted to see me, and how much he was grieving over Strunk.

Then there was the matter of Tanya Tucker. Since I had been with Glen, he had gone to Louisiana to see Tanya, which resulted in the police action he related earlier and national news reports. That had been heartbreaking and a source of embarrassment. My parents at first had been so thrilled that I was dating Glen, but then they grew apprehensive because of Tanya. I had assured them that it was over between Glen and Tanya, but my dad called me to tell me that he had read about their shouting match in Louisiana.

I don't think I ever knew a greater gentleman than Glen—until he drank. Then it was a Jekyll/Hyde transformation. When I eventually went to Lake Tahoe, I saw firsthand why he drank so much, and I'm not making excuses for him.

Alcohol was thrown at him from every direction. His dressing room was loaded with booze. His hotel suite was loaded with booze. His limousine was loaded with booze. Soon, Glen was loaded with booze. Whenever we went out, the waiters were carrying it to us, whether we ordered it or not.

I made up my mind right there in Lake Tahoe, with gambling, drunkenness, and other forms of indulgence all around, that I was not going to drink anymore.

Alcohol was everywhere, making it difficult to quit. But I did it nonetheless, and I haven't had a drink in ten years.

I had always been able to take or leave alcohol, but wound up drinking more than I ever had with Glen because I thought it would please him. I expected God to understand, because I thought God should appreciate my motive.

When I looked at Glen, I saw a man who, after fifteen years, was still on top of the entertainment world. His name was in lights and his annual cash flow was in seven figures. But his life was on the bottom, as defined by the absence of peace of mind. He was hooked on cocaine, smoked pot, and was usually drunk. I knew I couldn't help him get his life in order until I got my own straight. I had smoked pot with Glen a couple of times, and of course I quit that too.

I didn't realize, until I stopped everything, how messed up my own life had become. I had been living anything but a Godly life. That was October 1981.

I went with Glen to Phoenix to see the house he had bought, which is where we live today. I continued to accompany him on personal appearance tours. My parents didn't approve, although they never tried to stop me. My mother finally surmised, "Well, she loves this guy, and he travels all of the time, so if she wants to be with him, she's going to have to travel."

We went across the United States, to South Africa, and to England. We returned to Phoenix, and about a week before Christmas, Glen asked me to marry him. I said yes.

Was I afraid to marry a man who had been married three times previously and had had a notorious affair? The answer is no. I knew God could change Glen, and I knew He would. I had to let Him make His changes in me, and then maintain what He had changed without compromise.

Glen and I were married ten months later at the North Phoenix Baptist Church. I had been searching for a church because I wanted to be married in church, and because I wanted a church home for Glen and me. The North Phoenix Baptist Church seats fifty-five hundred people in the main sanctuary, and has more than twenty thousand members.

I was almost left waiting at its altar.

I was determined not to allow any alcohol at our wedding, afraid that Glen, his band members, and other friends would get drunk and spoil the reception, or the ceremony itself. I didn't mention to Glen that I had ordered no alcohol, but two days before the wedding he found out.

"You didn't order any booze?" he fumed.

"Oh, no," I said, pretending to be nonchalant.

He was angry because it was going to be a dry wedding, and angrier because I had made the decision without consulting him. So he left.

He got into a Mercedes 450 SL and left town without telling anyone he was going. His family from Arkansas was in town. My people from the East Coast were in town. But the groom was nowhere to be found.

"He'll turn up," said Shorty Campbell, Glen's brother. "Just be patient."

Glen spent the night out of town and never called anyone. He returned to Phoenix and spoke to a friend who owned a restaurant. His friend said he would provide alcohol to the wedding as his gift. So all was fine. Well, sort of.

Glen got drunk while Waylon Jennings sang "Amanda," one of his biggest hits. Then Glen and I danced to Waylon's lovely ballad. Waylon was accompanied by a blasted Steve Hardin on the piano.

I don't know what my mother thought about the antics, but they soon paled by comparison to Glen's announcement. He walked up to my mom, smiled through his intoxication, and asked her how she was going to enjoy being a grandmother. She didn't know what he meant, so he told her I was three months pregnant.

The youth pastor and another staff member at North Phoenix Baptist Church had wanted to come to the wedding, but had not been sent invitations. So they hid inside enormous electronic speaker closets inside the sanctuary. They could place their faces against the speaker cloth and see the proceedings, but the congregation couldn't see them. Perhaps they became hot inside the refrigerator-sized containers, because they came out just before the service officially convened. They ran into Glen as he was coming inside the church and asked if they could attend his wedding.

"Sure," he said. "Come on in." He was feeling no pain.

I enjoyed having them, but I'm glad Glen wasn't asked by a transient if he could come inside. Glen would have good-naturedly told him to bring all his hobo buddies.

The North Phoenix Baptist Church is awesome, but not so big that the presence of God can't fill it. It is a holy place. When Glen and I are in Phoenix, we always attend this church.

Many miracles, I discovered, happen gradually, not instantly. But they happen nonetheless. Glen's spiritual deliverance from drugs and alcohol came gradually. As of August 1993 he hasn't had a drink in six years. It's been even longer since he last used cocaine. But there were some trying and tearful times preceding his abstinence.

One evening I cooked dinner and Glen was late. He had played golf earlier in the day, so I called the country club. I asked for the Men's Grill, where a waitress answered and told me Glen was playing cards. I asked to speak to him, she put me on hold, and I remained there for fifteen minutes. Glen forgot that I was on the line. The dinner was burning, and so was I.

Our daughter, Ashley, was still a baby in diapers. I gathered her in my arms, loaded her into the car, and headed for the country club. Outraged, I marched with Ashley in my arms into a room where women, except for waitresses, were not allowed. But I didn't care.

There sat Glen, cards in his hands, cigar in his mouth, and cocktail at his side. He had an enormous smile on his face—until I unexpectedly appeared out of nowhere and handed him our baby. I virtually thrust the child into his arms.

He fumbled at the table, where other card players reeled in their seats. Suddenly, everyone in the room gave an audible sign of astonishment. "O-o-o-o-h-h," echoed through the opulent setting.

I ran into the rest room, where I sobbed. I had barricaded myself in the powder room, Glen and our baby were in the men-only room, and nobody was where I wanted them to be.

But Glen came home.

I was scared, knowing that I had crossed the line and that he would be furious. But he wasn't. Sometimes I still can't believe I did that.

Glen would sneak away from me after we were married to snort cocaine. I could always tell. But thank God for the wisdom He gave me in that I never lectured Glen about drugs or alcohol while he was using it.

Glen said earlier that he used to talk about God and the Bible while drinking and using cocaine. I saw this happen firsthand. He would get high on cocaine and be unable to sleep, then keep me up all night preaching the word of God. It was disgusting. Whenever he was wasted on drugs, he would preach a message of judgment. He would tell me what was wrong, in God's eyes, with my behavior and with his own. It was negative preaching from an altered mind and an impure heart.

Glen would get mad at members of his family whom I knew he loved very much. When he was sober, I would tell him what he had said about them and he would deny it and become angry.

His angry and defensive denial about drinking began while we were still dating. I spoke to Carl Jackson about it, and he insisted that Glen was never going to change.

"God can change him," I stressed.

Then, when Glen was sober, I would tell him to seek help about his drinking problem, and he would get furious.

Once, when we were staying in Malibu, California, we got into a discussion about his drinking and it fast became an argument. He was so angry and wild that he ended up putting his elbow through a pane of glass.

Glen claimed to honor my request that cocaine not be a part of our marriage. Mick Fleetwood came to town one night and he, Glen, and others stayed up all night in a recording studio. I was at home, pregnant with our first child.

Glen came home after daylight with Fleetwood, and as soon as I saw Glen I knew he was high but didn't mention it. Instead, I made breakfast for everybody.

"See, she's not mad," Glen kept saying.

In fact, I was furious and heartbroken.

It happened again after Cal, our first child, was born. That time I wasn't so quiet.

"I told you I didn't want cocaine to be a part of our marriage," I cried.

We argued, and then he blurted out, "Well, you're not taking my baby."

I realized how afraid he was about losing his child after having lost his son Dillon shortly after his birth.

"You can talk to my lawyer," I fumed.

Then Glen broke down. "I can't believe that I messed up one time and you're going to leave me," he said.

That was in late 1983. If Glen ever did cocaine after that, I never knew about it. I never saw anything in his behavior to make me think he was using cocaine, and I had learned all the signs.

The stopping of the drinking came later. When it came, it too came unequivocally.

In August 1986, Glen was in Hawaii for concerts with the Royal Philharmonic Orchestra. Glen and his conductor, T. J. Kuenster, were having drinks after a show, and Glen had another show to do the next day. He awakened with a terrible hangover, one of the worst he'd ever had.

"Lord, get me off of this stuff," he prayed. "Help me find a way to get away from this sin."

No doubt he had prayed many times previously, but God has His own timetable, and that was the time He chose to deliver Glen from alcohol. He hasn't had a drink since.

I think my frustration with the delay in the miracles of Glen's deliverance from drugs and alcohol had to do with his baptism. He and I had been baptized before we were married, and I somehow thought that the baptism would quicken Glen's victory over self-abuse.

Our baptism is a story in itself.

Glen had forgotten how cold it gets in Arkansas at Christmas, but it wouldn't have mattered. He wanted to be baptized in Saline Creek, at his childhood swimming hole.

On December 21, 1981, Glen and I flew to Little Rock, where

we rented a car for the drive to Billstown. Glen had earlier told his brother Lindell, the retired Church of Christ preacher, what we wanted.

"I can get a key to the baptistery," Lindell said. "The water's heated and we can do it there."

"No," Glen replied. "I want to be baptized outside."

Lindell wore chest-high wading boots and walked forcefully into the creek.

The temperature was two degrees above freezing. Glen wore jeans, and his entry into the ice water was not as rapid. The frigid water began to climb toward his stomach as he eased into the flow. He stiffened, as if walking into a liquid igloo.

Lindell put his hand on Glen's mouth, pronounced that he was baptizing him in the "name of the Father, Son, and Holy Ghost," and immersed him in the frigid water. Glen came out of the water singing, "Oh happy day, Oh happy day, / When Jesus washed my sins away."

I nearly froze to death too in the baptism. When you're young and in love, however, I guess you feel immune to the elements.

We shivered under blankets inside Lindell's pickup. Water ran down our shaking faces, and some of it mixed with tears of joy. I was almost frozen on the outside, but I had immense inner warmth. We had been baptized in a manner similar to Christians of old. It was wonderful.

I believed that Glen's drug and alcohol deliverance would come, but sometimes believing became hard, and I needed deliverance from my own lack of faith. I continued to pray. Sometimes I felt as though my prayers about Glen were getting no higher than the ceiling, but I prayed nonetheless. Then I did something else.

The Bible talks about the power of united prayer, and I enlisted that. Glen had told me not to tell anyone about his drinking. I did it anyway. I went to the pastors in our church. "Glen is drinking again," I would say. "Please pray." They did, and he never knew what Heavenly intentions were under way behind his back.

Meanwhile, I showed biblical scriptures to Glen, such as the admonition in Leviticus 10:9—"Do not drink wine, nor strong drink, thou, nor thy sons with thee when ye go into a tabernacle of the congregation, lest ye die: it shall be a statute forever throughout your generations."

Singer Johnny Lee's wife, Debbie, felt that he had a drinking problem. She asked me to ask Glen to talk to Johnny, as Glen believed he could quit drinking whenever he wanted. And Glen had told me he didn't want to drink anymore. Debbie visited me one day when Glen and Johnny Lee were playing golf. Glen was drunk when they returned.

I didn't know what to do. How could a drunk man speak to another man about his drinking problem? I'd thought Glen was ready for God to use him, but God wasn't finished with Glen yet.

I decided to conceal a tape recorder, and let Glen hear for himself the next day what he said and how he acted when he was drinking.

"I've got something I want you to hear," I said the next day, when he was sober.

I laid the recorder on the bed, turned it on, and walked out, knowing that if I stayed in the room he would become angry and turn the machine off. He must have been embarrassed by what he heard because he told me never to record him in that condition again. But I did—two more times.

And more and more he began to say that he had quit—that he had taken his last drink. The announcement never failed to raise hope in my heart.

Then we would go out for dinner, he would order a glass of wine, and my heart would sink.

"I thought you had quit drinking," I would say. "You said you had quit drinking."

"I quit drinking whiskey," he would say. "And I'm not drinking whiskey."

By that time I was at the point where I would burst into tears whenever I saw him take a drink. I seemed to be crying all the time, and that spoiled a lot of our time together. Many of what we had intended to be romantic evenings in restaurants or at home were anything but.

I even cried on our honeymoon in Australia, where Glen was

working. He got bad newspaper reviews after he and the key-board player, Steve Hardin, got drunk between shows. They ordered wine.

"Don't you think that one bottle is enough?" I asked.

"Shut up!" they fumed in unison, and ordered more wine.

Glen and I returned to our hotel room, where I poured cold water on him to get him ready for his second show. It didn't work very well.

Hardin didn't show up until the second show was halfway completed, and Glen had sung perhaps four songs. The rest of the time he told jokes.

As Glen has said, there are things that are "funny" now that weren't amusing at the time. They were heartbreaking to me, and I'm sure they hurt God more.

Glen, for example, would rise from bed while drunk, presumably to use the bathroom, but he wouldn't always return. Once he walked onto a hotel balcony while nude and locked himself out. I don't recall how long he was out there, because I was on the brink of sleep when it happened.

Other times he wouldn't return, and when I searched for him I would find him passed out in the bathtub. I was always afraid he would turn on the water and drown.

He sometimes mixed sleeping pills with alcohol, and there were nights when he would fall into a deep but restless sleep. His breathing would become incredibly heavy, and I would be afraid to go to sleep, for fear that he would stop breathing altogether. So I would lie there, softly crying and praying. He could have simply gone to sleep and never awakened again, as singer Keith Whitley did.

A deacon of our church, Bud Glaze, and our pastor, the Reverend Richard Jackson, were Godly men who shared Glen's passion for golf. I used to say that God let us move to Phoenix so Glen could play golf with those men and be under their wonderful influence.

Glen was so concerned that they not know that he was drinking, but I had been telling them the truth secretly, and they were praying privately.

Then Glen would stop drinking, but not really. He would be dry for a few days, then come home drunk. My hopes would rise, then my spirits would fall. It was as if we were taking one step forward, then falling back three. Living with his relapses was harder than living with the day-to-day drinking.

I remember one time when I thought we had put the drinking behind us but Glen came home drunk. He used to enjoy calling me a liar when he was loaded, and that night was no exception.

I tried to get away from him, but I couldn't. I went into one room, and he followed. This happened all over the house as he argued loudly with me and kept up his agitation. I opened a Bible and pressed it against my breaking heart. It was as if I needed to be physically close to God. I wanted Him to hold me. Then I put a blanket over my head and sneaked under our dining-room table. I surrounded myself with chairs so that Glen could not get to me. He knelt at the table's perimeter, but having that blanket over my head made it easier for me to tune him out.

There were times I felt my own faith seriously challenged. I felt inadequate as a wife, and as a praying Christian. I wondered if there was something about me that was prompting Glen's craziness.

When I was pregnant with our first child, Glen and I went to Palm Springs because he was entered in the Bob Hope Desert Classic. He was drunk for three days. Even though I had my self-imposed rule about not discussing his drinking with him when he was drunk, I could stand it no longer.

"Don't you think you've had enough?" I said finally.

He walked into the kitchen, tipped up a gallon of vodka, and began to swallow.

I tried to grab the bottle from his hand, and it fell to the floor and shattered. Broken glass and vodka covered the floor. I wiped up the broken glass as my falling tears mixed with the spilled vodka. I can't take this anymore, I said to myself. I really can't take this.

I told Glen that I was thinking about leaving, but not necessarily divorcing him. But then a scripture came into my mind: "I can do all things through Christ who strengthens me." As outrageous as our marriage had become, as traumatized as I was living with Glen's incessant drinking, I felt that if I left him, I would be displeasing God, and pleasing Satan. I was certain the alcohol and drugs would have their way with him if I left. Glen needed me. I felt as though God were using me, however slowly, and I claimed strength in Him.

Now, sometimes, when I see Glen on a Reverend James Robison crusade or hear his voice fill our home church, I can't believe it's the same man who used to break my heart while destroying his life. And Glen continues to grow as a Christian.

Most people would rather see a testimony than hear one. Glen lives his. He doesn't talk on and on about Jesus Christ in his concerts. Yet there is a special "feel" that is almost spiritual when he sings today. Others have noticed it too.

I sometimes sit in the wings and watch him close his eyes and open his soul while losing himself in song. Fans now say they are not only entertained but also blessed. They may not know why, but I feel it has to do with an anointing Glen has from the Holy Spirit, whose presence he seeks daily.

I've seen thousands of people rise to applaud Glen Campbell, towering in a spotlight. Yet I've never seen him stand taller than when he kneels with our children. I saw him agonize about whether he should write about his life, concerned that people dear to him will be shaken at how he once lived. I watched him put himself aside and place God first, thinking that others might be uplifted by the telling of his story.

I remain adamantly against the consumption of alcohol in our home. Glen's son Travis was married at North Phoenix Baptist Church, and he and his wife, Andrea, wanted to hold the reception at our house.

"We don't think it's fair that our friends can't toast with champagne at the reception," Travis said.

"Your friends can toast with champagne," I replied, "but not at my house."

They had an alcohol-free reception.

Glen, today, is flesh-and-blood proof that God can change a life. Glen once just lived, but today he is alive!

As Glen said earlier, "There's a strangely wonderful thing about God—He's not always on time, but He's never late."

Glen and I know.

Chapter 18

*W*e were in another airport, en route to another show. She was another wife of another would-be songwriter.

"Pardon me, Mr. Campbell," she said. "My husband writes and sings country songs and he's real good. I was wondering if you could give us some advice."

People approach me every place and in every circumstance. If I'm in a hurry or stressed, it's sometimes difficult to deal with, but I try to be kind. I remember my own days struggling to crack the music business veneer. I try to help others as inexperienced as I at first was.

"The first thing he'll have to do is move to Nashville, Tennessee," I told her. "Write to Marty Gamblin, the man who runs my music-publishing companies. Have your husband send his songs to him and see what he thinks."

Most songwriters I give that advice to never send anything. Those who do send songs that are mostly unusable.

The woman's husband wasn't like most songwriters. He didn't write, but he called Marty. He asked him if he might drive from his Atlanta home to play him some tunes.

"When do you want to do that?" Marty asked him.

"Well, I can't do it today."

"I can't do it for a couple of weeks," Marty told him.

"That will be all right. I'll come then," said the songwriter.

"If you're willing to drive up here, I'm willing to give your songs a listen," Marty said.

At twelve-thirty P.M. on August 15, 1985, Marty had his first appointment with Alan Jackson.

"I remember this long and lanky kid came in wearing a baseball cap," Marty said. "He was shy and real down to earth. I liked him. I was more drawn to his voice than to his songs. I asked if he had any tapes that featured his singing more than his songs. He had a tape that was taken from a soundboard in Atlanta, not in a studio. He told me it was rough and it was. He played me John Conlee's 'Rose Colored Glasses,' Conway Twitty's 'I'd Love to Lay You Down,' and David Allen Coe's 'The Ride.' I've never been a David Allen Coe fan, but the way Alan sang his song really knocked me out. I told him I thought he could be a star."

Marty, like many in my organization, is a strong believer in family and advised him to move to Nashville, but not if it meant breaking up his family.

Alan, whose wife, Denise, was a flight attendant, said she could be based out of Nashville as easily as she could Atlanta. Alan's wish was to move to Nashville and become a staff songwriter for one of my publishing companies.

Marty told him he couldn't immediately pay him a draw against future royalties.

"You're too green," Marty said, "and I couldn't justify giving you any kind of advance. If you move to Nashville, you'll have to get an outside job. You can't write if you're under financial pressure, so get a job doing something to support yourself and your family until your music begins to pay off."

Leery, Alan thanked Marty for his candor, walked quietly to the door, and closed it silently behind him. Three weeks later, Marty's telephone rang.

"I'm here!" Alan said. "I got a job in the mailroom at *Nashville Now*. What do we do now?"

"I don't know," Marty replied. "Usually, when I give people my move-to-Nashville spiel, I never see them again. But we'll think of something."

Marty immediately undertook the task of getting Alan a recording contract. He thought Alan would blossom first as a recording artist, then as a songwriter, but he pitched Alan's compositions anyway, including "Here in the Real World," "Chasing That Neon Rainbow," "Wanted," and "Someday" to several Nashville artists. No one wanted the songs. (Each would become a number-one hit after Alan recorded them a few years later.) Marty gave Alan a songwriting contract nonetheless. He believed in him when no one else did.

Alan returned to Marty and said he was unhappy because his wife was bringing more money into their household than he was. He asked if he might have fifty dollars a week as a draw against future songwriting royalties. Marty called Stan Schneider and asked for the fifty dollars a week, and Stan said, "Give him a hundred."

"It was a lot to ask for," Marty said. "I mean, at the time, you had guys in town like Skip Ewing, who had written hits, and their draws were only a hundred fifty dollars a week. Alan hadn't written anything that had been recorded, and none of his songs had even been placed on hold by any artists."

But Marty remained haunted by the notion that Alan could make it as a singer. He came to me and asked that I take Alan to the legendary record producer Jimmy Bowen. Marty had never come to me with a request like this, but I felt he would be doing Bowen a favor.

Alan, Marty, Bowen, and I had a meeting. Bowen told Alan to put ten songs together on a tape in the order he would sing them if he were doing a live show. He told Alan he wanted to live with the tunes for a while before making a decision about a recording contract. He also told Alan, after hearing his compositions, that he was about a year to a year and a half away from reaching maturity as a songwriter. That put the ball firmly in Marty's court.

"You're right," Marty told Bowen, "because all the songs you've heard from him were written about that long ago."

Bowen decided he wanted a new demonstration tape of Alan's songs, of better quality than what he had heard earlier. A demonstration session costs about four thousand dollars, and I agreed to pay it. It proved to be a tremendous investment.

A showcase for Alan Jackson was scheduled at Douglas' Corner Cafe, a popular Nashville listening room. All the record-company executives with the power to sign an artist were invited. Bowen rarely goes to showcases, but this time he made an exception.

"He walked in and a hush fell over the room," Marty recalled. "I honestly think his presence made the other label heads think, 'If Bowen is coming to see this kid, there must be something to him.'" However, Jimmy opted to pass on signing Alan to his label.

Marty managed Alan's career for a while, but ultimately realized his time was better spent on song publishing. He voluntarily and unselfishly removed himself from the career of a young man who would become a superstar. How much this cost Marty we'll never know. He took Alan to Barry Coburn, who had successfully managed Holly Dunn, who had just left him. Marty told Barry how much he believed in Alan. Barry decided then to represent Alan.

Luckily, Arista's Tim DuBois had also attended the showcase, and eventually the president of Arista, Clive Davis, would fly to Nashville to announce the formation of a country division and personally sign Alan to a deal, which launched the division.

"Had Alan not gotten a recording deal of his own," Marty surmised, "all of his great songs might never have seen the light of day."

My company published nine of the ten songs on Alan's first album, nine on the second, and seven on the third. Each of the three albums has gone platinum, meaning the sales were in excess of a million units.

The chance encounter at the airport translated into millions of dollars for all involved. Alan's fourth album could conceivably be a greatest-hits album, and go double or triple platinum, Arista predicts.

Alan, before the release of his first album, formed his own publishing company. I agreed to split the song publishing with him and let him take 50 percent of the royalties for his Mattie Ruth Music, named for his mother.

Barry Coburn, who was living in his office when Alan came into his life, today is probably wealthy. Alan, who had been living in a two-bedroom apartment under a house, now owns a Brentwood, Tennessee, mansion on eight acres, has a collection of cars and motorcycles, and is a multimillionaire.

There is a moral to this story that goes beyond Alan's lifelong dream becoming reality. It has to do with God's blessing me with the willingness to take the time for others. There was a time when I didn't. It also has to do with Marty's willingness to listen and persevere. And it has to do with Alan's songs, which were lyrically strong and impressive.

Country music's appeal, traditionally, lies in the lyrics. But today's lyrics, I feel, are inferior to those of years ago. Many modern country songs are shallow.

Three of the most popular tunes of 1993 were "Passionate Kisses," "Boot Scootin' Boogie," and "Achy Breaky Heart."

I'm sure you can figure the rest out for yourselves.

Coincidentally, the songs came along about the time Whitney Houston and Kevin Costner were starring in a motion picture called *The Bodyguard,* whose soundtrack featured Dolly Parton's "I Will Always Love You." That song was written in 1976, was number one in 1977, was performed in a movie with Dolly and Burt Reynolds in 1982, and rose to number one on the pop charts for Whitney in 1992. Will contemporary country songs enjoy such incredible tests of time? I think not.

In 1992, a major Nashville record label released a collection of Patsy Cline hits recorded in the early 1960s, including "Crazy," "I Fall to

Pieces," and "Sweet Dreams." The chances of today's hits being rereleased thirty years from now are very small, I think. If country or popular music ever emphasizes lyrics again, Jimmy Webb will have another explosive songwriting career.

Today's songs are often little more than glorified jingles. Perhaps the songwriters of old "lived" more, and therefore had more personal experiences from which to draw meaningful lyrics.

The country legend George Jones said he knows why today's tunes are so forgettable. There are more singers than ever before, and they place more demand on songwriters than ever before. Jones said the writers are churning out songs rapidly, at the expense of quality.

Perhaps today's songwriters simply lack inspiration. Many of today's singers unwisely try to write their own material so that they can earn more money. Their songs therefore have more commercial than creative value.

Trying to survive as a touring singer and songwriter is difficult since a songwriter needs peace, and a touring singer has little of that.

Good songwriting, I know from personal experience, relies on feelings. Sometimes they just won't come, or at least won't come when the writer wants them most. Maybe they do come and today's writers just don't recognize them.

I've always been, first of all, a singer/musician, and then a songwriter. Yet, thank God, I've tried to be receptive to feelings from any source at any time.

Once, while in a Canton, Ohio, radio station in 1965 for a promotional interview with the Beach Boys, I saw a sign on the wall that read, LET ME BE A LITTLE KINDER. Within twenty minutes, I had written: "Let me be a little kinder, let me be a little blinder, to the faults of those about me, let me praise a little more." And the verse concludes, "Let me think a little more of others, and a little less of me."

That bit of inspiration gave me a hit song, "Less of Me," and it was recorded by about thirty-five other singers.

I thank God for inspirations, and for the sensitivity He allows me to have toward them. Perhaps that kind of impulsive response is what's missing from today's songwriting. When the country-music industry was growing, writers wrote when the mood hit them. Today, they write on schedule. The majority of major music publishers in Nashville ask their staff writers to report to work at a certain hour and leave at another. Can heartfelt creativity be put on a time clock?

And then there are songs such as "Old Dogs, Children, and Watermelon Wine," which Tom T. Hall wrote on the back of an airsick bag on a twenty-minute flight from Atlanta to Nashville. He was inspired by an experience he had had the previous night watching an old black man during the Democratic National Convention. Tom was sensitive to that moment, and responsive to his feelings. He has written masterpieces from his personal experiences.

The same is true of my late friend, the genius Roger Miller. He was a wonderful combination of Shakespeare and Daffy Duck. I saw him write on the backs of napkins, bathroom tissue, matchbooks, whatever. He wrote for Tree International, one of the world's largest country-music publishing houses, for thirty-five years. I doubt that he ever wrote anything because he was supposed to come into his publisher's office and do it on command.

And I bring up one of my own compositions again, simply because I'm most familiar with my own work. I once wrote a song that was titled "Senses":

> The sense to see, and I saw you walk away
> The sense to feel, I feel lonelier each day,
> My senses tell me all I need to know
> It's over, but I don't have the sense to let you go.

That was written with the memory of romantic pain. I prefer to think it's substantial, and typical of thoughtful lyrics that were the heart of country music in the 1970s.

Country America magazine listed the one hundred most popular country songs of all time in October 1992. The list was based on the votes of fans; it had nothing to do with disc jockeys or radio airplay, although there probably wouldn't be much difference in opinions.

"He Stopped Loving Her Today" by George Jones was listed number one. It was also number one in a similar poll taken about the same time by *USA Today*. The song is about a man who loved a woman so much that it killed him. It was written in 1977. The fourth most popular song, "Crazy," was written in 1961; the fifth, "I Fall to Pieces," in 1960; the sixth, "El Paso," in 1959; the seventh, "Your Cheatin' Heart," in 1953; the eighth, "I'm So Lonesome I Could Cry," in 1949; the ninth, "Sixteen Tons," in 1947; and the tenth, "Lovesick Blues," in 1949. Only two of the top ten country songs of all time were written recently. They were "When I Call Your Name," the second most popular, written in 1990; and "The Dance," number three, written in 1989.

The irony is that more country music was sold in 1992 than during any other year in history. More than seventy million albums were purchased. Young people bought most of the records. Yet the most popular songs, according to a two-year-old magazine, are still the historical ones.

I think the youth factor also has something to do with today's songs having more style but less substance. Major companies and music-publishing houses are obsessed with signing young artists. Jimmy Bowen said that everything he's seen in his forty-year career is now reversed.

"There was a time when it was hard to get a new act played on the radio," he said. "Today, it's hard to get a veteran act played, because the radio stations are all playing the younger acts."

Recording legends such as Charley Pride, Merle Haggard, Tammy Wynette, Loretta Lynn, Barbara Mandrell, Johnny Cash, Willie Nelson, and others don't even have recording contracts. You can look at today's top one hundred country songs and count on one hand the number of artists over forty. Many are under thirty.

How can artists who have lived so little write significantly about life? And isn't country music primarily about life? And even more, isn't it primarily personal?

I was performing at a celebrity tournament in Tucson, Arizona, and Charley Pride was in the show. He had a song called "The Hand That Rocks the Cradle," about a man's love for the devotion of his mother. It was beautifully sentimental.

Charley and I worked it up and sang it for a bunch of veteran baseball greats: Yogi Berra, Mickey Mantle, Whitey Ford, Red Schoendienst, and others. One of the verses goes, "There ought to be a hall of fame for mamas." I looked out in the crowd and all those hardened old players had tears on their cheeks. I already liked the song, and that confirmed to me that it could be a hit.

I cut the track, but Charley never recorded his part. He got a new deal on Sixteenth Avenue Records and changed his mind about doing the tune. So I called Steve Wariner and he said yes. We cut the song, it was released in time for Mother's Day, and it received more airplay than any other country record of 1987. My mother, Carrie, died in December 1991. One of the things about which I'm most thankful is that she not only heard the record but I got to perform it live for her at the Roy Clark Theater in Branson, Missouri, in the summer of 1991, and earlier that year at a family reunion on July Fourth in Billstown, Arkansas.

I've joked many times that I seem to have a knack for finding writers who have one tremendous hit in them. Such was the case with Chris Gantry, who wrote "Dreams of the Everyday Housewife"; Larry Weiss, who wrote "Rhinestone Cowboy"; and John Hartford, who wrote "Gentle on My Mind." Each has written other successful songs, but only those blockbusters. And each of those songs grabbed me the instant I heard them. Yet, I insisted on living with each tune before I cut it. I wonder if contemporary artists are doing that.

I have carried a song around for as long as five years before recording it. I can think of only two or three songs out of hundreds I've recorded that I performed as originally written. I like to become intimate with the material, and change it to suit me. I invariably do that to the melody or chord progression.

The most instrumentally challenging song I've ever recorded was "MacArthur Park." There are many changes in that song, along with lots of minor and augmented chords.

I've done the *William Tell* overture a thousand times on my live show. That too is a challenge, and I don't think I've ever played it perfectly. If I ever do, fans might grow to expect it that way every time. I don't ever want to become predictable.

I think there is another explanation for today's simplistic music: The music business is more business than music. Too many times, the people who sit behind desks rather than stand behind microphones are selecting the songs that go onto albums and are released for airplay. Those same minds are also turning down hit songs. If a record company believes in an artist enough to invest money in him, promote his product, and subsidize his travel, it should also believe in him enough to let him select his own best work. There are also plenty of singers who aren't really artists and do need direction. But when a guy has proven his playing, writing, or singing the way it's been proven by Garth Brooks, Ricky Skaggs, Vince Gill, or Alan Jackson, why tell him what he should record?

This has been a great frustration to many artists, including myself. Record-company executives used to tell me, "We need a radio song, we need a drive song, we need a this song, we need a that song."

"How about a hit song?" I would reply.

The albums containing "Gentle on My Mind" and "By the Time I Get to Phoenix" were blockbusters because I had total control and recorded exactly what I wanted.

Today's record industry is more sophisticated and successful than at any other time in history. Nashville sees more gold records in one year than it once saw in twenty. It's easy to become intoxicated with all that flurry and forget that the song is still the hub of it all. I've been blessed with people on my payroll who can still hear a potential hit song, particularly Marty Gamblin. My own recording track record, bless God, speaks for itself. I think the record companies, no matter how big, will only get bigger if they relinquish creative control to most of the artists they sign.

Chapter 19

*T*he day was like most other days not spent on the road. I was at home, catching up on all the little things that are big deals to an often-absent father and husband. There was talk about how Cal, my oldest son by Kimberly, was doing in basketball, how Shannon was doing in school, and whether Ashley Noel would need braces after the loss of her baby teeth. There is always mail to be opened, and stories to be related about what I missed while I was touring from town to town in the nonstop pilgrimage that is my life.

I picked up an edition of *USA Today,* and leisurely sipped coffee as I unfolded the pages before me.

Then I began to cry. A headline screamed that on October 25, 1992, Roger Miller had died at fifty-six.

There is often a bonding among people of the same craft and that bonding is intensified if they had begun their careers together.

Roger and I started out together, and spent our lean years pulling for each other while pulling ourselves up by our bootstraps, and pulling ourselves apart with the frustrations of careers that were going nowhere in a hurry. We became as close as brothers. We laughed, cried, sinned, played music, celebrated, and regretted together, and had done so for three and a half decades.

Roger had a sensitive side, and in his later years became a devoted father to his small children and a loving husband to Mary, a woman who did as much to restore his sanity and save his life as Kimberly did for me.

And then there was the wit. Roger's mind was computer-fast and spontaneously hilarious. One-liners rolled fluently from his tongue. He was country music's answer to Robin Williams.

"I'd give my right arm to be ambidextrous."

"Did you ever notice that a chicken can gain ten pounds and never show it in his face?"

"Every day is Saturday to a dog."

I use many of his quips in my stage show today. I have always credited Roger publicly, just as I have praised the writing of Jimmy Webb and the imaginative compositions of Dolly Parton.

When Roger died I lost a friend. The world lost a genius.

Consider the fact that Roger, an eighth-grade graduate, was approached by a Yale professor and asked to write a Broadway musical. *Big River* ran for several seasons, toured, and won many Tony Awards. I've never put a lot of stock in book-learning if you have talent. Education can't hurt, but it isn't necessary. I have no formal education, yet I've been given an honorary doctorate degree in music from the University of California at Riverside. I appreciate the degree, but it hasn't helped my playing any.

Consider that Roger couldn't read a note of music, and had trouble with words containing more than three syllables. In 1965 he won five Grammy Awards and in 1966 he won six, including Song of the Year for "King of the Road." It beat "The Shadow of Your Smile," by Tony Bennett, and one of the most popular songs ever written—"Yesterday," by the Beatles.

A flood of thoughts runs uncontrollably through your mind after the death of a loved one. You realize that despite all your mental prepara-

tion for the passing, you were nonetheless unprepared. You find yourself dwelling on details that are seemingly inconsequential—some lame
thing the deceased once said, or what he wore the last time you saw
him—and you realize this is the first time you've thought about those
things. You wonder why you would think of something so trivial in the
wake of something so significant, then you realize you're not thinking
at all. You're just numb.

Roger had been suffering from cancer for about a year. He knew,
and knew his friends knew, that he wasn't going to live, despite his
valiant fight against that dreaded disease. Weeks before his passing, the
cancer spread to his brain. It was then no longer a question of if he
would die, but when.

So I braced myself for the day I would hear he had passed away. I'd
heard about his diminishing health from a cluster of mutual friends. We
would tell Roger Miller stories. We would laugh a lot, then the room
would suddenly fall silent, with nobody saying out loud what we were
all saying to ourselves—that Roger's time was ending.

Roger was booked for three days in August 1992 to join my extended
run at the Grand Palace in Branson, Missouri. He didn't show up and
gave little notice that he wasn't going to come. I think I know why.
With every ounce of strength within him, he had been determined to
make that show. Sometimes determination isn't enough, no matter how
intense.

I first met Roger in 1959 while playing in Albuquerque. He came
through town as a fiddle player and high-harmony singer for Ray Price.
That was back when Ray was billed as the "Cherokee Cowboy," and
he and the band wore the old country-star suits that were bedecked in
rhinestones and sequins. Roger called the members of the band "hill-
billy Liberaces."

Roger was a struggling songwriter then who subsidized himself as a
touring sideman. He had written a tune called "Invitation to the
Blues," and Price had made it a hit. I remember how Roger loved to

sing harmony to his own composition, and how he covered Price's vocal melody flawlessly on "Crazy Arms" and "Heartaches by the Number."

Roger and I liked to drink back in the late 1950s, and we went on a big drunk the night he came through Albuquerque. In those days, people in country music called having a hearty party "roaring." Roger and I roared loudly enough to echo all the way back to Nashville. He never made a secret about his infamous amphetamine problem. He was popping pills when I first met him. I've already mentioned that I had tried uppers once, and that they prompted me, after I changed my tire, to leave the jack and fender skirt on the highway. They also gave me a prostate infection. Roger had given me those pills.

The night after Roger and Ray Price left Albuquerque, they played Grants, New Mexico. Since it was a Sunday and I was off, I joined them and played guitar on their show. After that, the roaring resumed.

My break came in 1967 with "Gentle on My Mind," and Roger's preceded mine with the hit "Dang Me" in 1964. The song had come from an album he cut before leaving Nashville in disgust. He had pitched songs there unsuccessfully while working odd jobs, including one as a bellhop. Nothing had happened for him. He had a final shot at Smash Records, and figured he had nothing to lose, and he didn't.

"So this time, I'm going to record my music and record it my way," he told me.

His "way" meant combining meaningful lyrics with a zany delivery. In his early material, he wanted the listener to know that while the situation might be serious, the singer was not.

Here I sit high, gettin' ideas
Ain't nothin' but a fool would live like this
Out all night and runnin' wild
Woman sittin' home with a month-old child
Dang me, dang me, they ought to take a rope and hang me
High from the highest tree, woman would you weep for me?

Then he would scat in harmony with his guitar. He was a true stylist.

Singers and songwriters were more loyal when I entered the music business than they are today. Today's singers often want to sign contracts with a record company for one album, then renegotiate if the record hits.

Not so with Roger. Buddy Killen, retired president of Tree International, tells stories about Roger's tenure with Tree since his first days in Nashville. Roger signed with Tree in 1963 and never wrote for another publishing house. This was because Roger never forgot something Killen had done for him.

Nashville singers and songwriters in the 1950s and 1960s used to hang out at a dive called Mom's, which later became Tootsie's Orchid Lounge. Even the legendary Hank Williams frequented the place, and many hit songs were written on Mom's napkins. The joint sat directly across the alley from the Ryman Auditorium, home of the Grand Ole Opry until 1974.

Roger ambled into the place, where Killen was playing pinball. Killen said he watched Roger watch him for the longest time before the timid songwriter approached him, not knowing he was a music publisher. Roger told Killen that he and his wife were broke, and that they needed a place to stay. Without hesitation, Killen "loaned" Roger five dollars. When talk turned to songwriting, Killen invited Roger to bring his songs to Tree's offices the next day. Roger did, Killen listened, and he signed him to a writing contract. Tree went on to publish "Dang Me," "Engine, Engine No. 9," "King of the Road," "In the Summertime," "Husbands and Wives," and hundreds of other Roger Miller hits and standards. Tree made millions from Roger's work, Killen was never repaid his five dollars, and Roger Miller, despite other offers, was a staff writer for Tree International the day he died.

Roger had little use for the conventional life, before or after his songwriting and singing success. Killen told me a wonderful story about Roger being indebted to Tree for perhaps ten thousand dollars in advances against his royalties. He came into the office one day wanting three hundred dollars.

"But Roger," Killen told him, "you haven't written a song in a long time, and you're already into the company for so much money. I just can't let you have three hundred more dollars."

"But Buddy," he pleaded, "I've just got to have the money!"

Killen knew that Roger was behind on his rent and utility payments. He felt sorry for him, and against his better judgment gave Roger three hundred dollars, back when that was the equivalent of three thousand.

A day or so later, Killen asked Roger why he so badly needed the three hundred dollars.

"I found the most dandy riding lawn mower and I just had to have it," Roger said.

Roger didn't even have a lawn.

He remained a nonconformist until the day he died. There is a famous story in show-business circles involving Roger when he played the old MGM Grand, once the most lavish hotel-casino in Las Vegas.

Roger would take his chemical stimulants for days, going without sleep the whole time. I've heard people in the business say they'd seen him stay awake for as long as a week. It's a wonder that he never had a stroke. He was on one of his pill binges when opening night rolled around at the MGM. He was introduced, the music played, the applause began, and he sauntered to a stool at center stage. He sat down, hit one chord on his guitar, and promptly fell asleep. The first vocal sound the audience heard was his snoring.

I don't think Nashville ever produced a songwriter whose work was so consistently recycled. During the last five years of his life, Roger's songs that had been hits were hits again, this time by Highway 101, Ricky Van Shelton, and k. d. lang.

Roger was perhaps the most unpretentious person I've ever known in show business. His head simply wasn't turned, or swollen, by his success.

He had a 1976 Bentley when he and I lived in Los Angeles. I helped him move into a new house, and instead of calling movers or renting a truck, he loaded that luxury car with his personal stuff. The plush interior was littered with Roger's socks, guitars, shaving kit, and the like. Later, he moved to Santa Fe, where I visited him only to see the Bentley sitting on his front lawn with four flat tires. It had been there, he said, for three years, as if it were some kind of lawn furniture with a steering wheel. Roger had decided that a Ford Bronco was all he needed, and he just left the Bentley where it was. For all I know, the car is still there, a collector's item gathering dust and bird droppings.

I last saw Roger in the summer of 1992, when he and I were guests on a TV tribute to Minnie Pearl, who was convalescing from a stroke. Everybody who was anybody in country music was on the program. I looked in Roger Miller's face and knew I was seeing a dying man. His skin was puffy and the color of chalk. His once-flashing eyes were distant and glazed. Instead of being the life of the party, he was nearly silent.

Production ran long for what was eventually a two-hour show. Roger, although sick, was made to wait until late at night to videotape his solo. Then his part was cut from the program.

He had worked for Minnie Pearl, and talked to her regularly before and after her stroke. He spoke frequently to Henry Cannon, Minnie's husband. Roger's part in the program not only should have been retained, it should have been highlighted.

He had quit smoking, a habit some blamed for the throat cancer that ravaged him. He would be dead in less than six months, yet even in his final days, the wit and spirit of Roger Miller remained.

"I've given up so many bad habits," he told me, "that every time I reach for something, I quit it."

We talked about the national-election campaign, whose outcome Roger would not live to see.

Roger was cremated and I wasn't surprised. I've even wondered if he requested that with a joke in mind. He once told me about someone whose remains sat in an urn atop a piano. Someone mistakenly mistook the deceased's ashes for cigarette ashes, and occasionally flicked his tobacco ashes into the remains.

"Even after death, old so-and-so was gaining weight," Roger said, laughing.

I didn't go to Roger's funeral. I was working a show at Branson's Grand Palace, where I headlined throughout the summer and fall of 1992. But from those who were there, I heard it wasn't really a funeral at all. It was a celebration of a life that will be remembered forever because of the music it created.

Footage was shown on big-screen televisions from various country-music shows that Roger played when he was young, including *The Porter Wagoner Show,* country music's most popular syndicated television show in the late 1960s and early 1970s. Being on Porter's program was a big deal to any Nashville singer back in the days when selling a mere twenty-five thousand records could ensure a number-one song.

So, there was Roger, supposedly in his big moment. He stepped in front of Porter, blocking the host from the camera. Then he grabbed Porter's thigh, and Porter struggled to stand straight during his song. Meanwhile, a female vocalist in the background, aware of the hijinks but not able to see them, strained her neck to peer at the misbehaving men. Dolly Parton had no idea that Roger was goosing Porter on national television while she was on the screen.

There was far more laughter than mourning at Roger's memorial service, and I'm convinced that that's exactly what he would have wanted.

Nashville had not seen so many luminaries assembled for a memorial service since the passing in the mid-1960s of Patsy Cline and Jim Reeves. Speakers for Roger included Ralph Emery, Buddy Killen, Ray Price, Johnny Cash, Kris Kristofferson, Waylon Jennings, Jessi Colter, David Huddleston, Garrison Keillor, Don Meredith, Willie Nelson, David Steinberg, Mel Tillis, Marty Stuart, Roger Miller, Jr., and others. A newspaper account cited more than 250 celebrities and music-business executives in the audience. Chet Atkins accompanied Steve Wariner, who sang "Amazing Grace" for the hushed gathering, and Jessi Colter delivered a voice-and-piano presentation of "His Eye Is on the Sparrow."

Then there was a rollicking gospel medley from the Nashville Mass Choir, and finally everyone left the rickety old Ryman, where Roger Miller had premiered decades earlier. Those paying respects adjourned to Tootsie's Orchid Lounge for more stories about the man who had died but whose music never will. Roger had written his name on Tootsie's wall the night that he borrowed five dollars from Killen three and a half decades earlier.

Waylon Jennings is not known for being overly emotional or sentimental, although he has a sensitive side that many people have never seen. It showed the night of Roger's memorial.

"If Roger's looking, I'm sure he's getting a big bang out of this—me in a suit," Waylon told the crowd. "But a suit's all you get, Roger. A tie would be too much.

"The last time I saw Roger," Waylon continued, "he was in pretty bad shape. I was trying to talk the wheels off a Volkswagen, trying to give him encouragement. I guess I wore him out. He said to me, 'Boy, you look awful. Why don't you go home and take a nap.' So I did.

"You could never imitate him, you could never duplicate him," Waylon said. "I'm not even sure God could."

I believe God could. But I'm not sure He wants to. Perhaps one Roger Miller is all the rest of us are entitled to in our lifetime.

Chapter 20

*O*ne question I'm frequently asked these days is whether I plan to enter the ministry. My answer is that I'm already in it. While I have no plans to attend a seminary or seek ordination, I have a ministry in my music, much of which is focused on God and all of which is performed for God.

Parts of my show include the secular songs I've sung for twenty-five years, and I'm singing them better today than ever before. (I quit smoking on March 15, 1992.)

I once performed with a band, but today it's the band and the Holy Spirit. I can feel it when I'm onstage, I can hear it in recorded playbacks, and I can sense it in audience responses.

I have increased my appearances on evangelical television, and have appeared regularly on the Reverend Pat Robertson's *700 Club* as well as other shows on the Trinity Broadcast Network and Christian Broadcast Network. My appearances with Dr. Robert Schuller prompt more mail than any other television exposure I have. I had to decline, regrettably, an invitation from the Reverend Billy Graham to appear with him in April 1993 because of a previous commitment. I have sung before twenty thousand people during Christian conferences and conventions with the Reverend James Robison and in similar programs in Dallas, and at my home church, the North Phoenix Baptist Church. I was contacted in the early summer of 1993 by officials at cable television's Trinity Broadcast Network and asked to headline a program of gospel singers to be broadcast live from the Grand Palace in Branson, Missouri.

On May 21, 1993, I was given a tentative offer to appear sometime in 1994 in Israel for a concert promoted by a Christian radio station and the Israel Travel Bureau. I have never been to the Holy Land and look forward to going. I want to walk the way of the cross, and step in the same places Jesus did when He was led to His crucifixion. I want to visit Bethlehem and stand near the site of the manger where my savior was born. I want to "feel" His presence by being where He has physically been.

When I appear at Christian services today, I don't speak from a prepared text. I instead testify about my deliverance from alcohol, drugs, and tobacco, without the need of a detoxification or rehabilitation center. I sing. I tell jokes. I share.

I simply am the new Glen Campbell.

Kim reminds me of shows in which I was so drunk or high, I could sing only three or four songs and made lame attempts at comedy. It was really just so much babble, a drunken man who thought he was in control.

Some people in the Christian community do not know how to take the new Glen. They expect me to abandon my secular repertoire and all the hits upon which I built my career, wanting to hear only my contemporary Christian hits.

The audience gets both, and the format goes over well everywhere, especially in Branson, Missouri, where I had headline billing from April through October in 1992 and 1993 at the Grand Palace, the city's largest, most lavish theater. It's technically the best theater I've ever played in in the world. I shared the stage with various acts, most of whom work for two or three days, including Ronnie Milsap, Waylon Jennings, the Oak Ridge Boys, Emmylou Harris, Ricky Skaggs, Louise Mandrell, Randy Travis, the Bellamy Brothers, the Smothers Brothers, Doc Severinsen, and many others. The crowd is largely grassroots: believers in God, home, and country, who are receptive to my songs, which often include a patriotic number or two.

In October 1993 I signed a deal with a Branson investment group to build a new "Glen Campbell Goodtime Theatre." It will be a state-of-the-art 2,200-seat theater that will feature me, dancers, singers, my family members, and guest stars doing a totally new show. I'm looking forward to spending twenty-six weeks a year working at my own theater and doing my own thing.

My new show has no dirty jokes, which were a regular part of my program through 1981. Some of my show-business friends have had trouble understanding my new show and my salvation. They had no trouble being around me when I was drunk or high, but today some get uncomfortable when I talk about Jesus Christ.

I did a reunion tour of *The Glen Campbell Goodtime Hour* in 1991. Nicolette Larson, Jim Stafford, John Hartford, and I traveled across the nation singing songs from the twenty-five-year-old series, and it went over very well. On this reunion trip, Hartford, who I regard as a cornerstone of my early career, was the opening act in Sun City, Arizona, a suburb of Phoenix, where he used God's name in vain as part of his presentation. I wasn't trying to be holier than thou when I called him on it. I just don't want that kind of language in my show today.

Ronnie Milsap and I have been friends for years. He is a dynamic talent who I used as my opening act in the mid-1970s on his first overseas tour. He thrilled the audiences then, as he does now. When he played with me in Branson, I saw that his current show included a spoof of *Playboy* magazine and an impersonation of a television evangelist. He was asked by the management of the Grand Palace to delete those portions from his show.

When audiences leave my shows, I not only want them to feel entertained, I want them to feel like better people for having attended. I want them to be inspired, uplifted, blessed.

Jesus said, "If I be lifted up I'll draw all men to me."

I'm trying to lift up Jesus by raising my voice. I do not try to force my convictions on others, and yet I am charged by the New Testament's great commission and feel the responsibility to go into the world and preach the gospel. I'm trying to preach it by living it.

I don't want to try to do too much too soon in my Christian life. Some new Christians, God bless them, want to save the entire world, and do it before sundown. Haste is often associated with a lack of wisdom, particularly when it is involved with something as sensitive as people's spiritual lives. I think of B. J. Thomas, a sincere and talented Christian, who, after his spiritual conversion, rushed into a Christian music career. He wasn't established as a Christian singer, and his career was quickly jeopardized. The public became confused as to what kind of music to expect from him. He performed at Oral Roberts University in Tulsa, Oklahoma, where the audience was made up largely of Christians who thought they were going to hear religious music. B.J. sang his biggest secular hit, "Raindrops Keep Falling on My Head," and he was booed. Those Christians shouldn't have done that, and it had to be very discouraging to someone who was so new to his faith.

Similarly, I have felt sympathy for the Contemporary Christian singer Amy Grant, who, after years at the top of the Contemporary Christian surveys, accelerated her secular singing career a few years ago. She didn't leave her ministry. In fact, to my way of thinking, she expanded it. By incorporating secular music into her career, she attracted fans to the Christian message who might otherwise have never heard it.

It's surprising how many people in this nation know about churches, know about religion, and know about morality, but don't know that Jesus saves—the foundation of the Gospel of Christ.

Amy has been given notes from supposed Christians pompously telling her that she is going to hell for singing secular music and that she could still repent and save herself. "Judge not that ye be not judged," the Bible warns. I have to wonder about the salvation of a person who attacks someone whose life, music, and ministry are as overrun with proven integrity as Amy's.

I have been confronted as well because I don't perform only Christian music in the wake of my salvation. Doing so would probably attract only Christians to my concerts, and I don't want to spend my life and career espousing Christ to people who already know him. I want to expose Christ to people who don't. It's a waste of time to carry water to the sea when the rest of the world is thirsty.

I was hurt for Christians everywhere, including those involved, when scandal rocked the television-evangelism community a few years ago. Men with powerful international ministries were caught in sex scandals, and for a while it seemed as if the disclosures would never stop. Allegations of adultery were substantiated and, in one case, publicly confessed. Then accusations of homosexuality and financial payoffs surfaced. Millions of hearts were broken, and as many minds were disillusioned. The entire evangelical movement suffered, as people everywhere became suspicious of anyone preaching the gospel.

Anytime a man looks to another man for perfection he will find flaws. The only perfect man was Jesus Christ, and we're to keep our eyes on Him, not on those who talk and teach about Him. And God has a master plan. It was laid out long before the creation of the universe. The plan even included Judas's betrayal of Jesus Christ for thirty pieces of silver. None of the other disciples understood at the time. Later, some would when they saw how Judas's betrayal resulted in Christ's arrest by Roman soldiers. Had He not been arrested, He would not have been crucified. Had He not been crucified, He would not have risen from the dead—an act that showed unequivocally that He was the son of God. Christ's triumph over the grave, more than any other miracle, proved his role as the Messiah. And those thirty pieces of silver given to Judas indirectly purchased salvation for those who came into this world after Christ.

I don't ever want to become so Heavenly-minded that I'm no earthly good. Just because I'm a Christian does not mean I'm perfect. It merely means I'm forgiven. There is a joy that goes with that forgiveness. I simply want to share the joy, and let people know that it's theirs for the acceptance.

Yet, because Jesus Christ is more dear to me today than anything, it hurts me when people use his name in vain. I buried my mother in our family cemetery in December 1991. My father was buried there years earlier. Standing at their gravesides, I thought of things, big and small, that they had done for me. I wanted to tell them how much I loved them, but it was too late for that in this life. If I felt that sentimental about my earthly mother and father, how could I not feel the same about my Heavenly Father? I want to tell Him daily that I love Him, and I do. I would not tolerate anyone saying unkind things about my departed parents. Why should I tolerate negative talk about my Heavenly Father?

I recently played golf with a guy who would swing, see the shot go bad, and blaspheme the name of God. Besides using God's and Jesus' name in vain, his vocabulary was laced with the filthiest of profanities. He talked as I once did.

Was I angry about his speech? Mildly. But mostly I was hurt. It goes back to the love I have for God, and my not wanting to hear anyone talk badly about God, even though some might do it merely by force of habit.

On some occasions, when this kind of thing happens, I've felt compelled to say something to the offender. On this particular occasion, however, I prayed quietly and walked off the course.

I'm not going to condemn the speaker, and I'm not going to judge him. I'm also not going to play golf with him anymore. I told him to get a better routine. "You'll never improve by hitting the ball and then cussing," I said.

★★★

Before I became a Christian, I was unconcerned about morality and sin in anyone's life, including my own. Today, however, I have firm convictions, and stand up for what I believe. One of my beliefs concerns the most topical and controversial subjects of all time—abortion.

Before the 1973 United States Supreme Court ruling in the famous *Roe* v. *Wade* case, abortion was illegal in this country. Since the ruling, approximately 1.5 million abortions have been performed annually in the United States. Think about it. The total number of abortions performed in the United States since the Supreme Court decision is more than the population of Australia or ten American states. Almost 4,300 abortions are performed daily in the United States. Abortion has become the most common surgical procedure in America. Almost one child out of three is killed by abortion. With some exceptions, those abortions represent as many murders. Sometimes, they represent more.

Fifty years ago, in Houston, a child was born into poverty by a woman who had been raped. Because her pregnancy was unwanted, the distressed mother sought an abortion. Laws prevented it then, though they would allow it now. The mother gave her baby to foster parents, who raised the boy under the teachings of Jesus Christ. He accepted Christ as his personal savior at age fifteen. The formerly unwanted baby grew up to become the Reverend James Robison, one of the most prominent Baptist evangelists of our time.

The Reverend Robison's missionary work has fed and housed thousands of unwanted children in the former Yugoslavia. The children were born after their Croatian mothers were raped by Serbian captors. Many of the mothers abandoned their offspring at birth because they were thought to be symbolic of dishonor.

The Reverend Robison's Life Center in Croatia houses as many as one hundred children and mothers, and provides outpatient care for three hundred others. The Reverend Robison's LIFE Outreach International has provided shelter, food, and spiritual nutrition for thousands of people in the United States, Canada, and twenty foreign countries. My own life has been blessed for participating in his ministry. None of the lives spared by the Reverend Robison's efforts would have been had he been aborted half a century ago.

✭✭✭

In November 1992, Arizona voters considered a referendum to amend the state constitution to make abortion illegal except in cases of rape, incest, or those in which the mother's life was in danger. The measure was known as Proposition 110.

As Christians, Kim and I believe in the sanctity of life. We opened our home and wallets to campaign for passage of the proposition. Our financial contributions were into five figures, and we had a get-together at our house attended by more than two hundred supporters, speakers, and some members of the mass media.

I spoke on behalf of the rights of the unborn fetus, but had time to utter only a few clichés because there were so many others who also wanted to be heard.

"Every abortion stops a beating heart," Kim and I told our guests.

I don't understand the wording of the pro-choice movement that offers a woman the "choice" of whether she will abort her child or let it live. What choice? We're not talking about something as simple as choice; we are talking about human life!

It should be a woman's choice? It should be her choice to have a hysterectomy or to have her gallbladder removed. Those are her body parts. But a baby has its own genetic code. It has its own life. It has different blood within a different circulatory system. It has a different digestive system, and more. Abortion doesn't apply strictly to the mother's body; it also pertains to her baby's life. How hard is that to understand? Life begins at conception. Killing a baby inside a woman's body, therefore, is the equivalent of killing it outside her body.

I very much endorse the Christian Crisis Pregnancy Centers that are springing up all over the nation. They reach out to pregnant girls and women on a personal level. They do not force spiritual or moralistic views on anyone, yet they offer to show an actual abortion on videotape to women considering the procedure. Why shouldn't these young women, making a life-changing and possibly life-threatening decision, be allowed to examine abortion in every way possible, including through the camera lens? The best decision is an informed decision. The prospective mothers are then offered maternity clothes, cribs, diapers, and medical care.

My parents had twelve children. I've already mentioned that there was no way they could financially afford a family that large. I'm sure that my parents, at times, felt they couldn't afford us psychologically. They couldn't even afford the physical space for such a mammoth family in our various small shanties.

Abortion wasn't an option to my mother, and if it had been, she wouldn't have exercised it. My point is that people often consider giving up the unborn because having a child will be traumatic for a number of reasons. Almost no one today has reasons more pronounced to give up their unborn than my parents did. But thank God they didn't. The children who lived grew up to be productive, law-abiding citizens who make a contribution to their own lives and to the lives around them. The world is a better place because we lived.

I feel as though the abortion craze sweeping this nation is nothing less than a holocaust against the helpless. When Kim and I get to Heaven, I shouldn't be surprised if God asks us what we did to stop the slaughter of children commensurate to King Herod's attempt to take the life of Jesus by slaughtering babies. When we're asked, I'll be thankful to say we were active in the cause of life—a cause of Christ.

I find a terrible irony in the propaganda of those who advocate abortion. Many argue that the federal government should stay out of the abortion debate, but that it should pay for abortions. It's hypocritical for abortionists to contend that society has no right to tell a woman she can't murder her unborn child, but if she elects to do so, society should be obliged to finance the slaughter.

I think the abortion industry wants to talk about pro-choice simply to divert the issue. It has to talk about something other than abortion itself, as it can't defend abortion.

The same diversionary tactic was used during the United States clash over slavery. In the 1858 debates between Stephen Douglas and Abraham Lincoln, Douglas defended people's rights to own slaves, although he never portrayed himself as being proslavery. He simply said that slave ownership was a personal decision with no room for government intervention. He, in effect, called for pro-choice on the slavery issue. Douglas knew he couldn't defend his true convictions—the belief in slave ownership—so he camouflaged his convictions in the guise of pro-choice, the way today's abortion advocates hide their true convictions under the umbrella of pro-choice.

Abortion today is not strictly surgical. Advocates are asking the nation's Food and Drug Administration to make legal RU 486, an abortion pill. The purpose of that pill is to stop the beating of a developing baby's heart. Ironically, many pro-choice advocates don't want RU-486 in the United States, and for a very self-serving reason. They feel that licensing the drug in the United States will cause the closing of surgical abortion clinics. Should the pill prove to be dangerous, it will be difficult to get the surgical clinics reopened. So, the pro-choice bunch resists the killing pill for fear that it might ultimately result in less killing.

Ecclesiastes 11:5 says: "As you do not know the path of the wind, or how the body is formed in a mother's womb, so you cannot understand the work of God, the maker of all things."

☆ ☆ ☆

I don't understand those who want to ban private prayer from public schools, claiming that praying violates the separation of Church and State. Isn't praying a constitutional right also? One student's praying in no way compels another to pray.

Much of the public is in favor of sex education and the distribution of condoms in school. Many people think that students who smoke should have a designated area of the school grounds in which to do so. These people think that students with political convictions, no matter how dissident, should have the right to espouse them. But they don't think anyone should have the right to talk to God publicly. Freedom of speech does not allow the right to suppress someone else's freedom of speech.

An incident recently occurred at Stone Mountain Park, Georgia, site of the 1996 Olympic Games. An evangelist was refused the right to pass out evangelical literature by park officials who were employees of the state of Georgia. Parks have historically been the sites of free-speech forums and massive antiwar, pro-choice, and political rallies, including those held near the White House in Washington. But Georgia officials saw to it that it wasn't going to be that way in the Peach State.

The evangelist went to court, and park officials softened, allowing him to hand out his literature from two booths. He had two tiny spaces to espouse religion on a thirty-two-hundred-acre park.

On September 11, 1991, Massac County High School students in Metropolis, Illinois, were part of a national event called "See You at the Pole." They were among thousands of high school students throughout the nation who congregated around flagpoles to pray for their nation's leaders. The event went off without incident at most schools. But, due to a distorted interpretation of the separation of church and state, police arrested six students for praying in Metropolis. They were held in police vehicles and threatened with mace. The school board later apologized, but those six students' civil rights were violated, and a lawsuit was filed in defense of their liberty, according to literature distributed by the American Center of Law and Justice.

To me, it was just another indication of how Christians are being punished for what they believe and stand up for publicly. This punishment has manifested itself as discrimination, and touched me in my own home city.

On February 26, 1993, the *Arizona Republic* and *Phoenix Gazette* newspapers rejected a classified advertisement seeking a nanny for three children by parents who wanted a nonsmoking, Christian nanny. The newspapers' censorship committee said the ad was discriminatory.

I think the committee discriminated against the Christians. What if the advertisement sought an agnostic or homosexual nanny? Would the committee have declined the advertisement then? I think not. Many daily newspapers run personal advertisements for those seeking romantic partners with all kinds of characteristics, including certain sexual preferences. Isn't that discrimination? But those ads don't often mention Christianity, so there is no conflict with censorship committees. How regrettable.

★★★

The First Amendment allows freedom of the press. The people who publish the papers have the freedom to speak for themselves, and are not compelled to publish opinions that are in tune with the masses. Therefore, the thinking of a few is often inflicted on many, whether wanted or not. That is the terrible backlash of a free press.

I think that grassroots Americans with traditional, fundamental values are at last becoming weary of the propaganda espoused by the minority, liberal free press. In March 1993, the American Center for Law and Justice, in affiliation with the Reverend Pat Robertson, published a list of what I thought were encouraging findings. The survey included thirteen questions that drew responses from more than thirty thousand people. The fact that so many people took the time to respond to the survey indicates to me that people are getting restless and want to reach out in favor of the basic values upon which this nation was built.

More than 98 percent of respondents felt that private prayer in public schools should not be denied.

More than 98 percent felt that public school students should not be prevented from holding Bible studies or having Bible clubs during nonclassroom times.

92 percent agreed that religious art and musical expression is part of our national heritage and should not be censored.

More than 90 percent felt that all human life is sacred from conception to death, and that abortion and euthanasia should not be legally sanctioned.

97 percent felt that homosexuality should not become a civil right and that homosexual relationships should not be recognized as a lifestyle or a family unit.

98 percent agreed that the growing assault against the traditional family must be stopped.

More than 98 percent felt that the exploitation of people through pornography is morally and socially wrong.

More than 95 percent agreed that the public display of religious symbols on public property does not represent an "establishment of religion" as described in the First Amendment.

More than 98 percent agreed that efforts to eliminate God and morality from the public arena represent a serious threat to our nation's future.

98 percent agreed that Americans must have the freedom to demonstrate, speak freely, and exercise their First Amendment rights.

More than 97 percent agreed that the American Civil Liberties Union must be challenged as to its claims of being truly concerned with civil liberties and the protection of our constitutional rights.

More than 94 percent agreed that the recent trend toward "political correctness" on college campuses and in the media reflects a dangerous intolerance of traditional values.

More than 97 percent agreed that religious discrimination and harassment in the workplace must be exposed and punished.

Granted, the findings might have been drawn from selected survey respondents as opposed to a random sampling of people. But I still think most Americans are fast growing weary of the moral, social, and anti-God junk that inflicts itself on too many of our lives.

The most popular nonfiction book in the United States of America in recent times is a conservative overview of America written by Rush Limbaugh, whose immensely popular national television program is only two years old. There is nothing religious or spiritual about the show. Limbaugh has caught on because people are starved for fairness and decency and those who proclaim those values.

Mine is one more voice in a growing army. It will be until silenced by God Himself.

Epilogue

*A*t the end of 1991 I stood at the grave of my mother. Her health had been deteriorating for some time in her home in Billstown from a variety of illnesses, not the least of which was old age and fatigue from rearing a mammoth family before, during, and after an economic depression, and hurting for them through their emotional depression from pain that often resulted from recklessness or irresponsibility. I think the pain we bring to ourselves hurts more than pain that is accidental.

I stood with my brothers and sisters as we lowered my mother into a grave beside my father's. The death was expected, but I was unprepared nonetheless. The toughest hardship one experiences in this life, I feel, is the loss of a blood relative.

"You don't know about lonely," Vern Gosdin sang, "till it's chiseled in stone."

Standing on the winter-brown and wind-swept Arkansas landscape, I couldn't control the thoughts that raced through my head. Recollections of times happy and sad leaped to mind. I remembered how my mother would send me money in Albuquerque when I first went there because, as she said at a family reunion in 1991, "I thought if he felt a little support from home he'd stay with it, and I knew if he stayed with it he'd make it."

I thought about the times my mother and dad sang with me in Las Vegas or at the Houston Astrodome, along with all my brothers and sisters and anyone else who was remotely a Campbell. They loved to come see me perform, and I loved to call them onto the stage.

I looked over at my dad's tombstone on that frigid morning and thought about his precious country naïveté, which had remained intact despite the prosperity that found him late in life.

I shed tears, some in gratitude, for the rearing from two people who had the integrity of saints and the innocence of lambs.

My dad once visited me in Los Angeles, where he went into the bathroom and tried to eat the tiny pieces of decorative soap.

"Lonnie," he told Lonnie Shorr, "don't say anything to Glen, but don't eat any of them candies in the bathroom. They're spoiled."

I was in a restaurant with my dad and warned him to be careful with the seasoning sauce because it was hot. So he blew on it.

Once he was shopping in a rural Arkansas grocery store near where my sister worked. His false teeth hurt him, so he took them out and set them on a food shelf while reading the labels. When he checked out at the cash register, he couldn't remember where he had left his teeth. They were found by another customer, who was startled after she picked up a can and stared directly into the dentures.

I thought about the indescribable stress under which my dad lived when his children were young, not knowing from where the next meal would come. The easiest thing for him would have been to leave. So many men did during the Depression, after the stock-market crash of 1929. But no circumstance could have torn him away from the responsibilities that were his.

Standing over my mother's open grave, seeing her eased into the earth, I experienced another death that day: my own. I prayed that I might put thoughts of "self" to death and become more sensitive to the needs of those around me.

On February 2, 1993, my eldest child, Debby Campbell Olson, called Kim to say that my second wife, Billie, had died of cancer. It had been expected. Her body was brought back to Carlsbad, New Mexico, for the funeral.

As she lay dying in a Los Angeles hospital, one of my children, Kane, stole things from her house and sold them to buy drugs. He, at the same time, wrote checks on her account and forged her name. The infractions were the latest in a long series in Kane's life. He was arrested at the funeral.

I have spent money into seven figures on Kane's counseling. I don't know how much responsibility to feel for his situation. I know I was an absentee father. I know my priorities were wrong when he was growing up, as I was losing myself regularly in alcohol and drugs.

I can ask for God's and Kane's forgiveness. I can do better with the three young children I have today. I'm doing all I can.

Debby is perhaps the most mature of my children, not just because she is the eldest, but because she was reared in a less extravagant environment and went to work at various jobs shortly after her high school graduation. Tom Carter interviewed her for this book. With the tape recorder rolling, she voluntarily told him about the hardships of having been my daughter.

She was reared in England with her mother, and talked about the time when my career was red-hot. She never knew, she said, how many of her "friends" really wanted to be with her, and how many would hang around her just because she was Glen Campbell's daughter. She knew there were users in her life, even after she moved to Los Angeles to live with Billie and me one year before our divorce.

Debby's remarks gave me a new appreciation of the price of fame, and how that price applies itself not only to the famous but to their loved ones as well.

She wept during the interview and said that for the longest time she thought that I knew how to love but didn't know how to show it. She said that I'm living the kind of Christian life now that I want, "but he thinks everybody else has to live that way too. . . . I'm not saying that his way is not the right way, through the Lord," Debby said, "but we're only human and we have to go through changes. God knows he's gone through his, but it's okay now, because he's perfect now," she added sarcastically. "I don't blame him for not being a father," she said, "but it makes me try harder as a mom."

The only thing harder than hearing those words is repeating them here.

This book is a vehicle through which I can apologize to my children, my brothers and sisters, and anyone else who I might have hurt through ignorance and indulgence. My behavior, including lack of attentiveness toward my loved ones, was never motivated by a lack of love. My love wasn't misplaced; my priorities were.

I've made attempts to talk to or visit some of my children since undergoing my spiritual changes. I confess that it hasn't always been easy.

God saved me in a moment of prayer, but that didn't erase the effects of decades of mistakes on my part. God forgives us our sins, when we ask. But He doesn't erase the consequences of our sins.

I believe there are men on death row who have been forgiven by God for murder. But they will forever live in prison for their crimes, forgiven or not.

Healing is under way between my children and me. Most healings are gradual, so I know it will take time.

Debby lived with me for a while in the fall of 1992. She was hurting because of her own marital strife. I simply tried to let her know I understood her pain. I had been there. Kim and I shared with her what Christ has done in our lives, and Debby made spiritual decisions of her own.

Then God made some changes.

When Tom Carter called me in early 1993, Debby answered the telephone. "I'm not the same person you knew when we did our interview," she volunteered. "My life is better. I have Christ in it."

I said at the outset that I wouldn't preach, but just would share. I've been in the music business for so long that I can remember when it was more music than business. I've been prosperous for so long that the memories of poverty are less than vivid. I've been around the world as many times as most people have been out of state. I've been a lot of things to a lot of people—even when I was too little to myself.

But I've never been happier than I am now. I feel an internal glow that glistens. It's brighter than the glow of a rising—and recovering—rhinestone cowboy.

Discography

RELEASE NUMBER	TITLE

45's—Atlantic America

99525	"Call Home"/"Sweet Sixteen"
99559	"Cowpoke"/"Rag Doll"
99600	"It's Just a Matter of Time"/"Gene Autry, My Hero"
99647	"(Love Always) Letter to Home"/"An American Trilogy"
99691	"A Lady Like You"/"Tennessee"
99768	"Faithless Love"/"Scene of the Crime"
99893	"On the Wings of My Victory"/"A Few Good Men"
99930	"I Love How You Love Me"/"Hang on My Baby (Ease My Mind)"
99967	"Old Home Town"/"Heartache #3"

45's—Capehart

5008	"Death Valley"/"Nothin' Better Than a Pretty Woman"

45's—Capitol (Starting 1962)

4783	"Too Late to Worry—Too Blue to Cry"/"How Do I Tell My Heart Not to Break"
4856	"Long Black Limousine"/"Here I Am"
4867	"Truck Drivin' Man"/"Kentucky Means Paradise" (as the Green River Boys)
4925	"Prima Donna"/"Oh My Darlin' "
4990	"Dark As a Dungeon"/"Divorce Me C.O.D." (as the Green River Boys)
5037	"Same Old Places"/"As Far As I'm Concerned"
5172	"Through the Eyes of a Child"/"Let Me Tell You 'Bout Mary"
5279	"Summer, Winter, Spring & Fall"/"Heartaches Can Be Fun"
5360	"Tomorrow Never Comes"/"Woman's World"
5441	"Guess I'm Dumb"/"That's All Right"
5504	"The Universal Soldier"/"Spanish Shades"
5545	"Less of Me"/"Private John Q."
5638	"Can't You See I'm Tryin' "/"A Satisfied Mind"
5773	"Burning Bridges"/"Only the Lonely"
5854	"I Gotta Have My Baby Back"/"Just to Satisfy You"
5927	"My Baby's Gone"/"Kelli Hoedown" (unissued 45)
5939	"Gentle on My Mind"/"Just Another Man"
2015	"By the Time I Get to Phoenix"/"You've Still Got a Place in My Heart"
2067	"Hey Little One"/"My Baby's Gone"
2146	"I Wanna Live"/"That's All That Matters"
2224	"Dreams of the Everyday Housewife"/"Kelli Hoedown"
2302	"Wichita Lineman"/"Fate of Man"
2314	"Less of Me"/"Mornin' Glory" (with Bobbie Gentry)
2336	"Christmas Is for Children"/"There's No Place Like Home"
2387	"Let It Be Me"/"Little Green Apples" (with Bobbie Gentry)
2428	*"Galveston"/"Every Time I Itch I Wind Up Scratchin' You"
2494	"Where's the Playground Susie"/"Arkansas"
2573	"True Grit"/"Hava Nagila"
2659	"Try a Little Kindness"/"Lonely My Lonely Friend"
2718	"Honey Come Back"/"Where Do You Go"
2745	"All I Have to Do Is Dream"/"Less of Me" (with Bobbie Gentry)
2787	"Oh Happy Day"/"Someone Above"

*Denotes gold record certification.

2843	"Everything a Man Could Ever Need"/"Norwood (Me and My Guitar)"
2905	"It's Only Make Believe"/"Pave Your Way Into Tomorrow"
3062	"Dream Baby (How Long Must I Dream)"/"Here and Now"
3123	"Last Time I Saw Her"/"Back Talk"
3200	"I Say a Little Prayer"–"By the Time I Get to Phoenix" (medley)/"All Through the Night" (with Anne Murray)
3254	"Oklahoma Saturday Morning"/"Everybody's Got to Go There Sometime"
3287	"United We Stand"/"Ease Your Pain" (with Anne Murray)
3305	"Manhattan Kansas"/"Wayfarin' Stranger"
3382	"Wherefore and Why"/"We All Pull the Load" (unissued 45)
3411	"I Will Never Pass This Way Again"/"We All Pull the Load"
3483	"One Last Time"/"All My Tomorrows"
3509	"I Believe In Christmas"/"New Show on the Roof" (unissued 45)
3548	"I Knew Jesus (Before He Was a Star)"/"On This Road"
3669	"Bring Back My Yesterday"/"Beautiful Love Song"
3735	"Wherefore and Why"/"Give Me Back That Old Familiar Feeling"
3808	"Houston (I'm Comin' to See You)"/"Honestly Loved"
3926	"Bonaparte's Retreat"/"Too Many Mornings"
3988	"It's a Sin When You Love Somebody"/"If I Were Loving You"
4095	*"Rhinestone Cowboy"/"Lovelight"
4155	"Country Boy (You've Got Your Feet in L.A.)"/"Record Collector's Dream"
4245	"Don't Pull Your Love—Then You Can Tell Me Goodbye"/"I Miss You Tonight"
4288	"See You on Sunday"/"Bloodline"
4376	*"Southern Nights"/"*William Tell* Overture"
4445	"Sunflower"/"How High Did We Go"
4515	"God Must Have Blessed America"/"Amazing Grace"
4584	"Another Fine Mess"/"Can You Fool"
4638	"Can You Fool"/"Let's All Sing a Song About It"
4682	"I'm Gonna Love You"/"Love Takes You Higher"
4715	"California"/"Never Tell You No Lies"
4769	"Hound Dog Man"/"Tennessee Home"

*Denotes gold record certification.

4799	"My Prayer"/"Don't Lose Me in the Confusion"
4865	"Somethin' 'Bout You Baby I Like"/"Late Night Confusion" (A-side with Rita Coolidge)
4909	"Hollywood Smiles"/"Hooked on Love"
4959	"I Don't Want to Know Your Name"/"Daisy a Day"
4986	"Why Don't We Just Sleep on It"/"It's Your World" (A-side with Tanya Tucker)
6886	"Temple De Acero"/"Hava Nagila" (A-side is "True Grit" in Spanish)
7-9966	"Walking in the Sun" (promo 45 only; commercially issued as cassingle)

45's—Capitol-Starline Reissue Series

6133	"By the Time I Get to Phoenix"/"Hey Little One"
6134	"I Wanna Live"/"Dreams of the Everyday Housewife"
6135	"Wichita Lineman"/"True Grit"
6136	"Galveston"/"Where's the Playground Susie"
6137	"Gentle on My Mind"/"Arkansas"
6138	"Less of Me"/"Let It Be Me" (with Bobbie Gentry)
6190	"MacArthur Park"/"My Way"
6201	"Try a Little Kindness"/"It's Only Make Believe"
6202	"Honey Come Back"/"Dream Baby (How Long Must I Dream)"
6203	"All I Have to Do Is Dream"/"I Say a Little Prayer"–"By the Time I Get to Phoenix" (A-side with Bobbie Gentry; B-side with Anne Murray)
6230	"Rhinestone Cowboy"/"Country Boy (You've Got Your Feet in L.A.)"
6260	"Southern Nights"/"Sunflower"

45's—Ceneco

1324	"Dreams for Sale"/"I've Got to Win"
1356	"I Wonder"/"You You You"

45's—Crest

1087	"Turn Around, Look at Me"/"Brenda"
1088	"Buzz Saw"/"Annie Had a Party" (Gee Cees)

1089	"From Here to Nowhere"/"Rockin' & Rollin' " (Dick Bills)
1096	"The Miracle of Love"/"Once More"
1101	"Song of New Orleans"/"Theme for the Young and Blue" (Jerry Capehart)

45's—Compleat

| 113 | "Letting Go"/"Letting Go" (B-side instrumental) |

45's—Everest

| 2500 | "Delight Arkansas"/"Walk Right In" |

45's—MCA

41305	"Pecos Promenade"/"The King of Country Music" (Tanya Tucker)
41323	"Dream Lover"/"Bronco" (Tanya Tucker, A-side with Glen Campbell)
52474	"Slow Nights"/"Midnight Love" (Mel Tillis, A-side with Glen Campbell)
53108	"The Hand That Rocks the Cradle"/"Arkansas"
53172	"Still Within the Sound of My Voice"/"In My Life"
53218	"I Have You"/"I'm a One-Woman Man"
53245	"I Remember You"/"For Sure for Certain for Always"
53426	"Light Years"/"Heart of the Matter"
53493	"More Than Enough"/"Our Movie"

45's—Mirage

| 3845 | "I Love My Truck"/"Melody's Medley" (B-side instrumental) |

45's—Starday

| 853 | "For the Love of a Woman"/"Smokey Blue Eyes" |

45's—Universal-MCA

| 66024 | "She's Gone, Gone, Gone"/"*William Tell* Overture" |

45's—Warner-Viva

49609   "Any Which Way You Can"/"Medley" (instrumental)

GROUPS:

Crickets 45's—Liberty

F55541   "Don't Ever Change"/"I'm Not a Bad Guy"

Folkswingers 45's—World Pacific

391   "Black Mountain Rag"/"This Train"
394   "Don't Think Twice (It's All Right)"/"This Land Is Your Land"
396   "12-String Special"/"Amor A Todos"
4-1812   "12-String Guitar" (jukebox EP)

Gene Norman Group 45's—GNP Crescendo

361   "Masters of War"/"Don't Think Twice"

Mr. 12-String Guitar 45's—World Pacific

77803   "All I Really Want to Do"/"Subterranean Homesick Blues"

Sagittarius 45's—Columbia

44163   "My World Fell Down"/"Libra"
44289   "Hotel Indiscreet"/"Virgo"
44398   "Another Time"/"Pisces"
44503   "Truth Is Not Real"/"You Know You've Found a Way"
44613   "I'm Not Living Here"/"Keeper of the Games"

EPs—Capitol

SU 2928   *Bobbie Gentry & Glen Campbell* (jukebox)
SU 103   *Wichita Lineman* (jukebox)

SU 210	*Galveston* (jukebox)
SU 752	*Glen Campbell's Greatest Hits* (jukebox)
CP 54	*Mary in the Morning* (plus 2 others)
CP 55	*By the Time I Get to Phoenix* (plus 2 others)

LPs—A&M

WR 5293	*No More Night* (contracted)

LPs—Atlantic-America

90016	*Old Home Town*
90164	*Letter to Home*
90483	*It's Just a Matter of Time*

LPs—Capitol

T/ST 1810	*Big Bluegrass Special* (mono/stereo) (*The Green River Boys Featuring Glen Campbell*)
T/ST 1881	*Too Late to Worry—Too Blue to Cry* (mono/stereo)
T/ST 2023	*The Astounding 12-String Guitar of Glen Campbell* (mono/stereo)
T/ST 2392	*The Big Bad Rock Guitar of Glen Campbell* (mono/stereo)
T/ST 2679	*Burning Bridges* (mono/stereo)
T/ST 2809	*Gentle on My Mind* (mono/stereo)
T/ST 2851	*By the Time I Get to Phoenix* (mono/stereo)
T/ST 2878	*Hey Little One*
ST 2907	*A New Place in the Sun*
ST 2928	*Bobbie Gentry & Glen Campbell*
ST 2978	*That Christmas Feeling*
ST 103	*Wichita Lineman*
ST 210	*Galveston*
ST 8-0263	*True Grit*
STBO 8-0268	*Glen Campbell Live*
SW 8-0389	*Try a Little Kindness*
SW 443	*Oh Happy Day*
SW 475	*Norwood*

*Denotes gold record certification.

SW 493	*The Glen Campbell Goodtime Album*
SW 733	*The Last Time I Saw Her*
SW 752	**Glen Campbell's Greatest Hits*
SW 869	*Glen Campbell & Anne Murray*
SW 711117	*Glen Travis Campbell*
SW 11185	*I Knew Jesus (Before He Was a Star)*
SW 11253	*I Remember Hank Williams*
SW 11293	*Houston (I'm Coming to See You)*
SW 11336	*Reunion—Sings the Songs of Jimmy Webb*
SW 11389	*Ernie Sings and Glen Picks*
SW 11407	*Arkansas*
SW 11430	**Rhinestone Cowboy*
SW 11516	*Bloodline*
ST 11577	*The Best of Glen Campbell*
SO 11601	**Southern Nights*
SWBC 11707	*Glen Campbell Live at the Royal Festival Hall*
SW 11722	*Basic*
SOO 12008	*Highwayman*
SOO 12075	*Somethin' 'Bout You Baby I Like*
SOO 12124	*It's the World Gone Crazy*

LPs—Word

895410NX	*No More Night* (bookstores)

INDEPENDENT, REISSUED, AND REPACKAGED LABELS:

LPs—Buckboard

BBS 1010	*Plays 12-String Guitar*

CD

RCD-110	*Glen Campbell's Greatest Hits and Finest Performances* (Reader's Digest Compilation)

*Denotes gold record certification.

LPs—Capitol

93157	*Limited Collector's Edition*
94469	*Gold Medal Award, The Artistry of Glen Campbell*

LPs—Customtone

BE 49	*Guitar Gold* (with Stan Capps)

LPs—Koala

AW 14169	*Way Back When*

LPs—Longines Symphonette Society

LS 218a/SYS	*Golden Favorites* (5-LP Box [5403–5407] with Bonus Album)
SYS 5408	*Gentle on My Mind* (Bonus Album)

LPs—Pickwick

PC/SPC 3052	*12-String Guitar of . . .*
SPC 3134	*A Satisfied Mind*
SPC 3274	*The Glen Campbell Album*
PTP 2048	*The Goodtime Songs of Glen Campbell*
SPC 3346	*I'll Paint You a Song*
SPC 3701	*Galveston*

LPs—Starday

SLP 424	*Country Soul*
SLP 437	*Country Music Star #1*

LPs—Surrey

S/SS 1007	*Country Shindig* (mono/stereo)

LPs—World Pacific

WP/ST 1812	*12-String Guitar*
WP/ST 1814	*12-String Guitar Volume 2*

WP/ST 1833   *The Electric 12*
WP/WPS 2 1835   *Mr. 12-String Guitar*

BUDGET ALBUMS:

Capitol

SL 6699   *Christmas with . . .*
SL 6754   *Glen Campbell & Dean Martin*
SL 8113   *The Greatest Hits of Glen Campbell* (2-LP Set, TV
                     Offer)
SL 8164   *The Glen Campbell Collection* (TV Offer)

Pair

PDL 2-1089   *Favorites by Glen Campbell* (2-LP Set)

CASSETTE ONLY:

Capitol

4XL 9015   *The Night Before Christmas*
SL 6926   *Christmas with Glen Campbell & Sonny James*

MCA

42099   *Still Within the Sound of My Voice*
42210   *Light Years*

New Canaan/A&M

7019977634   *Favorite Hymns*

Stack-O-Hits

A.G. 9020   *Melody Ranch Presents Glen Campbell*

Other Albums:

TITLE	RELEASE DATE
Walkin' in the Sun	1990 Liberty 93884
Unconditional Love	1991 Liberty 90992
Show Me Your Way	1991 New Haven 20011-2
Wings of Victory	1992 New Haven 20021-2
Somebody Like That	1993 Liberty 97962

GLEN CAMPBELL lives in Arizona and Branson, Missouri, with his wife, Kim, and their three young children.

TOM CARTER was an award-winning newspaper reporter and has been a stringer for *Time* and *People*. He co-authored Ronnie Milsap's and Ralph Emery's autobiographies and is currently working with Reba McEntire. He lives in Nashville, Tennessee.